MAX HASTINGS is the author of many of them about twentieth-cen Let Loose, Catastrophe, Vietnam an a correspondent, he reported on eleven conflicts, including Vietnam and the 1973 Yom Kippur and 1982 Falklands wars for BBC TV and newspapers. A former editor-in-chief of the *Daily Telegraph*, he has won many awards both for his journalism and books, including Journalist of the Year, Reporter of the Year, Editor of the Year, together with a Somerset Maugham Prize and two RUSI Westminster Medals. He contributes to *The Times*, reviews books for the *Sunday Times* and writes a column for Bloomberg Inc. He and his wife Penny live in West Berkshire where they garden enthusiastically. He has two very grown-up children and two grandchildren.

OPERATION BITING

THE *SUNDAY TIMES* #1 BESTSELLER
A *Times* Best History Book of the Year
A Waterstones Best Book of the Year

'There are few things in life more dependable than a war story told by Hastings ... He's a master of drama, a writer intimately familiar with the mind of the soldier ... Hastings is a superb military historian with a delightful talent for gossip ... *Operation Biting* is not a typical war story. War histories are usually studies in failure. So many catastrophic mistakes. So many needless deaths. What a relief then, joy even, to be able to read about a battle with a happy ending and genuine heroes – a day that went well' *The Times*

ALSO BY MAX HASTINGS

REPORTAGE
America 1968: The Fire this Time
Ulster 1969: The Struggle for Civil Rights in Northern Ireland
The Battle for the Falklands (with Simon Jenkins)

BIOGRAPHY
Montrose: The King's Champion
Yoni: Hero of Entebbe

AUTOBIOGRAPHY
Did You Really Shoot the Television?
Going to the Wars
Editor

HISTORY
Bomber Command
The Battle of Britain (with Len Deighton)
Das Reich
Overlord: D-Day and the Battle for Normandy
Victory in Europe
The Korean War
Warriors: Extraordinary Tales from the Battlefield
Armageddon: The Battle for Germany 1944–45
Nemesis: The Battle for Japan 1944–45
Finest Years: Churchill as Warlord 1940–45
All Hell Let Loose: The World at War 1939–45
Catastrophe: Europe Goes to War 1914
The Secret War: Spies, Codes and Guerrillas 1939–1945
Vietnam: An Epic Tragedy 1945–1975
Chastise: The Dambusters Story 1943
Operation Pedestal: The Fleet That Battled to Malta 1942
Abyss: World on the Brink – The Cuban Missile Crisis 1962

COUNTRYSIDE WRITING
Outside Days
Scattered Shots
Country Fair

ANTHOLOGY (EDITED)
The Oxford Book of Military Anecdotes
Soldiers: Great Stories of War and Peace

MAX HASTINGS

OPERATION BITING

**THE 1942 PARACHUTE ASSAULT
TO CAPTURE HITLER'S RADAR**

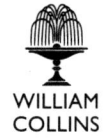

WILLIAM
COLLINS

William Collins
An imprint of HarperCollins*Publishers*
1 London Bridge Street
London SE1 9GF

WilliamCollinsBooks.com

HarperCollins*Publishers*
Macken House, 39/40 Mayor Street Upper
Dublin 1, D01 C9W8, Ireland

First published in Great Britain in 2024 by William Collins
This William Collins paperback edition published in 2025

1

Copyright © Max Hastings 2024

Max Hastings asserts the moral right to be identified
as the author of this work in accordance with the
Copyright, Designs and Patents Act 1988

A catalogue record for this book is
available from the British Library

ISBN 978-0-00-864220-4

All rights reserved. No part of this publication may be
reproduced, stored in a retrieval system, or transmitted,
in any form or by any means, electronic, mechanical,
photocopying, recording or otherwise, without the
prior permission of the publishers.

Without limiting the exclusive rights of any author, contributor
or the publisher of this publication, any unauthorised use of
this publication to train generative artificial intelligence (AI)
technologies is expressly prohibited. HarperCollins also exercise
their rights under Article 4(3) of the Digital Single Market
Directive 2019/790 and expressly reserve this publication
from the text and data mining exception.

Maps by Nicolas Bucourt BEM
Set in Minion Pro

Printed and bound in the UK using 100%
renewable electricity at CPI Group (UK) Ltd

MIX
Paper | Supporting
responsible forestry
FSC™ C007454

This book contains FSC™ certified paper and other controlled
sources to ensure responsible forest management.

For more information visit: www.harpercollins.co.uk/green

With love and admiration for
Margaret MacMillan OM, CH, OC,
who possesses every quality as a historian
to which others of us aspire.

Contents

	List of Illustrations	ix
	Introduction	xiii
	Note on Timing	xxi
1	Reg	1
2	Dickie	20
3	Boy	38
4	Rémy	55
	1 'THE MOST EXTRAORDINARY SECRET AGENT I EVER MET'	55
	2 BRUNEVAL	75
5	Johnny	82
	1 C COMPANY	82
	2 TILSHEAD AND INVERARAY	92
6	Charlie	106
7	'Party' Planning	114
	1 'PICK'	114
	2 THE ENEMY	123

8	The Jump	141
9	Henry	166
10	Junior	189
11	Cook	208
12	The Prizegiving	227
	1 CELEBRATIONS	227
	2 THE WHEEL OF FORTUNE	239

APPENDIX I:
Maj. John Frost's Orders for Operation
Biting February 1942   261
APPENDIX II:
Order of Battle for C Company 2nd
Parachute Battalion 28 February 1942   271
APPENDIX III:
Maj. Gen. Frederick Browning's After-
action Report on Operation Biting,
March 1942   279
APPENDIX IV:
Extracts from the Report of the
Telecommunications Research
Establishment on the German
Technology Captured at Bruneval   297

Acknowledgements	327
References and a Note on Sources	329
Bibliography	341
Index	345

Illustrations

First plate section
Tony Hill's shot of a Würzburg *gerät* (*Airborne Assault Museum, Duxford*)
Men of C Company, 2nd Parachute Battalion (© *IWM*)
PRU pilot Tony Hill
Dr Reg Jones (*University of Aberdeen*)
'Rémy' (*Bruneval: Opération Coup de Croc by Colonel Rémy*)
'Pol' Roger Dumont (*Bruneval: Opération Coup de Croc by Colonel Rémy*)
'Charlemagne' Charles Chauveau (*Bruneval: Opération Coup de Croc by Colonel Rémy*)
Daphne du Maurier with Maj. Gen. Frederick Browning (*Keystone-France/Getty Images*)
Early 1942 RAF aerial view of the battlefield of Operation Biting (*Courtesy of Nicolas Bucourt*)
'Dickie' Commodore Lord Louis Mountbatten (© *IWM*)
Frost's men practise their exit by landing-craft (*Airborne Assault Museum, Duxford*)

Second plate section
'Bobby' Marquis de Casa Maury at his 1937 wedding to Freda Dudley Ward (*TopFoto*)

Lt. Col. Johnny Goschen with Major John Frost (*Airborne Assault Museum, Duxford*)

An Edwardian image of the almost sheer defile (*Nicolas Bucourt*)

'Lone House' (*Photograph courtesy of Nicolas Bucourt via Alain Millet*)

'Beach Fort' (*Photograph courtesy of Nicolas Bucourt via Alain Millet*)

A modern view of the beach from the sea (*Photograph courtesy of Association Bruneval Raid: Operation Biting, France, via Thomas Bucourt*)

MGBs – motor gunboats (© *IWM*)

Admiral Sir William James (*National Maritime Museum, Greenwich, London*)

The admiral as he is best known to posterity (*V&A Museum*)

Wing-Commander Charles Pickard (© *IWM*)

Luftwaffe personnel off-duty (*Photograph courtesy of Cédric Thomas*)

German troops parade through the town's streets (*Photograph courtesy of Cédric Thomas*)

An RAF Whitley dropping paratroopers under training (*Airborne Assault Museum, Duxford*)

Third plate section

RE Captain Dennis Vernon (*Airborne Assault Museum, Duxford*)

F/Sgt. Charles Cox (*Airborne Assault Museum, Duxford*)

A Würzburg in action (*Das Bundesarchiv*)

Some of the Biting attackers test-fire Boyes anti-tank rifles and Bren guns (*Airborne Assault Museum, Duxford*)

The hapless *Gefreiter* Schmidt (*Airborne Assault Museum, Duxford*)

ILLUSTRATIONS

Luftwaffe personnel from the La Poterie site
The route by which the men of Charteris's missing section skirted the village (*Photograph courtesy of Nicolas Bucourt via Alain Millet*)
HMS *Prins Albert*
The ALCs as they would have looked on their retreat from the beach (© *IWM*)
One of the returning triumphant MGBs (*Airborne Assault Museum, Duxford*)
Lt. Euan Charteris (*Photograph courtesy of Association Bruneval Raid: Operation Biting, France, via Charteris family*)
Pte. Hugh McIntyre
Exultant paratroopers, showing off a German helmet to Charles Pickard (© *IWM*)

Fourth plate section
Pte. Peter 'Walker'
Lt. Cdr. Fred Cook, RAN (*Australian National Maritime Museum*)
Sgt. Dave Grieve
Air Commodore Norman quizzes Corporal Jones with Charlie Cox (*Airborne Assault Museum, Duxford*)
Fusilier Tewes and Heller (*Trinity Mirror/Mirrorpix/Alamy Stock Photo*)
An admiring friend watches Pte. Mark Ginsberg (*Airborne Assault Museum, Duxford*)
The King and Queen visit 51 Squadron at Dishforth (*Airborne Assault Museum, Duxford*)
A US paratrooper stands with John Timothy (*Airborne Assault Museum, Duxford*)

Three of the British prisoners captured at Bruneval (*Photograph courtesy of Association Bruneval Raid: Operation Biting, France, via Lechevallier family*)
The impeccable 'Boy' Browning
The British prisoners in Normandy (*Photograph courtesy of Nicolas Bucourt*)
RSM Gerry Strachan at his 1943 wedding to army cook Ivy (*Airborne Assault Museum, Duxford*)
John Frost at Buckingham Palace (*Airborne Assault Museum, Duxford*)

Introduction

A conversation took place during the small hours of 26 October 1941 between Winston Churchill and General Sir Alan Brooke, for the convenience of the nocturnal prime minister, though inconvenience of his diurnal companion. Churchill observed that a man's life is akin to a walk down a long passage with closed windows on either side: 'As you reach each window, an unknown hand opens it and the light it lets in only increases by contrast the darkness of the end of the passage.' In those bad days of the Second World War – and ahead of Pearl Harbor, they were still almost unremittingly bleak for Britain – even the prime minister with his passion for offensive action could identify scant opportunities for initiating big operations against the Axis. The 'end of the passage' – the path to Allied victory – remained opaque. Four days after Churchill's remark to Brooke, he felt obliged to write to Gen. Sir Claude Auchinleck in Cairo that 'Whipcord', a plan to invade Sicily, must be abandoned as 'beyond the compass of our stride'.

The greatest conflict in human history was not conducted at an even tenor of ferocity, anguish, sacrifice. In every belligerent society with the possible exception of Russia, there were lulls in the slaughter – significant periods when nothing momentous took place. The term Phoney War was coined to describe the period between September 1939 and April 1940, when the French and German armies, together with a relatively small British Expeditionary Force, confronted each other in passivity. But there were other 'phoney wars' later, when not much happened, measured against the standard of Stalingrad '42 or Normandy '44.

Following 1940 defeat in France, Britain remained fiercely engaged at sea and in the air. On land, however, while relatively small imperial contingents fought the Germans and Italians in the desert, and thereafter also the Japanese in South-East Asia, most of the British Army was confined to its home islands, rearming and training for a resumption of the continental struggle against major German armies which would not take place until the final year of the war. This did not mean that Britain's warlords were idle. Alan Brooke, who became Chief of the Imperial General Staff in December 1941, faced the relentless strain inseparable from strategy-making and the new partnership with the United States. Nonetheless many would-be battlefield commanders were left chafing in remote regions of the United Kingdom, eager to engage the foe and exercise the career opportunities that war had opened to them, while having no scope to do so as they merely inspected training, supervised exercises and awaited the deliveries of weapons, vehicles and equipment which alone could fit their formations to fight the Germans or Japanese.

At all costs, however, and being especially mindful of American public opinion, Churchill was insistent that Britain's home army should not be seen to be entirely idle. He pressed for raids on the continent, pursuing objectives which might fulfil useful purposes, or sometimes attacking targets that had no value at all – they were merely accessible to small amphibious forces. Many generals recoiled from this sort of petty piracy, and on the other side the Wehrmacht declined to bother with it. German doctrine held that wars were won by big battalions, on great battlefields. Hitler's commanders rejected perceived sideshows and trivia, and so did most of their American counterparts.

Britain's prime minister, by contrast, loved adventures, whether personal or national. In January 1942, a raid was proposed which promised a genuine prize. The British and Germans were locked in an electronic conflict, to empower their own air forces and frustrate those of the enemy, through ever more potent refinements of radar. New installations had appeared upon the Channel coast of France, which were obviously vital to Hitler's defences against the RAF's bombing campaign. Neither aerial reconnaissance nor Ultra decrypts, nor even monitoring of German pulse transmissions, could tell Britain's 'boffins' all that they needed to know about these latest weapons – for radar was, of course, a weapon.

Thus, Scientific Intelligence at the Air Ministry proposed an assault on the German installation at Bruneval,* a wooded hamlet twelve miles north of Le Havre. The burgeoning Combined Operations Command seized on the scheme. It seemed practicable, even allowing for the straitened resources of Britain's army, navy and air force of those days – 'within the compass of our stride', to recall Churchill's phrase. Bruneval was not far from home, barely ninety miles across the Channel from Portsmouth. A descent on the site promised opportunities to test new men, tactics, weapons, equipment – indeed

---

* Some local people in Normandy are irked that Operation Biting is always linked with Bruneval, when technically both the Freya and Würzburg radars were sited within the village boundaries of La Poterie-Cap d'Antifer. Bruneval is merely the hamlet above the defile leading to the beach, nonetheless its name is now indelibly associated with the 1942 raid, and it seems too late to undo this.

revolutionary means of making war. Churchill enthused. The chiefs of staff agreed. Plans were made and preparations set in train for a night assault codenamed Biting, to be launched during February's full moon, which should illuminate the battlefield in a fashion indispensable to success. Engineers would be sent, to dismantle and carry home components of the Würzburg, while a company of the newly-formed 1st Parachute Brigade shielded the treasure-hunters. An assault of this kind was ideally suited to a glider landing, but in January 1942 Britain's embryo glider force was nowhere near ready to go into action: parachutists must do the job.

In the absence of a British campaign on the continent, such small business consumed the attentions of big men. Later in the war, when the destinies of armies and of nations were disputed daily on vast battlefields, forays on the scale of Bruneval would pass unnoticed in the operations rooms of the great. Men would fight and die in their thousands without much disturbing the digestions of the conflict's directors. In February 1942, however, when the British and American peoples were being served a relentless diet of defeats, such a venture as Biting assumed a significance attainable only in that time and place. It was as if the floodlights of a great football stadium were turned upon a match played within lines painted over a mere fraction of its turf. Such glamorous figures as Commodore Lord Louis Mountbatten and Maj. Gen. Frederick 'Boy' Browning competed for its laurels. The operation later became famous as an early demonstration of the courage and enterprise of the fledgling French Resistance movement, of which Gen. Charles de Gaulle was the inspiration and figurehead.

Biting seemed to me to offer an opportunity not merely to relate a small British triumph, but to set the story in the wider context of the personalities, each fascinating in a different way, from the brilliant Scientific Intelligence officer R.V. Jones, through Mountbatten, Browning, France's 'Colonel Rémy' and his comrades, the RAF's drop leader Wing-Commander Charles Pickard, airborne forces' first star Major John Frost, and Flight-Sergeant Charles Cox – a plucky little twenty-eight-year-old radar mechanic who allowed himself to be 'volunteered' for the key role in Jones's technological adventure. All my books aspire to tell 'people' stories, because these are what history is about. This one is especially so.

I should begin by paying tribute to my delightful friend the late George Millar, himself a wartime warrior as well as a fine journalist. George authored a 1972 account of Bruneval, enriched by opportunities to conduct personal interviews with some of those who took part, then mostly alive and very much kicking. Mountbatten, still preening himself about Biting, contributed a foreword in which he wrote of how 'we in Combined Operations pulled off a small but completely successful raid under the noses of the Germans'.

I have drawn significantly on George's narrative, while also using personal testimonies that are held in the Imperial War Museum archives and at the Airborne Assault Museum at Duxford, together with copious material in the National Archives. Much information is now available, above all the secret military reports, which reposed in files that remained closed when George wrote. Among published sources I should pay special tribute to the 2012 *Raid de Bruneval: Mystères et vérités*, by Alain Millet and Nicolas Bucourt BEM, which offers a mass of detail about Biting, especially the German side, some of which came new to me. While there are points in it to quibble about, this French account is by far the most comprehensive study by authors on either side of the Channel. In September 2023 Nicolas proved an enchanting and boundlessly knowledgeable guide to Bruneval, which increased my debt to him. It deserves saying that only a personal visit to the scene makes the Biting story fully comprehensible, because no photograph or map can properly reveal the intractability of the terrain, especially on the steep approaches to the evacuation beach.

I am grateful to Julian Jackson and Robert Gildea for identifying to me some notable recent French accounts of wartime Resistance, especially Philippe Kerrand's 2022 biography *L'étrange colonel Rémy*, which has been invaluable. I profited from having interviewed in 1980 for my own early book *Das Reich* some thirty former *Résistants*, from whom I learned much about wartime France that astonished me, both for good and ill. In *Finest Years*, I discussed at length Churchill's enthusiasm for what I dubbed military theatre, a significant element of Britain's war effort when bigger things were unachievable. In *The Secret War*, I addressed Resistance across Occupied Europe.

In 2019 soldiers of the modern 2 Para staged a reconstruction of Biting for army instructional purposes. The resulting film, today accessible on YouTube, gives something of the flavour of the action on the night of 27/28 February, though it is marred by the absence of the snow that carpeted Normandy in 1942, and makes little of the blunders and mishaps which took place. These are inseparable from any battle, but an understanding of them is important, to those who seek to grasp the real events behind the Bruneval legend.

Appendix IV, the British analysis of the German technology captured at Bruneval, will be incomprehensible to most readers, as are its details to me, but it seems important to the completeness of the narrative of the raid, for the benefit of techno-cognoscenti.

It may add fractionally to my own credentials as a chronicler that in 1963, as an officer cadet with 10 Para TA, I completed the Parachute Regiment's basic training and jump course, and mingled with hoary veterans of John Frost's generation. I became familiar with the weapons used by C Company at Bruneval, and once participated in a 3 Para mass night drop in Cyprus, which convinced me that airborne assault always has been, and always will be, a chancy business. I remember, as if it was yesterday, the moment when the men about to board our RAF Argosy in November twilight were given the sobering warning by our company commander that refusal to jump was a court-martial offence. Almost twenty years later, I served as a shivering spectator at one of 2 Para's battles in the Falklands war, in which the battalion performed in a fashion that showed its men worthy successors to John Frost and his band. I have seldom felt more privileged than on the night in 1992 when I was among guests at the great dinner in the Guildhall, attended by many veterans of World War II, to celebrate the Parachute Regiment's fiftieth anniversary. My son once asked to borrow for a fancy dress party my old airborne smock, last worn on marches across East Falkland. He observed, justly enough, that I would never need it again. Nonetheless I declined in the tones of a grumpy old man, saying: 'That's not the point.'

The Bruneval raid was a thrilling action that had important consequences. The plan for the attack, conceived by Mountbatten's and Browning's staffs, should never have worked. It demanded that the defenders should sleepwalk through the attackers' Channel crossing; acquiesce relatively passively in the presence for three hours in France of a small, ill-armed force which a serious German counter-attack would have crushed with ease; then indulge the raiders' slow-motion escape across the Channel, unmolested by the Luftwaffe and Kriegsmarine. Yet Biting, for some extraordinary reason, defied all the probabilities of disaster, such as befell many other wartime special operations. Its story lifts the spirit, because it is that of ordinary people doing fine and difficult things well. I am a sceptic about the word 'hero', daily prostituted in twenty-first-century newspapers: when I served as an editor, people were branded as 'heroes' or 'heroines' in our pages only with my explicit consent. But those who contributed to the little victory at Bruneval, many of whom were killed later in the conflict even though they survived the night of 27/28 February 1942, were indeed heroes, whom it is a joy to celebrate here.

MAX HASTINGS
Chilton Foliat, West Berkshire, and Datai, Langkawi, Malaysia
November 2023

Note on Timing

In 1942 continental clocks were set one hour ahead of British ones, as they are today. In this narrative all timings, including those in German reports, have been standardized on UK time and the twenty-four-hour clock as employed by the armed forces, so that 9 a.m. is 0900, and so on. Nonetheless timings given in the text below for events in France are unreliable because of conflicting or imprecise evidence, sometimes only circumstantial. They merely represent the best guesstimates I can contrive.

1
Reg

Far from the battlefields of the Second World War, an invisible conflict was waged by rival intelligence services, navies, air forces and scientists, in pursuit of advantage in the electronic contest which assumed ever-growing importance in determining outcomes, especially at sea and in the air. Although in the earlier 'Great War' wireless interception had played a significant role in the Anglo-German naval struggle, only now was technology evolving that enabled belligerents to locate enemies far beyond reach of the naked eye or telescope. Warships acquired means to pinpoint threats both on the surface and beneath it. 'Bomber barons' were progressively empowered by navigation aids and aiming devices. Even more critical, especially in the eyes of governments desperate to shield their homelands, were the incremental advances in defensive radar that first warned of approaching foes, then tracked airborne attackers for destruction by anti-aircraft guns or fighters.

Those British people privy to the secrets of 'RDF' or 'Radio Direction Finding' – the deceptive cover name given to British radar – took enormous pride in their country's achievement of having devised this technology, then linked it to a communications network with defending fighter squadrons just in time to win the Battle of Britain. Nationalistic conceit made many, even senior officers, slow to acknowledge that the Germans might have created similar devices and be exploiting them against British fighters and bombers intruding upon Nazi-occupied Europe. They chose to ignore such evidence as the identification of a radar aerial on the foremast of the German pocket battleship *Graf Spee*, scuttled off Montevideo in December 1939.

One who harboured no doubts, however, was the Air Ministry's Assistant Director of Intelligence (Science), Dr R.V. Jones – Reg to his family and friends – an authentic wartime star, and a fascinating human being. Born in 1911, this brilliant young physicist escaped from a humble family background through a series of scholarships, first to Alleyn's School in Dulwich and then Wadham College, Oxford, where he secured a first-class degree in the era when this was a rare distinction. His father had been a sergeant in the Grenadier Guards, and his son wrote: 'My childhood was steeped in the Regimental tradition of discipline, precision, service, endurance and good temper.' Reg possessed a miscellany of virtues of which the most conspicuous were brains, curiosity, open-mindedness, articulacy, energy and self-confidence. The debit side of this last quality was an arrogance that exasperated some important people, especially if they were less intelligent than the pushy scholarship lad. Most, however, recognized Dr Jones as uncommonly bright.

No lonely genius he, Reg was compulsively gregarious, a practical joker with unexpected hobbies and interests. For a time, he pursued glass-blowing. Then he acquired a pistol, and made himself a deadly shot. A rich Oxford student friend introduced him to the family stately home in Staffordshire. There Jones, who became a regular guest, roamed the countryside, gun in hand: 'My bag was mainly rabbits but over the years I also shot hares, stoats, pigeons, crows, jays' – and once a fox. By the outbreak of war, the scientist's private arsenal embraced six pistols and a rifle. Intensely romantic, his England was 'that of Rupert Brooke and [polar explorer Captain] Robert Falcon Scott ... If the time came, this England would be worth fighting for.'

Jones began his professional career under the umbrella of a fellowship in astronomy, though he never practised in that discipline, but in 1934, when he was twenty-three, he was retained by an American inventor to work on possible methods of infra-red detection. Although it would be years before this science was applied to British defence, Jones became a pioneer. He worked for some time at Oxford's Clarendon Laboratory, supervised by Professor Frederick Lindemann, 'the Prof', Churchill's familiar, ennobled in 1941 as Lord Cherwell. Jones achieved the difficult double of earning the matching regard of Sir Henry Tizard, Lindemann's great rival and indeed focus of that tennis-playing bachelor's enmity. The young man found himself increasingly engaged in the study of radar – and of intelligence. It was a reflection of the village character of Britain's scientific community that in the autumn of 1939 Jones fell into conversation at a bus stop on Oxford High Street with a colleague who talked to him about the discovery of nuclear fission – the possibility that a Bomb might one day be built; the danger that the Germans might be exploring the same path, with terrible potential consequences.

The secretary of the Tizard Committee on air defence, which played a critical role in the evolution of Britain's radar-based air defence system, noticed that from 1936 onwards R.V. Jones, though still working mostly at Oxford, 'continually got himself mixed up with Intelligence matters'. In many countries, notably including Germany, such cross-pollination would have been resented and probably frustrated. It was an important part of the genius – and genius it was – of this element of what became the British war machine that where scientific and technological talent and flair were identified, they were nurtured.

When Dr Jones was invited to accept a salaried post that bridged the Air Ministry and the Secret Service, investigating the role of science and technology in the enemy's armed forces, he responded with characteristic impulsive eagerness: 'A man in that position could lose the war! I'll take it.' He was given a share in a small office in the Air Ministry, being formally identified as 'a scientist with a special interest in German weapons'. On 4 November 1939 the British naval attaché in Oslo found himself the recipient of a packet of documents describing various secret weapons at Hitler's command. These included two types of radar; large rockets; rocket-propelled gliding bombs and much else. The author described himself as 'a friendly German scientist'.

MI6 rejected the 'Oslo report', as it became known, as an enemy 'plant'. The Secret Service's senior figures, never celebrated for their imagination, argued that no one person in Germany could have known so much about weapons across such a diverse spectrum. Fred Winterbotham of MI6 passed a copy of the report to Jones. The latter, almost alone, was soon convinced the document was genuine, and benign in intent. He wrote wryly later: 'In the few dull moments of the war I used to look up the Oslo Report to see what should be coming along next' – and which often did. Only long after the conflict was Jones able to confirm that the document had indeed been the work of a noble anti-Nazi physicist, Hans Ferdinand Mayer.

One of many written broadsides that Jones fired at the powers-that-be deplored British ignorance of what was happening scientifically on 'the other side of the hill', chiefly because spymasters and service chiefs had no idea what to look for.

Submitted on 7 December 1939, the report's language, outspoken as were few Whitehall documents, reflected the character and erudition of its author: 'A serious disparity in Scientific Intelligence between England and Germany almost certainly exists ... due in part to the extra secrecy precautions observed in Germany, and in part to the lack of coordinated effort in our acquisition of information.

'Parallels have frequently been drawn between the Peloponnesian War and that between England and Germany, but rarely more accurately than in the present connection. A similar disregard for Scientific Intelligence exists now in England to that which existed in Athens. Pericles, in a classic exposition of Athenian policy, stated: "Our city is thrown open to the world, and we never expel a foreigner or prevent him from seeing or learning anything of which the secret if revealed to an enemy might profit him" (Thucydides II, 39). Athens lost the war.'

Tizard congratulated Jones on the report and his proposals for strengthening scientific intelligence, though some service officers bridled at being harangued about their business by a brash young civilian. Jones nonetheless prospered, not least because of his extraordinary network of contacts and relationships. One of the worst aspects of the wartime conscription of intelligent people for uniformed service was that many found themselves obliged to serve in roles that chained them to the chariots of more senior figures, sometimes tyrants, who were much less clever. By contrast, among the admirable features of Britain's 'boffin war' was the manner in which many scientists flitted between services and technical facilities, exchanging ideas and information. Jones, as one of these, enjoyed a privileged war. He worked alongside his intellectual peers, in pastures fertilized by mutual respect between those who grazed them. The Secret Service chiefs did not cause him much trouble, because he was protected by powerful mentors.

He felt equally at home in the Air Ministry, MI6 headquarters in Broadway beside St James's Park Tube station, 'Station X' at Bletchley Park, RAF photo-intelligence at Medmenham ... and even – thanks to 'the Prof's' startling, because rarely proffered, goodwill – the Cabinet Office and Downing Street. Jones once attempted the impossible, to broker a reconciliation between Lindemann and Tizard. The latter asked his young friend to carry a message to the darkly brooding prime ministerial favourite: 'Tell him from me that I should be glad if we could stop this ridiculous quarrel at least for the period of the war, and concentrate on fighting the Germans.' The other eminence, however, would have none of this. When Jones reported Tizard's words, Lindemann merely snorted contemptuously: 'Now that I am in a position of power' – as Churchill's scientific adviser – 'a lot of my old friends have come sniffing around!'

In 1940 Jones married Vera Cain, physically half her husband's considerable size but a formidable woman in her own right, whom he had met while both were working for the Admiralty Intelligence Branch, where she captained the women's hockey team. They made their first home in a flat in Richmond from which he commuted daily to Whitehall. The couple would have three children during the course of the war.

In June, amid the Battle of Britain, Lindemann, as 'the Prof' then still was, summoned Jones to the Cabinet Office to quiz him about whether he believed the Germans had radar, a notion which many important people dismissed. The following month, Jones first reported to the chiefs of staff on enemy radar development, following the pinpointing of what appeared to be a scanner at Lannion in northern Brittany. Doubts were cast on the identification of this technology, however, by sceptics who pointed out that the array was not mounted on a high tower, such as the British found indispensable for their own installations. Yet Jones linked the photographic images from Lannion with Luftwaffe signals intercepted by Bletchley Park, which made reference to Freya, a Nordic mythological figure. The scientist was prompted to investigate this creature's biography, scouring both memory and his books.

The goddess Freya had turned to a lover in place of her husband, in order to secure a magic necklace called Brisingamen, guarded by Heimdal, a servant of the gods, gifted with powers to see a hundred miles in daylight and darkness alike. Since British practice strictly forbade the use of a codename for any operation, weapon or device that might reveal its purpose to the enemy, Jones was initially sceptical that the Germans might be employing the designation Freya for a long-range radar. The scientist remained firmly convinced, however, that Freya was radar-related. He finally reported: 'It is unwise to lay too much stress on this evidence, but these are the only facts that seem to have any relation to our previous knowledge. Actually Heimdal himself would have seemed the best choice for a code-name for RDF but perhaps it would have been too obvious ... It is difficult to escape the conclusion therefore that the *Freya-Gerät* is a form of portable RDF. Freya may possibly be associated with Wotan – she was at one time his mistress – although it would have been expected that the Fuhrer would have in this case chosen Frigga, Wotan's lawful wife.'

This was an example of a characteristic Jones missive that caused critics to vent irritation towards him, as too clever by half. Nonetheless, he was right. The Germans called radar D/T – *Dezimeter Telegraphie*. As is so often the case with discoveries, their scientists had worked on its development in parallel with their British counterparts, though likewise in ignorance, once the Nazi era began and international cross-fertilization ceased. The nineteenth-century German physicist Heinrich Hertz could claim to have been the first to demonstrate the nature of radio waves, pursuing a path earlier explored by Faraday and Maxwell in Britain. Karl Ferdinand Braun invented the cathode-ray tube, while Ambrose Fleming made the pioneer radio valve, much improved by the American Lee de Forest.

Two other Americans, Gregory Breit and Merle Tuve, in 1924 devised means for transmitting a succession of radio pulses, and in 1929 a Japanese scientist established a technique for emitting radio signals on a narrow spectrum. By 1933 a German Navy scientist was experimenting upon a primitive radar installation with a dish aerial, mounted on a balcony overlooking Kiel Harbour. Within three years, Hitler was being briefed about this technology, which was detecting warships at a range of twelve miles. Also in 1936, Germany produced the first so-called Freya array, capable of spotting aircraft at ranges of up to seventy-five miles. Almost simultaneously, the Telefunken company created the first short-range height-finding set, codenamed Würzburg.

Essentially, until the last of the interwar years German radar development advanced at roughly the same pace as that of the British, which was powerfully influenced by Robert Watson-Watt. The latter then leaped ahead not with the science, but in its practical application to defence against bomber attack. A.P. Rowe, Sir Henry Tizard and their colleagues conceived a system for harnessing radar to fighter direction, which was enthusiastically embraced by the RAF. It was this system, not superior technology, that gave Churchill's nation its decisive advantage in the Battle of Britain. The Germans, meanwhile, began to fall behind both with the science and its application because in 1939–40 their leaders, and especially Luftwaffe chief Hermann Goering, were little interested in means of defence. Their thinking in those months of victories focused almost exclusively upon the offensive, to which they deemed radar to have scant relevance.

In the late summer of 1940 the War Cabinet, after assessing the evidence from the Lannion photos and from Jones, rejected the notion that the enemy might have matched British development of radar through home-grown expertise. Government luminaries preferred instead to believe the Germans had captured a set in France, and exploited this. The prime minister was then assured that no RDF had been lost to the enemy, though this was untrue. A British apparatus had fallen into German hands near Boulogne; been duly examined by Luftwaffe experts, and judged to be much inferior to their own Freya, which they considered an advance upon anything the RAF was using on such frequencies. It is striking to notice that, after the flurry of 1940 British activity and curiosity about enemy radar, thereafter amid huge events and with so many other demands upon Scientific Intelligence, for months investigation was permitted to lapse. While in Jones's compelling 1978 memoir, one revelation follows the last in a sequence of pages, a study of the dates he cites shows how protracted the intervals could sometimes be between landmark developments and discoveries.

In the early days of the Luftwaffe blitz, Jones won Churchill's ear and admiration by urging his conviction, against the views of RAF chiefs and many scientists, that German bombers were exploiting electronic guidance beams to navigate to Britain. The triumphant vindication of this theory, together with his subsequent success in devising means of countering the enemy technology, conferred upon Jones exceptional credibility, especially in the eyes of the prime minister. He retained critics, especially in MI6, who regarded the scientist as a presumptuous young man with too much to say. He himself wrote later: 'The path of truthful duty is not easy; there were several attempts to get me removed from my post because of my insistence on unpalatable facts being faced. I survived – but I might not have done had the situation' – beneath the Luftwaffe blitz – 'not been so serious.' By 1941 Jones's star blazed high, his energy apparently limitless, his grasp of Germany's air defences becoming more impressive by the day. He interrogated prisoners, especially Luftwaffe aircrew. He pored over photographs of enemy installations on the continent, snatched by high-flying Spitfires. He communed with the eggheads and mathematical geniuses of Bletchley Park about the significance of intercepted Luftwaffe signals.

Yet some senior officers still discounted the importance of radar and electronic navigation aids, whether in the hands of the Germans or the RAF. Those outside the technical branches argued – wrongly, because in reality Bomber Command's aim was wildly erratic – that British aircraft were locating and attacking targets in Germany without any of the elaborate equipment the Luftwaffe seemed to find necessary for its own bombing. The air marshals were almost all men who had attained high commands in the fledgling RAF following youthful army service, rather than after completing apprenticeships in aerial technology, which evolved rapidly through their subsequent service careers. Such men seemed less interested in the enemy's radar capabilities than were Dr Jones and his colleagues. In February 1941, for instance, Air Vice-Marshal Sir Arthur Harris, then assistant chief of air staff, minuted: 'Are we not tending to lose our sense of proportion over these German beams? We have endless prisoner of war reports pointing out that they do not and cannot rely on beams to any very great extent because we monkey about with them so successfully ... Lack of beams will not stop the Boche and in my opinion will not even embarrass him.'

Other RAF brass, however – the names of Philip Joubert and Edward Addison recur constantly in correspondence with scientific wizards such as Tizard and D.R. Pye – were more enlightened. So was the new assistant chief of air staff for intelligence, Air Vice-Marshal Charles Medhurst, who approached Reg Jones on being appointed early in 1941. 'He told me how impressed he had been by my work on the beams,' said Jones, 'and said that he would like me to take over responsibility for analysing how the German night defences worked.'

The scientist immediately determined to focus his attention on radar, 'because I was sure that the Germans would find, as we had found ourselves, that ... they would have to depend on it for night-fighting'. By 1941, to an extraordinary degree this young scientist represented not merely a component of intelligence studying German air defences, but almost *all* scientific intelligence – among the few people in Britain possessed of the specialist knowledge and imagination to ask the right questions, then to divine answers. As the British bomber offensive slowly gained momentum, the Luftwaffe was developing techniques for marrying radar to searchlights, flak guns and fighter direction. Suddenly the technologies that had seemed to Goering mere curiosities a few years earlier became the focus of intense interest and mass production, vital to the air defence of the Fatherland.

Jones understood some of this when he received his brief from Air Vice-Marshal Medhurst. He started his investigation with the single fragmentary clue that the enemy was known to be exploiting Freyas. He had by now acquired an assistant named Derek Garrard, who had previously worked on radar at the Telecommunications Research Establishment – TRE – at Swanage in Dorset. In the latter's first weeks as an intelligence-gatherer, he conducted some experimental electronic trawls for German transmissions, and from a listening position near Dover pinpointed unexplained signals on 375 megacycles. Further research identified these as related to German *Seektakt* naval radar, employed to direct gunfire against British shipping in the Channel. Evidence was mounting everywhere, especially in the minds of Jones and Garrard and some airmen, that the Germans had technology of a sophistication comparable with that of the British.

They needed to know much more. There were three channels through which relevant evidence could be gathered, and Jones had access to all of them. First were 'most secret sources', Luftwaffe messages decrypted at Bletchley Park, for which he was on the tiny authorized reading list. He had already found repeated mentions in Luftwaffe decrypts of the technology codenamed Freya, associated with the big receivers of which a network was growing: by late 1941, Scientific Intelligence had plotted twenty-seven scanners on the north coast of France.

Other decrypts indicated the Germans were also bringing into service a second type of radar, dubbed the 'Würzburg apparatus'. In March 1941, transmissions from the French coast were intercepted on wavelengths of 53 centimetres. As Jones explained in his subsequent report, 'they showed pulses characteristic of RDF, and giving a maximum range of about 40 kilometres. These transmissions were independent of the main long range coastal chain of "Freya" stations ... and were thought to form an inner chain, probably extending inland in the form of a carpet.'

The RAF's electronic eavesdroppers monitored German emissions through both ground-based and airborne listening units. On 8 May 1941, a 'Ferret' electronic eavesdropping Wellington bomber of 109 Squadron noted that in addition to the now-familiar signals from Freya arrays, operators were also picking up short-range transmissions from other such installations on a frequency of 570 megacycles. A third vital tool of British intelligence thereafter came into play, though only sluggishly, over a period of months: aerial photographic reconnaissance. Jones knew roughly what to look for, because late in 1941 benevolent neutrals, one American and one Chinese, presented the British with copies of photographs snapped near Berlin's anti-aircraft defence towers. These showed a big circular disc aerial which seemed almost certainly related to the direction of the local AA guns.

Nothing like it had then been identified on the French coast. However, Charles Frank, now working beside Garrard on Jones's staff, had an inspiration. Frank, exactly the same age as his chief and likewise newly married, was equally gifted and imaginative. He had a prodigious memory and fluent German acquired during youthful studies at Berlin's Kaiser Wilhelm Institut für Physik. Now, studying medium-altitude photographs of a Freya site at Bruneval, north of Le Havre, Frank identified a big farmhouse and buildings nearby which he guessed, correctly, were being used as quarters for its crew. His eye and magnifier shifted a few inches, to an isolated château on a clifftop grazed bare by cattle, and approached by a well-worn track. This would probably be used for officers' billets, Frank surmised, or possibly as a headquarters. Another much-used track led north from the big house almost to the cliff edge. This ended in a small, unidentifiable black dot, which might be a latrine or a bunker entrance. But it might also be another type of radar scanner, albeit much smaller than that which had been photographed near Berlin Zoo.

Jones now requested low oblique images of the Bruneval site, such as might show the nature of the equipment sited on the cliff edge. The RAF's specialists, squadrons of the PRU or Photographic Reconnaissance Unit, had adopted a technique which the pilots called 'dicing' – as with death. When very close photo cover of an objective was needed, an unarmed fighter streaked in at tree height. Such tactics required luck, courage and the fine judgement to expose images at the right split-second opportunity. PRU Spitfires were using the technique so often several of their wing undersides had been repainted pink, which made them less conspicuous at low level than the previous duck-egg green shading.

The voluminous correspondence in the archives, stretching over two years, testifies to the sluggish pace at which the German radar story, or rather the British response to it, progressed through Whitehall and the service departments. Hereafter, however, everything accelerated. In the winter of 1941, Jones's networking skills once more played a role in what became the Bruneval saga. The PRU was based at Benson airfield, between Wallingford and the edge of the Chilterns. The photographic interpretation centre was located fifteen miles away at Danesfield, a wisteria-clad mansion which became famous in wartime RAF legend as Medmenham – the name of the nearby village – where some of the great British intelligence discoveries of the war were made, more than a few of them by women of the WAAF who played key roles in the centre's evolution.

Jones had befriended S/Ldr. Claude Wavell who, within the Danesfield operation, ran G Section, dedicated to the study of enemy radar and wireless installations. The scientist had also struck up an acquaintance with one of the Benson pilots named Tony Hill, with whom one day he went drinking in a local pub. Though Jones never avowed this, it does not seem fanciful to suppose that he felt the inescapable part-envy, part-awe, of a groundling, living a relatively safe war, towards contemporaries and especially aircrew who faced the enemy daily at mortal risk. Hill was twenty-seven, old to fulfil the fighter pilot's requirement for lightning reflexes. He was a colonel's son who had attended Harrow public school before becoming a director of a small brewery near his home in Hertfordshire. He had learned to fly with the RAF Volunteer Reserve just before the outbreak of war, and was now piloting a Spitfire over Europe nearly every day, both at extreme high altitude and ultra-low level, almost clipping French trees.

Hill told Jones he had a problem. He was unafraid of hedge-hopping over German positions in his Spitfire, but his photos often proved a disappointment. He was, in his own words, 'a bit slow'. His camera was located behind the cockpit, pointed sideways and slightly astern. When tasked to film a given objective, a pilot was obliged to dive, watch the target vanish beneath the Spitfire's beautiful broad, thin wing, then press the shutter release. Again and again, Hill was late doing this, and thus came home without some of the required images. Jones and Hill discussed 'dicing' technique exhaustively, then the scientist made suggestions for solving the pilot's timing problem by trial and error experiments. In the year or so of life left to Hill, in the tragically attenuated human experience which was commonplace for wartime fliers, the young pilot went on to take some of the finest and most significant photographs in the PRU's record books.

One day in late November 1941, Hill chanced to drive over from Benson to Danesfield with his fellow pilot Gordon

Hughes, who needed to chat to Claude Wavell. Hill lingered outside while Hughes disappeared into the rabbit warren of offices. Wavell was almost twenty years older than the airmen. He had gained immense experience of photographing terrain from planes during a decade working on a survey of Brazil. He was also a fine mathematician, and on this winter's day showed Hughes the use he had been making of spherical trigonometry. He had perfected a new device he dubbed the 'Altazimeter', for gauging the height of objects from aerial photographs. This could be determined, he explained to Hughes, by multiplying shadow length by the tangent of the sun's altitude. An interpreter needed only to know the latitude of a location, the scale and orientation of photos, and the date.

Wavell then began to talk to Hughes about the new German radar which was exciting the curiosity of Jones and his colleagues. He placed two medium-altitude photos of a length of French coast in his stereoscope and showed them to the pilot. The ill-defined object at the bottom of the photos might, just might, be what the boffins – or perhaps 'spooks' would be a more appropriate term – were seeking. Hughes suggested Tony Hill should be brought in to examine the pictures. Others were produced from Wavell's collection, showing – for instance – how a variation in shadow had first enabled Charles Frank to spot a Freya, indeed to convince doubters within the RAF that the Germans possessed radar.

Back to the newer pictures: could these show the dish-shaped aerial of what Jones and his colleagues had started to call a 'Würzburg'? Hill asked: 'Where exactly is this place Bruneval?' Wavell told him, and the pilot said decisively, 'I'll get you your answer tomorrow.' Sure enough, next day the phone rang in his office from Benson. Tony Hill said: 'You were right. It must be a parabolic whatnot, and the Jerries were round it like flies ...

It's like an electric bowl heater and about ten feet across.' The bad news, however, was that as the Spitfire had streaked low over the French coast at 350 mph, Hill had failed to catch the relatively tiny object on film. 'But don't worry. I'll have another go tomorrow.'

Now came yet another example of how Britain's war effort, and explicitly the RAF's part in it, could sometimes indulge astonishing personal initiative, creative indiscipline – choose your own phrase. Next morning Hill took off once more for Bruneval, breaching an entirely sensible rule that no PRU pilot could photograph the same objective – repeat a 'dicing' sortie – two days running. Moreover the formal request from Jones for images of Bruneval had now filtered through to Benson, and the mission had been allocated to another of its squadrons. Subsequent legend held that Hill warned his rivals off flying anywhere near Bruneval, which he now regarded as 'his'. Be that as it may, and whether or not – as is sometimes alleged – ground personnel at the airfield questioned his right to take off, what is certain is that Tony Hill flew to France, captured a series of outstanding images of Bruneval, and returned safely. The pictures, examined by Jones and his colleagues, showed a dish-shaped aerial, obviously atop a Würzburg, smaller relation of the apparatus photographed at Berlin Zoo, of which in the months that followed Hill and his comrades would photograph more examples along the coast of the continent.

The manner in which Jones, aided by the several branches of British intelligence, identified this German radar, already constituted a thrilling and fascinating detective story. Yet developments thus far proved to represent only its first chapter. Scientific Intelligence made an informed guess that the enemy then deployed around four hundred Würzburgs, as a key element of their defences against intruding British fighters and bombers. Methods of countering the technology, they concluded, could be devised only following a physical examination of a set. Here was a vital enemy weapon, so near and yet so far from Reginald Jones. Or was it, instead, a case of so far and yet so near? To be sure, the radar site was located ninety miles from Britain, in Occupied Europe. But the little clifftop fishing hamlet of Bruneval lay at the very outer rim of Hitler's empire, on the Channel coast within a few minutes' flying time, a few hours' sailing, from Churchill's land. Might it be possible not merely to snatch images of a Würzburg, but to steal its secrets?

When Reg Jones and Charles Frank studied the PRU photos, the former traced his finger along a cliff defile, leading up from the narrow beach. 'Look, Charles,' he said eagerly. 'We could get in there!' A deep gully was marked on pre-war French maps as '*descent des anglais*'. Here was obviously a route by which, in times gone by, English smugglers, tourists, occasionally sailors and soldiers, had ventured in and out of France. This time, the track might be employed to reach up and snatch an enemy's jewels. Jones frankly admitted, though, that despite his natural impulsiveness he was at first reluctant to promote a raid. He recoiled from accepting responsibility for risking the lives of other men – the prospective raiders. Moreover, he was vain enough to take pride in his many successes judging the significance of new German technology by sheer brainpower, without the need to explore its physical properties.

Very soon after Jones started to flirt with the notion of raiding Bruneval, however, he chanced to meet Wilfrid 'Ben' Lewis, deputy superintendent of TRE, and an expert on Doppler effects. Lewis was yet another remarkable character, a thickset Cumbrian thirty-three at that time, who would later assume direction of Canada's nuclear research programme and become one of North America's most distinguished scientists. In 1941, he was preoccupied with improving radar-controlled night-fighter interception, as a means of defence against Luftwaffe bombers. Jones confided his musings about Bruneval, and what might be done there. The Cumbrian immediately responded: if a plan to assault the radar site and snatch its Würzburg was put forward, he and TRE would support it. This was an important conversation: it stirred Jones to take a next step. He put the idea to the Air Staff, and also mentioned Bruneval to Lord Cherwell; which meant, of course, that the prime minister became privy to it.

The outcome was that the Air Staff proposed an attack on Bruneval to Combined Operations HQ, directed by Commodore Lord Louis Mountbatten. It was almost a year since Jones and his colleagues had first spotted traces of the new German radar, and specifically of the Würzburg. The story had been slow to unfold. But in January 1942 Britain's capabilities by land, sea and air were significantly greater than they had been when Bletchley Park noticed in Luftwaffe signals mentions of a Nordic goddess and her kindred. Mountbatten the naval officer was panting for an opportunity to carry his war to the enemy, and embraced the proposal at once. His staff set to work, to translate Jones's fantasy into a plausible reality. An assault was discussed at the first of a series of conferences at COHQ in London's Richmond Terrace on 12 December 1941. Mountbatten chaired a 12 January meeting attended by all the possibly interested parties, to agree a draft scheme. Less than two weeks later, on 21 January 1942, an operational plan to assault Bruneval was submitted to the chiefs of staff. And approved.

2

Dickie

The raid on Bruneval became the most important operation of the war thus far to be launched by Churchill's piratical creation, Combined Operations. This had its inception on 4 June 1940. Amid the catastrophe of Dunkirk, Churchill wrote a memorandum to Maj. Gen. Hastings 'Pug' Ismay, his chief of staff, which afterwards became famous as an earnest of his burning commitment to offensive action, rather than mere reaction to German assaults. He began by saying it was right for Britain to be much preoccupied with the threat of a Nazi invasion, and to address this danger energetically: 'But ... some may feel inclined to ask the question – why should it be thought impossible to do anything of the same kind to [the Germans]? The completely defensive habit of mind, which has ruined the French, must not be allowed to ruin all our initiative.

'It is of the highest consequence to keep the large numbers of German forces [committed] all along the coasts of the countries they have conquered, and we should immediately set to work to organize raiding forces on these coasts where the populations are friendly ... What we have seen at Dunkirk shows how quickly troops can be moved off (and I suppose on) to selected points if need be. How wonderful it would be if the Germans could be made to wonder where they were going to be struck next, instead of forcing us to try to wall in the island and roof it over! An effort must be made to shake off the mental and moral prostration to the will and initiative of the enemy from which we suffer.'

Two days later, in the same vein, Churchill wrote: 'Enterprises must be prepared with specially-trained troops of the hunter class, who can develop a reign of terror down [enemy-occupied] coasts ... I look to the joint Chiefs of Staff to propose the measures for a vigorous, enterprising and ceaseless offensive against the whole German-occupied coastline.' Among the first fruits of the prime minister's musing was the appointment, on 14 June, of fifty-eight-year-old Royal Marine Lt. Gen. Alan Bourne as 'Commander of Raiding Operations on coasts in enemy occupation' and Adviser to the Chiefs of Staff on Combined Operations, with a headquarters in the Admiralty. At the same time the brilliant maverick Col. Dudley Clarke, who would later become celebrated as a master of deception in the desert, convinced army chief Gen. Sir John Dill that Britain needed a specialist raiding unit, of the kind Churchill characterized as 'men of the hunter class'. The first 'Commando' was formed, its name – suggested by the South Africa-reared Clarke – borrowed from that of the Boer guerrillas who had fought the British to such effect four decades earlier. On 23 June, Clarke himself led a pathetic little raid on the French coast, by men transported in RAF air-sea rescue launches. They landed at three points around Boulogne, killed two Germans and came close to terminating Clarke's own career when a careless friendly-fire bullet almost severed his ear. On 14 July another such venture failed against occupied Guernsey, with the loss of all those involved.

The prime minister said crossly: 'Let there be no more silly fiascoes like those perpetrated at Boulogne and Guernsey.'

Eight months would pass before the next such operation, during which Churchill pressed for action to form, arm and equip units capable of doing more serious damage to the Germans. As early as 22 June, impressed – indeed, much over-impressed – by the contribution of Luftwaffe paratroops to Hitler's conquest of the continent, he ordered the creation of a matching British force. On 7 July he likewise addressed the Ministry of Supply, asking what was being done to design and build landing-craft capable of carrying tanks. This last initiative produced vessels which, eventually copied by the US Navy, conveyed Allied armour into amphibious assaults through the victorious years of the war.

On 17 July Churchill decided that Gen. Bourne lacked the clout for his appointed role and replaced him at the head of Combined Ops with Admiral Sir Roger Keyes, a sixty-seven-year-old veteran of many battles. During the 1901 Boxer Rising this then-junior naval officer had forced a Chinese railway engine-driver to do his bidding by travelling on the footplate himself, holding a revolver at the man's ear. Keyes went on to become prime mover and director of the April 1918 naval raid on Zeebrugge. Churchill had always admired the admiral as a mischief-maker as well as a professional hero: the new chief had the stature and public image which Bourne lacked. One of Keyes's first initiatives was to demonstrate the independence of his old service by moving Combined Operations out of the Admiralty and into requisitioned houses in Richmond Terrace, a few steps across Whitehall from Downing Street. The veteran seadog, despite his age, was full of energy. In March 1941 his command mounted its first raid that was deemed a success, against Norway's German-occupied Lofoten Islands. But the old man at the head of Combined Ops was vain, petulant, quarrelsome. While famous for his courage, he was not equally celebrated for brains. Although Churchill was respectful of presumption and often tolerant of insubordination, he tired of Keyes's inability to work with others, and of his manifest lack of judgement.

The prime minister wanted Combined Ops to be led by a star, but he now acknowledged that such a figure should be identified with the current war, not the previous one. He cast around for a younger model than Keyes. In the autumn of 1941, Captain Lord Louis Mountbatten, destroyer leader and friend of Hollywood film stars, was in America waiting to put to sea once more, on the bridge of HMS *Illustrious*. This was the nation's finest aircraft-carrier, under repair in a US shipyard after suffering extensive bomb damage in the Mediterranean. The prime minister dispatched a signal to 'Dickie', as Mountbatten was universally known, demanding his immediate return to London, relinquishing command of *Illustrious*, to assume a role that his Downing Street admirer was confident would prove rewarding. To Churchill's irritation, the order did not prompt instant compliance. Mountbatten, with the serene self-confidence conferred by his semi-royal status as a great-grandson of Queen Victoria, said he could not drop everything and dash across the Atlantic. Pressed, he cited a pending invitation to a White House dinner. When he did catch a plane home, he used the president as an air-raid shelter from Churchillian wrath, having prompted Franklin Roosevelt to soothe Britain's 'former naval person' with assurances that Dickie had been most useful to him.

All this took place some weeks before Pearl Harbor and US entry into the war. Mountbatten finally presented himself at Chequers on 25 October 1941, when he learned of Churchill's intention to appoint him to succeed Keyes. He was blessed with matinee idol looks and boasted cousinship with King George

VI, together with charm, ambition and some intelligence, impaired by a childlike vanity. Born in 1900, he was the sort of professional hero whom the prime minister liked, advanced and was not infrequently deceived by. Yet Churchill was not wrong that glamour had a part to play in sustaining the spirit of peoples in adversity at war, and there was not much of it around: consider how the US government and chiefs of staff felt obliged to defer to that prince of charlatans, Gen. Douglas MacArthur, because he possessed star quality.

Now, however, Mountbatten with his usual hubris baulked at the prime minister's proposal. He asserted that he would prefer to remain afloat. Always in his mind was the ultimate ambition to become First Sea Lord. Churchill responded furiously: 'What can you hope to achieve, except to be sunk in a bigger and more expensive ship? Here, I give you a chance to take a part in the higher leadership of the war!' Churchill said that while the immediate role of Combined Operations was to organize mere raids, its ultimate and most important purpose was to prepare for the re-invasion of France, which would perforce become the greatest combined operation in history: 'You are to give no thought to the defensive. Your whole attention is to be concentrated on the offensive.'

Mountbatten allowed himself to be persuaded. Only afterwards was a title agreed, that of Commodore, Combined Operations, which meant a step in rank for him. He was crestfallen, however, to be briefed by the chiefs of staff about their own much less grandiose vision of his role: 'You are to be technical adviser on all aspects of, and at all stages in, the planning and training for combined operations.' The chiefs were determined to keep Mountbatten in his place. They failed, though, because the man himself declined to defer to mere rank and seniority. The prime minister's backing, reinforced by the new commodore's social attack and salesmanship, trumped mere service hierarchy.

Mountbatten would hereafter become one of the most famous British figures of World War II, though it is still disputed whether he was a substantial one. Adrian Smith, one of his biographers, has written: 'The Chief of Combined Operations always remained an agent, never a real player.' Mountbatten controlled no army, air force or fleet, beyond a few commandos and landing-craft. To implement its plans, his organization depended upon the goodwill of the three service chiefs to loan men, ships and planes on an operation-by-operation basis. Yet it is impossible to dispute the celebrity and influence which the new commodore achieved. Nobody, except perhaps his country's admirals, could deny that Dickie thrived under floodlights. If he lacked depth of intellect, he compensated with a driving enthusiasm that bore him far towards the greatness he craved. His ambition was given early impetus by the injustice done to his father, Admiral Prince Louis of Battenberg, deposed as First Sea Lord in 1914 because of his German lineage. Doubts persist whether Battenberg was, in reality, the great naval leader and strategist that his younger son – the family name changed amid conflict with Germany – claimed. Prince Louis was certainly badly treated, but the first-generation Mountbatten's own hunger for glory needed no stimulus of parental grievance to prompt him to try hard.

Bereft of any capacity for reflection, less still self-doubt, Mountbatten in his youth drove through the lower ranks of the Royal Navy like some advanced motor torpedo-boat under uncertain control. After World War I service as a midshipman in Beatty's battlecruiser *Lion*, he became a lieutenant with a reputation for technical efficiency and ease in handling men. Close friendship with Edward, then Prince of Wales, together with a 1922 marriage to Edwina Ashley, possessor of a vast fortune as granddaughter of Edwardian financier Sir Ernest Cassel, earned suspicion and resentment from some colleagues and superiors, as did his playboy lifestyle off duty, among a louche, racy social set.

On the polo field, as a pilot, as a seaman, success did not come to him from natural genius. Instead he hauled himself up the Royal Navy through professional dedication, an infinite capacity for taking pains. Critics of his nightlife could scarcely fault an officer who never failed on duty to give of his utmost; who passed out top of his specialist signals course and displayed a passionate interest in new technology. His courage was matched only by lust for recognition. 'What an opportunity for anyone to earn an Albert Medal!' he wrote in frustration after a young seaman fell overboard from *Warspite* and drowned while he himself was unluckily below. 'Wish I'd been on deck.'

Mountbatten adored being rich – his wife inherited the equivalent of £100 million in modern money at a time when his naval pay was £610 a year – and indulged himself in servants, cars, boats, homes. His London bedroom was remodelled to resemble a naval officer's cabin, with a porthole which revealed a diorama of Malta's Grand Harbour, featuring model ships that could signal to each other. When this atrocity was completed, he held a press viewing which confirmed his seniors' view that Mountbatten was no gentleman, as the Royal Navy understood the word, but instead a cad and bounder not unlike Beatty, the great naval star – though by no means naval genius – of the previous generation.

Dickie and Edwina's weekend guests at Broadlands, their stately home in Hampshire, were issued each evening with a proforma which they were obliged to fill out and return to the staff, saying what they wished to do on the following morning and afternoon. A second docket invited them to indent for available cars, horses, boats, fishing facilities. No extravagance was too vulgar, no presumption excessive, that enabled Mountbatten to boost a polo team, win a race, secure a medal or gain an appointment.

Mountbatten weathered the 1936 Abdication Crisis without being compelled to make the dangerous gesture of serving as best man at the now-Duke of Windsor's subsequent wedding to Wallis Simpson, though he was loyal enough to offer. His social and political connections were unmatched, fostered by lavish hospitality in London and Hampshire. Admirals not infrequently found themselves being wined and dined by young Captain Mountbatten on a sybaritic scale which they would have been less than human not to find irksome. His severest critics were drawn from his own Service. Nor was their disdain the product of mere social exasperation.

'He possesses a naïve simplicity combined with a compelling manner and dynamic energy,' declared his 1938 confidential report on completing a posting at the Admiralty. 'His interests incline mainly towards the material world and he is, therefore, inclined to be surprised at the unexpected; he has been so successful in that sphere that he does not contemplate failure. His social assets are invaluable in any rank to any Service. His natural thoroughness is extended to sport. Desirable as it is to avoid superlatives, he has *nearly*' – [author's emphasis] – 'all the qualities and qualifications for the highest commands.'

Noel Coward's feature film *In Which We Serve*, which was being shot at Denham Studios even as preparations were made for the assault on Bruneval, made Mountbatten and his destroyer *Kelly* famous, though both their experience and the names were lightly fictionalized. Noel adored Dickie, saying, 'He is a pretty wonderful man, I think.' Years later Mountbatten wrote disingenuously to his thespian friend, looking back: 'I have been greatly criticised, chiefly among my brother officers, for being a party to the making of a film which was apparently designed to boost me personally.' It was assuredly true that Mountbatten himself never tired of screenings, hosting one in Richmond Terrace for COHQ's staff. On such occasions, he kept up a running commentary for audiences, not least a party at Buckingham Palace that included Mrs Eleanor Roosevelt, about the personal history on which the film was based.

Yet his record in command of *Kelly* was at best exceedingly unlucky. When he drove the ship gratuitously fast in heavy seas she was struck by a wave which heeled her fifty degrees to starboard, inflicting severe damage and almost causing her to founder. Repairs were scarcely completed before the destroyer hit a mine in the mouth of the Tyne. After eleven weeks in dry dock, she emerged to be badly damaged in a collision with another warship. In the Norwegian campaign, *Kelly* was torpedoed and almost sunk after rashly using her signal lamp at night in hostile waters. When Churchill – always Dickie's friend, as well as then First Lord of the Admiralty – sought the award of a DSO to her captain for getting the crippled ship home, the navy would have none of it. The C-in-C Home Fleet wrote acidly that 'owing to a series of misfortunes ... *Kelly* had only been to sea for 57 days during the war, and that any other captain would have done the same'.

In the Mediterranean, Mountbatten incurred severe criticism from his C-in-C Admiral Andrew Cunningham for his performance in the days before *Kelly* was finally sunk by German aircraft: 'The trouble with your flotilla, boy,' the merciless 'ABC' later told one of Mountbatten's subordinates, 'is that it was thoroughly badly led.' Philip Ziegler, Dickie's best biographer, declares this a harsh judgement but himself agrees that

'Mountbatten was not a good flotilla leader. It is perhaps not too fanciful to compare his performance on the bridge with his prowess behind the wheel of a car. He was a fast and dangerous driver.'

Mountbatten's sexuality was an object of speculation among his contemporaries and to posterity. Edwina never provided him with the intimate companionship for which he yearned, though she acted out impeccably the public role of consort when, as was increasingly often the case, her husband appeared on platforms, under spotlights. He himself later said: 'Edwina and I spent all our married lives getting into other people's beds.' It was certainly true that Lady Mountbatten boasted a legion of lovers, yet Ziegler comments of her husband: 'He conducted at least two protracted love-affairs [with women] outside his marriage, to the apparent satisfaction of both parties, but he was never promiscuous. Though he liked to imagine himself a sexual athlete, he seems to have had in reality only slight enthusiasm for the sport ... if asked to choose between seduction by the most desirable of houris and a conversation on service matters with a senior officer of influence, he would unfailingly have chosen the latter.' There has been gossip that he was a closet gay, but ambition was surely too dominant a force for him to have risked a sexual scandal which, in those days, must have been terminal. He was certainly an extreme narcissist. He seems unlikely, however, to have indulged in active homosexuality.

After the loss of *Kelly* in May 1941, Mountbatten toured America describing his experiences, both in public and in private, to US leaders. He enjoyed a huge success. Americans always liked him, responding to the showmanship that sometimes irked his compatriots. It did no harm that he was sort-of-royal and could have been auditioning for Hollywood;

and that he, in his turn, appreciated Roosevelt's people. One of his strongest cards, when he reached the highest ranks, was that he empathized with Americans as most upper-crust British men did not.

On arrival in Richmond Terrace to take up his role at Combined Ops, he inherited a staff of only twenty-three. This he expanded exponentially, with Combined Ops spilling out of its poky headquarters to occupy most of nearby Scotland Yard. The chiefs of staff were wary of him from the outset, and dismissed many of the CCO's wild proposals as unrealistic. But Dickie's rhino-hide skin preserved him from being bruised by the snubs and put-downs of generals, admirals and air marshals. He commanded the support of the man who mattered, the prime minister. He set about establishing Combined Operations as the film set on which not only would heroic deeds be enacted for the benefit of the British war effort, but these would also elevate the fame and fortune of himself, their executive producer.

Philip Ziegler wrote: 'Mountbatten delighted in the planning of these adventures, took an interest in every detail and fretted obsessively while they were in progress … The more outrageous the methods used, the more he relished them.' A raid on Brest was once being discussed, involving the landing of tanks and the rolling of depth charges into the dry dock. A staff officer who recoiled from such an assured bloodbath said wearily: 'Let's forget about all this nonsense and catch the 5.15 from St Malo!' The commodore promptly seized on this as a wonderful idea, calling for a plan to hijack a train and drive it to Brest's harbourside.

It became a persistent gibe in the corridors of uniformed power that Mountbatten's outfit was a mere tennis match – 'all rackets and balls'. Many able officers were reluctant to join its staff, seeing it as a career cul-de-sac. A senior army functionary, Col. Cyril Lloyd, observed to Robert Bruce Lockhart that while he liked Mountbatten personally, 'the PM is ruining him by exalting him in the way he has done. His position has been made impossible with the Chiefs of Staff and the service departments generally, and his own staff is the laughing stock of London.'

Mountbatten could be ungenerous, even vindictive, to subordinates not on his favourites' list. He appointed Sir Harold Wernher, a brother-in-law twice removed, as 'Controller of Ministry and Service Facilities'. Churchill grumbled: 'Isn't he some sort of relation of yours?' Mountbatten, unabashed, responded tartly: 'Not so close as Duncan Sandys' – a Churchill son-in-law newly appointed to government office – 'is to you.' Wernher proved one of the commodore's most successful appointments, but others were much less inspired. He chose as his chief of intelligence 'Bobby' Marquis de Casa Maury, for which this pre-war polo crony's credentials were hard to discern. Casa Maury was a forty-five-year-old Cuban-Spanish aristocrat who had owned the Curzon cinema in Mayfair. After an earlier divorce he married Freda Dudley Ward, long-serving mistress of the Duke of Windsor when Prince of Wales. The Casa Maurys now occupied a grand house in Hamilton Terrace, St John's Wood.

A well-known racing driver before the war, the marquis had also become an RAF reservist. He was serving as an intelligence officer at West Country fighter stations when Mountbatten plucked him forth to join his own court at COHQ. Casa Maury inspired mistrust among the intelligence organizations as an outsider and foreigner, acknowledged to the man himself by Brigadier Robert Laycock, later Mountbatten's successor as CCO – and, incidentally, married to Freda Casa Maury's daughter Angie – as 'a wholly irrational prejudice against you in that you are a marquis and your name is … not Smith, Jones or Robinson'. Casa Maury was now accorded a leading role in planning the Bruneval raid.

Here was evidence to support the worst charge against Mountbatten, which would dog him until the end of his life: that he clogged his entourage with toadies and favourites, among whom Casa Maury's name was often mentioned; and that he was obsessed with his own self-aggrandizement. Alan Brooke wrote of Mountbatten's contribution that 'he certainly played a remarkable role as the driving force and mainspring' of Combined Operations, but the CIGS adopted a harsh view of Mountbatten's subsequent appointment to the Chiefs of Staff Committee: 'There was no justification for this move … he frequently wasted both his own time and ours … at times he was apt to concern himself with matters outside his sphere … The title "Chief of Combined Operations" was also badly chosen, since every operation we were engaged in was a "combined" one.' Harold Macmillan reflected on Mountbatten years later: 'A strange character … who tries to combine being a professional sailor, a politician and a royalty. The result is that nobody trusts him.'

Yet among those who could forgive his defects, Mountbatten inspired respect and loyalty as well as affection. Whatever the sailor lacked as a director of military or naval operations, he sought to make good by a genius for public relations. At this stage of the war, when Britain stood inescapably on the strategic defensive, it was important to create at least a façade of activity, attack, initiative. In the winter of 1941, it is hard to imagine anyone better-suited to do this than Mountbatten, though it was much less assured that he was fit to bear responsibility for men's lives in action.

He worked enormously hard, often sleeping in the office – as also, to do him justice, did his friend Casa Maury. He showed an imagination that, if often fantastic – for instance, his later enthusiasm for Habakkuk, an iceberg aircraft-carrier – was an antidote to the congenital pessimism that afflicted many of Britain's service directors, including Alan Brooke. In the first months after the United States entered the struggle and began to work with British brass, Roosevelt's service chiefs displayed grave doubts about whether they had entered the right war with the right ally. Thus, the value should not be underestimated of the liking and respect that Mountbatten generated among Americans. US general Al Wedemeyer accompanied George Marshall on an early 1942 visit to Britain, and wrote later: 'Mountbatten was by all odds the most colourful on the British Chiefs of Staff level. He was charming, tactful, a conscious knight in shining armor, handsome, bemedalled, with a tremendous amount of self-assurance. Because of his youthfulness ... it was obvious that the older officers did not defer readily to his views. They were careful, however, to give him a semblance of courteous attention. After all, he was a cousin of the King and, no doubt about it, a great favourite of the Prime Minister.'

Churchill wrote to Admiral Sir Dudley Pound, as chairman of the chiefs of staff, about Mountbatten: 'I want him to exercise influence upon the war as a whole, upon future planning in its broadest sense; upon the concert of the three Arms and their relation to the maintaining of strategy; upon Combined Operations in the largest sense, not only those specific Operations which his own organization will execute.'

Later in the struggle, indeed later in 1942, Mountbatten's tenure at Combined Operations would be permanently tarnished, his reputation justly scarred, by the disastrous raid on Dieppe. But ten months earlier, when he assumed his role, that failure lay in the future. Both Dickie and his embryo organization had everything to play for. Beyond recruiting personnel and touring training facilities, with his usual diplomatic skills he wooed Hugh Dalton, the minister of economic warfare who was responsible for the Special Operations Executive. Dalton envied Mountbatten's privileged relationship with the chiefs of staff, and his later membership of their committee, but he, too, found himself seduced by Dickie's famous charm.

Naval capability, and above all the means to convey troops to a hostile shore, would obviously be a key element of Combined Operations. The boat-builders Thornycrofts were commissioned to create some prototype shallow-draught landing-craft, forty feet long, constructed from mahogany then armour-plated, with a maximum speed of ten knots. The new organization also acquired several former cross-Channel ferries including *Prins Albert*, a 370-foot-long, 3,000-ton Belgian vessel capable of twenty-two knots, which could carry eight landing-craft and 250 troops, and became mother ship for the embryo flotilla. A base and training centre was established in the Household Brigade Yacht Club at the mouth of the River Hamble in Hampshire, which by 1942 had become home to almost a thousand personnel 'terrifically keen', in the words of their CO, most of whose officers were amateur yachtsmen posted immediately on completion of a brief naval indoctrination at the shore training base HMS *King Alfred*. They acquired an assortment of vessels, and exercised mostly with requisitioned leisure craft.

A thirty-seven-year-old lieutenant-commander, seconded from the Royal Australian Navy, was appointed to direct the base and its operations. He christened it HMS *Tormentor*, with a flea his curious choice for its crest, justified by Combined Operations' supposed mandate to make the Germans itch. Fred

Cook from Victoria became a naval cadet at thirteen. Since the war started, on secondment to the Royal Navy he had been among just four hundred survivors following U-47's October 1939 torpedoing of the battleship *Royal Oak* in Scapa Flow. Seven months later, he was serving as second-in-command of the light cruiser *Curlew* when she too was sunk, by German air attack off Norway. Soon after that experience, he was posted to the embryo Combined Ops, where his enthusiasm won warm approval. He first met Mountbatten in November 1941, when the new commodore came down to watch landing-craft exercises in the Solent. Later, Cook designed what became the badge of Combined Operations, featuring an albatross borrowed from the Australian Air Force crest, a tommy gun and a RAN-pattern kedge anchor.

Combined Ops' first significant action under Mountbatten's direction was mounted in the last days of December 1941. Army commandos paid a return visit to the Norwegian coast, briefly occupying the islands of Vaagso and Maaloy, where they wrecked German facilities, killed some enemy soldiers and brought home to England scores of Norwegian volunteers for the Allied forces. The raid was noisy and disorganized, but yielded a propaganda success, at a cost of modest casualties. Churchill was not impressed, however, writing testily to Ismay on 7 January that it 'must be judged a marked failure, as it was abandoned hastily and without any facts being apparent which were not foreseen at the time of its inception'.

Even less happy was Operation Flipper, a November commando assault on Rommel's supposed headquarters in North Africa, though planned by Eighth Army in Cairo rather than in Richmond Terrace. The iconic commander of the Afrika Korps proved to be elsewhere. Roger Keyes's son Geoffrey was among the casualties, apparently accidentally shot dead by one of his own men, a mishap compensated by a posthumous Victoria Cross. It was widely felt in the army that the decoration was designed to make everybody feel better about a fiasco, not the first or last time a VC has been awarded under such circumstances.

But such pinprick operations as these failed to fulfil Churchill's intemperate demands for European coastal action, such as would seriously trouble the Boche, the World War I term by which he often referred to the enemy. The Air Ministry produced a mildly facetious memorandum, explaining how Combined Operations was to work with the three services. 'Procedure: CCO [Mountbatten] has bright idea and discusses with Commanders or Commands concerned. Commands submit their comments on feasibility or otherwise.' 'Otherwise' would feature extensively in Whitehall debate during the months and years that followed. Mountbatten and his staff rummaged for ideas; planned furiously. They were obliged to discard a score of fanciful schemes that exasperated Churchill's senior officers without ever coming to the attention of Hitler's generals and admirals.

A cheeky staff officer composed a doggerel which, to the commodore's credit, he himself sometimes quoted:

Mountbatten was a likely lad,
A nimble brain Mountbatten had,
And this most amiable trait:
Of each new plan which came his way
He'd always claim in accents pat
'Why, I myself invented that!'
Adding when he remembered it,
For any scoffer's benefit,
Roughly the point in his career

When he'd conceived the bright idea,
As 'August 1934'
Or 'Some time during the Boer War'.

Then in December 1941 the Air Staff, at the behest of Reg Jones and the Telecommunications Research Establishment, offered Combined Ops its proposal for an assault on Bruneval; the kidnapping of a Würzburg. As soon as Dickie heard of it, he loved it. When the chiefs of staff signed off the mission, in January 1942, the CCO hastened to mobilize means to launch the operation. It would need planes, ships. And a revolutionary force in warfare: paratroops.

3

Boy

As he traced the defile at Bruneval with his fingertip on Tony Hill's sensational photo, Reg Jones had said to his assistant Charles Frank, 'We could get in there', and Mountbatten's first impulse was similar. The moment his planners set to work, however, they were obliged to tell their nautically-minded commodore that a seaborne assault was 'not on'. German troops guarded the coast and radar site. They had enjoyed eighteen months of occupation in which to entrench, wire and probably mine the Channel approach. If British troops landed on the beach below Bruneval, they would be dead long before they could scale its cliff or force a passage up its narrow ascent path.

The only credible method of attacking the installation would be to deliver men by air and by night atop the high white cliff on which the Würzburg stood. Somebody pointed out that even the Germans, pioneers of parachute warfare, had never attempted an operational drop in darkness, but the leaders of Britain's new airborne forces believed such an assault now to be within the powers of their own men. If the attackers achieved surprise, they might overrun the position; hold it while engineers stripped the radar set of its vital components, then descend the defile to make their escape to the beach, for a rendezvous with Mountbatten's landing-craft.

A huge amount of luck would be needed to get a force in, then keep it ashore for two or three hours, without the Germans rallying their considerable local strength to overwhelm it. But Churchill was eager, Mountbatten was enthusiastic, and there was impatience to test in battle Britain's parachute soldiers, men of the embryo Airborne Division. This was led by another famous figure of those times, Major-General Frederick Browning. 'Boy', as he was known within the army, anticipated his own and his formation's first hour of glory quite as eagerly as did Dickie Mountbatten that of Combined Ops.

At the inauguration of Browning's command, in the autumn of 1941, his formation's staff was dubbed by their chief 'the Dungeon Party', because its officers spent some weeks in office accommodation two floors beneath Westminster's King Charles Street, before removing to cheerier quarters. Until Churchill assumed the premiership, the British armed forces' experience of parachuting related solely to its usefulness as a means of escape from a doomed aircraft. Even this was a concession to modernity brought into general service by the RAF only after 1918. While the 'Great War' was being fought, though German pilots were equipped with parachutes and occasionally enjoyed opportunities to use them, among their British counterparts only observation balloon crews were issued with these indulgences. Such equipment, commanders reasoned fantastically, might if universally provided encourage 'windy' airmen in action to abandon their cockpits prematurely.

In the 1930s the British Army learned that the Russians and Germans had created substantial bodies of paratroops, but took no steps to emulate them. Airborne units demanded extravagant resources, not least of scarce aircraft. They must perforce be lightly armed, and thus vulnerable, especially as they descended. Once on the ground, they could move no faster than their feet would carry them. As the ground forces expanded sluggishly, there seemed many higher priorities.

Then, in the summer of 1940, Britain's dominant warlord committed himself to airborne warfare, just as he embraced combined operations. Churchill ordered that the army should form 'a corps of at least five thousand parachute troops'. The War Office decreed the creation of a specialist training centre, the Central Landing Establishment. It was to be located at Ringway, near Manchester, chosen because it was far removed from the coastlines threatened with invasion, and no impediment to the busiest fighter and bomber airfields of southern and eastern England. Its first RAF commander was baronet Sir Nigel Norman, a reserve officer whose considerable gifts had been deployed before the war on the design and construction of civil airports, including Gatwick and Birmingham. Unfortunately, however, Ringway was plagued by its region's poor weather. During the ensuing years many training days would be lost when low cloud or high winds made parachuting impossible. The school's early months were also dogged by resistance from the Air Ministry to the provision of dedicated aircraft, and by a lack of enthusiasm among senior soldiers for yet another new gimmick which the erratic prime minister had wished upon them. John Frost wrote long afterwards: 'The endemic trouble with British Airborne Forces was that the Army never really believed in them.'

On the airfield, after some frightful early accidents, several of them fatal, order slowly evolved from confusion. Nothing, though, could alter the fact that time-expired Whitley bombers, which were all the air marshals would allocate to Ringway, were little suited to dropping parachutists. Their construction required that men exit from a hatch cut in the floor, to avoid hitting the plane's double tail boom. A careless jumper struck his teeth on the rear lip of the aircraft's 'arsehole', with painful consequences – a so-called 'Whitley kiss'. Men with false teeth, of whom there were then many, were debarred from service because it was thought these must be lost in a drop. Only much later in the war did the superb American C-47 Dakota, with a door exit matching that on the German Junkers Ju-52, become available in quantity, and dominate 1943–45 airborne operations.

The RAF assumed responsibility for teaching soldiers to parachute. This was seldom less than a nerve-racking, because life-threatening, activity. While all US Army paratroopers carried reserve 'chutes strapped to their chests, British wartime jumpers did not. A 'roman candle' – the compacted silk cylinder beneath which a man found himself descending at literally breakneck speed when an ill-packed canopy failed to deploy – was not survivable. Once, after exiting the hole an officer's rigging lines became entangled in the plane. All efforts to retrieve him failed and in the end the pilot flew as slowly as possible out over the sea, where he was cut loose 'in the hope that he would not hit the water too hard'. This flash of optimism proved unjustified.

Ringway's RAF instructors nonetheless developed a fine reputation for skill, courage and powers of reassurance. Almost none of that generation of trainees had previously taken to the skies, even as aircraft passengers, before they embarked on airborne training. Yet now, on their first ventures above the ground, they were invited to quit first a balloon cage – for the two initial jumps of the training course – and five times thereafter an aircraft in mid-flight.

Before the war was ended, Ringway's instructors came to include former schoolmasters, professional footballers, boxers;

a cycle champion and a circus acrobat; a 'Wall of Death' motorcyclist and a ballet dancer. One instructor accumulated a score of fourteen hundred descents, including sixteen in a single day, setting an unbroken record. Their senior officer, F/Lt. John Kilkenny, dubbed 'ringmaster of Kilkenny's circus', was himself a veteran of sixty-eight jumps.

This tall, thin, faintly camp but fatherly ex-NCO became famous to successive classes of trainees. He introduced them to airborne warfare with an enthusiastic oration before they made their first descent, from a captive balloon winched upwards until four hundred feet above the airfield: 'Gentlemen, someone once described parachute-jumping as "dicing with death" in the skies, a frightful phrase, quite apart from being grossly untrue. You simply do exactly the same as you [have practised in ground training], the only difference being that you have a parachute and there's a bit farther to fall. I have it on good authority that our parachutes are good ones – they ought to be, at sixty quid apiece. I know that tomorrow you'll jump simply beautifully out of the balloon … It's a piece of cake. One final word of advice. This neighbourhood is rich in pubs, and it's quite easy just by walking the hundred yards to the [civil] airport to get very drunk. Do so by all means, but not the night before a jump. That's all – and good jumping tomorrow!'

The army's initial paratroop unit was one of the newly-formed army Commandos, No. 2, which was arbitrarily rebranded as the '11th Special Air Service' battalion – usage that pre-dated Lt. Col. David Stirling's later appropriation of the title in the North African desert. Because the new art was perceived as at best exotic, at worst highly dangerous, it was decreed that all those who jumped must be volunteers. A rule was introduced that any man who, during training, decided in a balloon cage or aircraft that he could not go through with a descent should be permitted to return to his former unit without disgrace. This was a privilege of which thirty trainees availed themselves during Ringway's first months. On school flights ever since an occasional pupil has flinched, when confronted with the vacant sky beyond the aircraft door – refusals in a given 'stick' or sequence of jumpers can be infectious. Once a man completed the course, however, and became a qualified parachutist with embroidered wings sewn beneath the shoulder of his tunic, it was a court-martial offence to refuse to jump, because of the disastrous disruption such conduct must inflict upon an operation. British Army parachutists were paid a cash bonus for each of their early descents, and then received a small addition to their pay for having secured the qualification, just as they did for passing an Arabic or Gurkhali exam.

An early parachutist described an exit from a Whitley, seized by the slipstream and momentarily dragged horizontal: 'It simply and almost, it seems, apologetically, whisks you away from the plane on the end of your parachute ... Then, if you are the right way up, your legs are whipped up so that you seem likely to kick your own nose, and you feel as if your fall has been arrested by a giant hand grabbing your braces.' A Grenadier officer reported on his first jump, with fellow officer Henry Wright. After leaping from the aircraft, he wrote, 'the next recollection I have is of Major Wright with parachute open and canopy fully filled, some one hundred and fifty feet above me. My parachute, sir, had not then fully opened, and I had the gravest doubt as to whether it would function before it had been repacked. I was unable to devise a method of repacking it in the limited time at my disposal. As I was also unable to think of any satisfactory means of assisting the contraption to perform the functions which I had been led to suppose were automatic, in my submission I had no alternative but to fall earthwards at, I believe, the rate of thirty-two feet per second, accelerating to the maximum speed of one hundred and seventy-six feet per second ... This I did ... And having dropped a certain distance, my parachute suddenly opened, and I made a very light landing.'

And so to battle. In February 1941 thirty-eight officers and men were dropped in southern Italy to destroy the Tragino aqueduct, which supplied water to two million Italians. This was a mildly absurd operation, codenamed Colossus, conceived chiefly to revive the flagging morale of 1st Parachute Battalion – then still known as 11th Special Air Service – whose soldiers were weary of an idleness which had corroded their spirit. The raid achieved little: damage to the aqueduct was swiftly repaired; all but one of the paratroopers was captured. Their Italian interpreter, a forty-five-year-old former head waiter at London's Savoy Hotel named Fortunato Picchi, was most unfortunately shot as a traitor to Italy, though a naturalized Briton. Churchill's people, when informed of Colossus, were impressed to learn that their armed forces had acquired some parachutists, even if the mission had been less than an unqualified success. The Tragino aqueduct assault was an exercise in public relations rather than strategy, but served its limited purpose in keeping alive hopes that the British Army might usefully build a corps of paratroops, and that it was not wholly inactive, beyond the North African desert.

By November 1941 No.1 Parachute Training School, as the Manchester base was now known, qualified a hundred jumpers a week, their right shoulders adorned with coveted 'wings', though a substantial proportion found graduation delayed by suffering landing injuries. One trainee wrote later: 'The RAF at Ringway, from the station commander to the lowliest aircraftsman, extend a welcome to would-be parachutists that is probably unique in the three services. In the surrounding pubs they are feted. Yet it is not so difficult to understand. The men who go there are under few illusions about the type of war they are going to. The fact that they have chosen one of the most dangerous ways of going to the war explains the willingness of the RAF instructors to make the preparation for this solemn undertaking as pleasant as possible. We noticed this most forcibly in the dining hall. At our first dinner we were confronted not by odiferous stew and sour-faced army cooks but instead by delectably cooked meals that looked, smelt and tasted excellent, served by young women in white overalls and coquettish chefs' caps ... They smiled with a serenity that was a joy to behold, and dispensed second helpings with a goodwill that was nothing short of amazing.'

Those were the days before the Parachute Regiment was formally embodied: its maroon beret would be introduced only in November 1942. Meanwhile volunteers for airborne service retained the headgear of their former regiments, including the bonnets of Scottish units. In September 1941, 11th SAS was abruptly redesignated 1st Parachute Battalion, founding element of 1 Para Brigade, which soon also acquired a second battalion. The men's new allegiance was distinguished merely by shoulder lanyards of different colours, that of 2 Para being yellow.

In October 1941, Frederick Browning was appointed to command what was to become a full-blown airborne division, of mixed parachute and gliderborne units, and thereafter expand to corps strength. A Guardsman to his fingertips, for the next three years Browning would play a central role in the development of Britain's sky warrior force. Most immediately, he acted as a guiding influence on the Bruneval raid, selecting and training the men to execute it. His staff, in conjunction with Mountbatten's people in Richmond Terrace, took over detailed planning for the ground assault and subsequent withdrawal to the beach, where the navy, in the person of Fred Cook, would become responsible for their escape back across the Channel.

Most wartime histories which feature Browning focus upon his service record, mentioning as an aside that he was married to the novelist Daphne du Maurier, author of *Rebecca* and other great romantic bestsellers. Yet their relationship was extraordinary, and influenced the general he became, at the climax of an enduringly enigmatic life. Never less than flawlessly turned out, he was viewed by his contemporaries as the pattern of a Guards officer: decisive, assured, patrician, brave. But the outer man masked one of the most complex and indeed troubled personalities ever to reach high command.

Born in 1896, to a successful wine merchant father, he grew up in a large house behind Harrods store in Knightsbridge. He passed through Eton and Sandhurst – for which he failed the entrance exam before being admitted thanks to Grenadier regimental influence – then in 1915 joined a battalion in France. After only two months on the Western Front in which nothing especially memorable or terrible happened to him, Browning was invalided home under circumstances that have never been explained, diagnosed with nervous exhaustion. The cause appears to have been a condition known in the family as 'Tommy's tum' – at home 'Tommy' was his nickname. At irregular intervals throughout his childhood, he was convulsed by agonizing stomach pains. These eventually receded, as they did in the course of 1916. In September that year, Browning was again passed fit for service, and returned to France. He found that only six of those with whom he had served a year earlier were still in the line: his absence had spared him from participation in the summer bloodbaths of the Somme.

The ensuing year was – by the murderous standard of the Western Front – for him relatively uneventful. Everything changed, however, at the end of 1917, season of Passchendaele. Browning's battalion was committed to seize a German position, Gauche Wood, across an open field. Casualties were devastating. He, still only a lieutenant, found himself sole unwounded survivor among seventeen officers. He assumed direction of the remains of three companies, which deployed on the left end of the wood after five hours of fierce hand-to-hand fighting. They repelled a German counter-attack and endured devastating incoming shellfire before being relieved. Browning received a DSO, and for the rest of his career enjoyed a hero's reputation, which erased comrades' memories of his peculiar 1916 medical travails, such as might have condemned a private soldier of that era to the glasshouse, or worse.

Yet the emotional scars of Gauche Wood never healed. For the rest of Browning's life he suffered what is now known as post-traumatic stress. Though always attractive to women, after the war he seemed unable to form lasting relationships: the 'right girl' eluded him. In the autumn of 1931 he was a thirty-four-year-old major passing his leave sailing with a fellow bachelor officer along the south-west coast in his twenty-foot cruiser *Ygdrasil*, when one evening they tied up at a mooring off Fowey in Cornwall. They were observed from the shore by twenty-four-year-old Daphne du Maurier, a budding novelist, who was completing one of many idyllic summers in that haven, writing *The Progress of Julius*, a quite extraordinary work for a young woman to have created, a bleak tale of a heartless monster.

Du Maurier was struck by Browning's dark good looks. But, contrary to the plot of a proper romantic yarn, the couple did not meet to speak on that trip, nor indeed until the following April. When they did so, she was smitten. Browning possessed both the physical attributes and apparently dominant personality which she demanded from a man. Though she had already had several affairs, she always struggled to define her own sexuality – and, come to that, her rightful gender. Now Browning seemed to meet all her requirements, and she made plain her eagerness to go to bed with him.

This prompted a new twist in the couple's courtship: confronted by a beautiful and fascinating young woman one of whose novels he had already chanced to read, the major turned her down – to borrow P.G. Wodehouse's phrase – like a blanket. Affairs, Browning said, were 'sleazy'. 'Nice girls' didn't do 'it'. Du Maurier's difficulty was that she had always despised 'nice girls'. She realized, however, that she must have Browning on his terms, or not at all. Three weeks after they met, she wrote to a friend: 'He is the best-looking thing I have ever seen, lives for boats and all the things I live for … He is one of these people with terrific "ideals" and I'm scared of giving him a shock.'

During the weeks that followed, the besotted du Maurier sought in vain to persuade the Grenadier officer of the joys of Bohemian romance. He, on the other hand, 'is trying to teach me that those ways of living are messy and stupid and very, very young'. It had to be marriage – or nothing: 'It will take at least five brandy-and-sodas, sloe gin and a handkerchief of ethers to push me to the altar rail.' Yet in the summer of 1932, the romantic novelist herself proposed to the major – and was accepted, once he recovered from the shock of finding Daphne seizing the initiative. Friends who asked her father Sir Gerald, the famous theatrical actor-manager, how he felt about the alliance were told of his relief: 'My dears, I am delighted – I thought she would have had a baby with a Cornish fisherman by now!'

Their subsequent marriage was notably complex but intermittently happy, though she never reconciled herself to the army. She 'couldn't see the sense in military life ... bugles and khaki and people yelling all the time and saluting'. 'Tommy', however, was 'the most charming person in the world'. They were not rich, because the Browning family money had vanished in the 1929 crash. Fortunately, though, Daphne's novels were already on a path to achieving the bestsellerdom which she craved. Her income dramatically raised the bridegroom's standard of living.

Emotional issues nonetheless persisted. She wrote to her mother: 'I feel I mustn't leave Tommy too much ... He has these awful nervy fits of misery, ten times worse than Daddy's old horrors; all harking back to that beastly war ... He clings to me just like a terrified little boy, so pathetic, it wrings one's heart.' She noted the contrast between Major Tommy at Pirbright, his tunic blazing with medals, barking out orders, and the sobbing retarded adolescent who sought solace in the night – a comfort which she found hard to provide, because she had always recoiled from acquiring emotional dependants. In the words of her biographer: 'She wanted what she thought she had married, an utterly self-reliant war hero, somebody calm, solid and stable ... The nurturing side of Daphne was almost non-existent and it horrified her to have any kind of care demanded of her.'

She described Tommy's departures for duty as being like those of 'a miserable boy being sent to school'. She also shrank from his enthusiasm for stately home weekends, when she wanted only to mess about in boats. She scorned the duties of an army wife: 'Can you picture me going around the married quarters and chatting up forty different women? "And how is the leg, Mrs Skinner?" "Dear little Freddie, what a fine boy he is" (this to a swollen-faced object obviously suffering from mumps).' In 1936, when she wrote her first big bestseller *Jamaica Inn*, Tommy was commanding his battalion. In the following year, she began to create *Rebecca* while enduring misery as the now colonel's wife during an Egyptian posting.

The approach to war found her a stellar literary success on both sides of the Atlantic, while her husband raged at the unpreparedness of the British Army and the 'incompetent nincompoops at the War Office'. Only Winston Churchill, he told Daphne, understood the nation's unfitness to fight. He himself was once again suffering attacks of 'Tommy's tum', of which she was impatient, just as her shortcomings as a homemaker irritated him. In the autumn of 1940, when Browning was commanding an infantry brigade, she wrote to a friend confessing her recent behaviour had been that of 'a sour old army wife in an Indian hill station, who has a disapproving eye on all gaiety'. Yet she and Tommy had been less than ten years married. She began to conduct a flirtation, which in the summer of 1941 turned into an infatuation, with Christopher Puxley, owner of the big house in which the Brownings were billeted, even as she penned another huge literary success, *Frenchman's Creek*.

It was not easy for a woman to be at ease with an ambitious, thrusting, energetic army officer preoccupied with his own role in a world war, even as she herself became alienated from all these things. She wanted only peace, Cornwall, her children and especially her new-born son, together with her rightful existence as a writer. According to her biographer: 'She didn't understand half the things he talked about, and some of the tasks allotted to him were so secret he couldn't talk about them anyway. But she knew, all the same, how very important Tommy was becoming, and what a Herculean task he had just been given – the formation of First Airborne Division.'

Even as the Bruneval raid was incubating, a domestic melodrama unfolded. Christopher Puxley's wife Paddy discovered her husband in the arms of Daphne. Soon afterwards, and inevitably, the Brownings quit the couple's house. Daphne and the children decamped to Cornwall. Her intimacy with Puxley continued, however, though she was at pains afterwards to insist – scarcely credibly – that it had not then been fully consummated.

Browning supposedly knew nothing of this. He wrote almost daily adoring little notes to his 'beloved Mumpty' and the children. He filled his few leisure moments by sketching boats he would have built for them with her earnings, once the war – 'this filthy business' – was over. Posterity's image of the general is dominated by his role at Arnhem, the 1944 battlefield disaster for which he bore a heavy responsibility. Yet in 1941–42 he was perceived as an effective, imaginative and intelligent officer, a gifted organizer and martinet, a rising star. Not long after his appointment to First Airborne, Browning commissioned the artist Edward Seago to design its shoulder badge, which became a sky-blue Bellerophon astride Pegasus the winged horse. Col. Charles Carrington, a shrewd observer of wartime senior officers, admired Browning, obviously without discovering much of the inner man. He described the general as 'ebullient ... indeed a *beau sabreur*, bursting with health and high spirits and self-confidence, an Elizabethan type looking just like Sir Richard Grenville of the *Revenge*, and perhaps aware of the resemblance'.

In the twenty-first century, however, Browning's role in Biting becomes far more interesting when it is understood that, even as he hastened from meeting to exercise area, supervising training and attending operational conferences, he was privately haunted by demons and a profoundly troubled relationship with his wife. To be sure, complications in wartime marriages were common enough. But Browning's exceptionally uneasy private persona goes some way to explain his often irascible behaviour. He deserves more credit than he nowadays sometimes receives, for his role in those early days of British airborne warfare, when he exercised senior commands while battling secret stresses. Geoffrey Powell, who later served under him, wrote of Browning, 'He possessed all the virtues as well as some of the defects of his background. He was devoted to the interests of his men, and they in their turn both liked and admired him, despite a barrier of reserve which few succeeded in penetrating.'

An important factor is often missed, about the conduct of commanders in conflict. To civilians – the mass of the world's population – war seems the ultimate horror, causing them to recoil from its prospect and even more from its reality. Yet it offers to professional warriors the most significant opportunities of their careers, which they eagerly exploit. In the Second World War many officers of all three services, who had struggled through decades of duty to secure sluggish upward steps in rank, achieved meteoric advancement. America's Dwight Eisenhower entered the struggle as a fifty-one-year-old colonel, and emerged from it three years later as a five-star Supreme Commander. Bernard Montgomery was in 1940 a mere divisional commander, at fifty-two relatively old for such an appointment in war, but within four years he was a field-marshal and Britain's most famous soldier.

Likewise on the much smaller canvas of Bruneval, all those involved, especially Mountbatten and Browning, saw in the raid a notable opportunity to enhance their own laurels. This was in no way discreditable, but a cynic should notice that among the martial orchestral theme in those days – aircraft engines, shouted orders, gunfire, the tramp of marching boots

– also discernible were the voices of ambitious men, competing to be heard, heeded, promoted.

In mid-January 1942, it was decided that Operation Biting, as the assault on Bruneval was now codenamed, should be executed by a single company of 1 Para Brigade, whose tasks would be to suppress the German defences; to protect engineers charged with dismembering the Würzburg set; then to cover their retreat to Mountbatten's landing-craft, which would close upon the little beach below the cliff to evacuate the raiders and their prospective prizes. A hundred-odd fighting soldiers should suffice to do the business. Browning consulted with the brigade commander, Richard Gale, who said that of all his companies in training, though 1 Para was more experienced, he thought 2 Para's C Company, overwhelmingly composed of Scots, was shaping best.

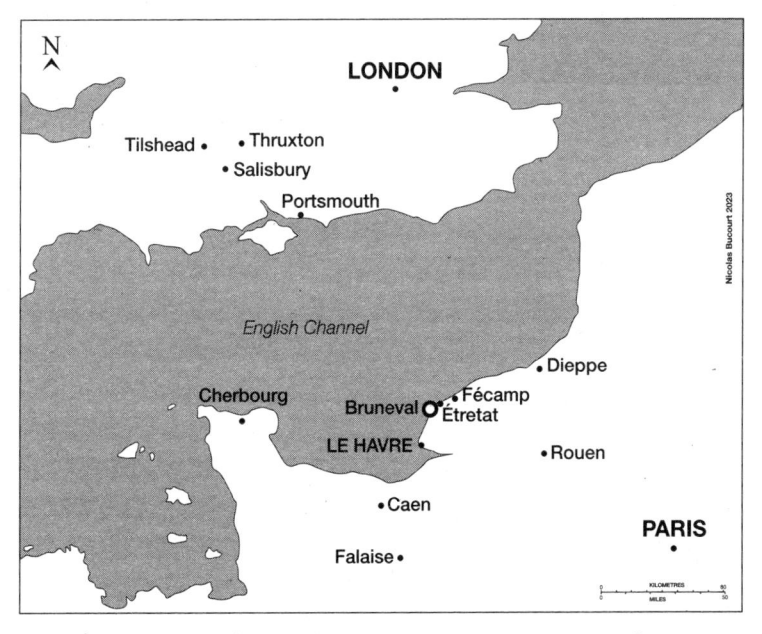

The scene of cross-Channel operations against Bruneval

It was decided these men should be shifted from the battalion's camp at Hardwick Hall in Derbyshire to Tilshead in Wiltshire, five miles west of Browning's new divisional headquarters at Syrencot House, and within reach of the south coast, where most of the rehearsals with the navy must take place. They could take off for the operation from Thruxton, an airfield near Andover of which the runway was newly completed. On 14 January, ten days before the chiefs of staff approved Biting, C Company was told to prepare for detached duty – 'special training in Combined Operations'.

And even as these novice warriors armed and prepared for a task which commanders knew – though the paratroopers did not – should happen by the end of February to conform to the need for a full moon and enough tide to ensure the landing-craft did not strand, there was a further vital requirement before anybody could jump anywhere: intelligence. The Spitfire photographs of Bruneval had enabled Reg Jones to identify its Würzburg. To mount a successful attack, however, the planners needed pinpoint information about the local defences. How many German troops were deployed within reach of the site? Were the approaches or the beach below mined? How quickly might the immediate defenders be reinforced? These questions could and must be answered not by cameras or signal decrypts but instead by observers on the ground – old-fashioned spies, going about their business in the fashion practised for countless centuries, and now being learned anew by men and women of the French Resistance.

4

Rémy

1 'THE MOST EXTRAORDINARY SECRET AGENT I EVER MET'

At the end of January 1942, following a request from Combined Ops, MI6, Britain's Secret Service, asked the BCRA – the Bureau Central de Renseignements et d'Action, intelligence section of 'Free France', the exile regime in London presided over by Gen. Charles de Gaulle – to seek information about Bruneval. The enquiry did not mention Operation Biting, because Free French security was notoriously porous. It merely sought details of the defences around certain German installations in upper Normandy. The planners already had access to pre-war holiday photographs and postcards of Bruneval beach and cliffs, long since gathered following a BBC public appeal for such images after Dunkirk, covering the entire coastline of France. This yielded thirty thousand images immediately, and eventually ten million. For the raid, however, they needed much more, and thus caused a wireless signal to be dispatched to de Gaulle's principal organizer in northwest France, later known as 'Colonel Rémy', though Gilbert Renault never held a uniformed command in his life.

Renault was an impassioned follower of the general. But his daring and initiative were not matched by discretion. Rémy's survival in Occupied France was even more miraculous than that of most secret agents in enemy-held territory. The mission to Bruneval to which he now committed two of his men, in response to London's request, nonetheless proved one of his finest hours of the war, and became a small triumph of intelligence-gathering.

Two years later, when Allied victory was obviously assured, the French Resistance would experience a surge of recruits, indeed a tidal wave, generated by people eager to identify themselves with the winners. In 1942, however, many months before Stalingrad, Hitler's fortunes appeared at their zenith. While few French people welcomed the German occupation of half their country, with a puppet Vichy government ruling the other half, most saw no choice save to collaborate. The Germans had not then introduced the hated STO – *Service du travail obligatoire* – which from February 1943 forced 600,000 French workers to join a million PoWs labouring in Germany, while STO evaders fled to the maquis.

Many French people disliked and resented the British. After the wildly inaccurate RAF bombing of the Renault factory outside Paris, which killed 367 French people, *Résistant* Jacques Lecompte-Boinet recorded his housekeeper saying, with the same bitterness that many of her compatriots had displayed after the 1940 destruction of the French fleet at Oran: 'The English are pigs, just like the Boche – always happy to trample on poor people.' Only a small minority of French men and women displayed in 1941–42 the inclination, as well as the extraordinary courage, necessary to reject acquiescence in their fate – collaboration; instead, to assist the Allied cause.

London's January 1942 Bruneval request was transmitted via one of the three Free French wireless-operators then active in the German-occupied regions. On receipt, Renault passed it to one of the network of amateur spies – they were all amateurs then – whom he had recruited and now managed. What followed represented the fruits of long and mortally dangerous labours, since the fall of France. His personal vicissitudes were, in significant measure, those of Resistance at large. Anyone who knew his history might have been forgiven for believing it was more likely the Bruneval quest would fail than that it should succeed.

The principal personalities of de Gaulle's movement were, from start to finish, almost all misfits, the 'awkward squad'. In the words of Emmanuel d'Astier de La Vigerie, they were the *'mauvais coucheurs'* and *'farfelus'* – literally the 'poor sleepers' and 'charlatans'. Relatively few of society's 'haves' were willing to risk their possessions as well as their lives to work against the Germans and the Vichy government, presided over by Marshal Philippe Pétain, with their many organs of surveillance, control and repression.

Resistance instead recruited many doctors, teachers, peasants, trade unionists. 'None fitted the conventional picture of the respectable good citizen,' wrote the famous historian of the Occupation Henri Amouroux. The characters of many 'rendered them perhaps ill-adjusted to a normal profession in a normal world at a normal time'. There were also practical considerations. The point is often missed that to be a committed *Résistant* deprived a person of their job, and thus of an earned income. Until later in the war, when large sums were made available to subsidize those who participated actively, it was hard for people at the bottom of society, with families to support, to give up everything to work for the cause. 'At the beginning of 1942,' wrote the later network leader Jacques Lecompte-Boinet, 'Resistance was still, and for a long time to come, ill-organised. The *Résistants* (if we can give them that name) were obliged to fund themselves and to spend without taking heed of the cost in time and money.'

Gilbert Renault was born at Vannes in 1904, eldest of ten children of an academic. A devoted Catholic, he became also a right-wing monarchist, for a time antisemitic, albeit also anti-German. All his life he sulked on Bastille Day, which he believed to commemorate a national tragedy, the fall of the Bourbons. His pre-war career was heroically unsuccessful in every department save that of procreation. In 1929 he married Édith Anderson, daughter of a Scottish immigrant, with whom he had an eventual nine children. He worked for some years in banking, serving briefly in Gabon. Returning broke from Africa, he and his wife lodged in her parents' house. He occupied for a time a humble role in insurance; was sometimes reduced to selling household belongings, including Édith's piano.

Then he made an essay into film financing, where his most notable achievement was to turn down French rights in Disney's *Snow White and the Seven Dwarfs*, which might have made his fortune. He travelled to Spain during its civil war, forging friendships with prominent Franco supporters that later proved important. His only financial success – a near-lifesaver – was that in 1938 he won the big prize, half a million francs or around £5,000 sterling, in the national lottery. But his most recent biographer Philippe Kerrand observes that at the time of the German invasion of France, Renault 'lacked all social status ... means even to put a decent roof over the heads of his family'.

The pivotal moment of his life came in June 1940, when he and his brother Claude made an abrupt decision not to remain at home as the German panzer juggernaut swept towards Vannes, but instead to hasten abroad, abandoning Édith, again an expectant mother, together with his eight children, to the care and support of her parents. He later claimed that both brothers were always committed to go to England, but some evidence suggests their preferred option was to head for French North Africa, had not the only available means of escape from Nantes, their nearest accessible port, been the Norwegian cargo boat *Liste*, bound for Falmouth, where it berthed on 22 June, four days after France surrendered. Renault and his fellow fugitives sobbed unashamedly as they pored over English newspapers reporting Pétain's decision to quit the war: 'We were betrayed, dishonoured.' Then, he recorded later, 'a hand touched my shoulder and I turned to see an old woman who looked like a caricature from *Punch*, with a huge flowery hat and wearing a pince-nez. She smiled upon me and said: "Don't worry, my boy. Everything will be alright." Her expression was so kindly that I could not help myself smiling back. She then insisted: "Have a cup of tea".'

Renault was thirty-five years old, an unimposing, portly figure who had held no paid employment for over a year and was equipped only with a salesman's patter and wildly exaggerated self-importance. Once arrived in London bent upon offering his services to de Gaulle, who had raised his exile standard just a few days earlier, in his famous broadcast to the French people on 18 June, the newcomer nonetheless expected to be received with open arms. Instead he was bussed with his fellow travellers to the Camberwell centre where MI5 screened refugees. He was eventually freed to travel to the home of a connection in Gerrard's Cross, where he lingered for a week, a restless guest.

Consumed with impatience and enthusiasm, he presented himself at the temporary headquarters of Free France, St Stephen's House in Westminster. There he met for the first time another remarkable personality, twenty-nine-year-old career soldier Captain André Dewavrin, a former instructor in fortification at the military college of St Cyr. Dewavrin himself had met de Gaulle for the first time only a week or two before, when he was quizzed by his new chief about his personal history. Strikingly boyish, even innocent, in appearance – and thus belying a notably enigmatic and even mysterious personality – the captain possessed three qualities deemed indispensable to aspiring members of de Gaulle's court: patriotism, brains and an impassioned personal commitment to the general, who told another early 'rallier' in those days: '*Nous commençons à zéro.*'

At the conclusion of this, their first meeting, de Gaulle said tersely to the young career soldier: '*Bien.* You will be my chief of intelligence. *Au revoir. À bientôt.*' Dewavrin saluted, and their conversation was terminated with the general's accustomed brusqueness. The captain adopted a *nom de guerre* borrowed from that of a Paris metro station: 'Colonel Passy'. He then set about conducting job interviews with prospective recruits who knew no more and no less about the business of intelligence than did their appointed chief. Dewavrin addressed his task, in de Gaulle's own later wondering words, 'with a sort of cold passion'. He became one of a handful of men who remained mainstays of Free France for the rest of the war.

And now here was Renault, an unknown figure newly arrived from Vannes, offering to return to the continent as a secret agent, a role for which he had no qualifications whatsoever, unless one counted the Catholicism which three-quarters of de Gaulle's early adherents professed. Renault described how the young officer 'fixed me with his cold blue eyes' and demanded why he thought he might make a spy. He replied limply: 'I have worked in business. I have a lot of contacts who could be useful.

I know a lot of radio broadcasters.' The older man admitted later: 'I was making up my story as I went along.' In truth, Renault's most significant selling point, especially in the eyes of the British Secret Service which must facilitate and fund any mission that Dewavrin sponsored, appears to have been his pre-war connections among Spanish Francoists. At a time when it was extremely difficult to infiltrate agents direct into France, Renault could travel to neutral Spain on a civilian flight. Dewavrin finally sent this eager volunteer back to his temporary quarters in Buckinghamshire, saying that he might hear more.

In the weeks that followed, Renault formed a chance acquaintance with Maurice Schumann, later to be dubbed 'the voice of France', who was then making pioneering Gaullist broadcasts for the BBC's French Service. On the evening of 21 July, Schumann invited Renault to deliver a personal message to his wife over the air waves – anonymously, of course, to protect her security. The words chosen by this new recruit to Free France were as theatrical as was much of the rest of Renault's life: 'Today it is more than a month since I held you in my arms for the last time ... I have since often asked myself if it was not my duty to return to protect you not only from the Germans, but also from worse enemies: those French people who are now seeking to create a new regime modelled on a monstrous one. [Yet] we have here [in London] a Chief. Under his orders, we shall prevail.'

By an astounding chance, at the dinner table of Renault's mother-in-law's home in Vannes, an almost disbelieving Édith heard the broadcast; received the message. She had already endured much at the hands of her rackety, improvident husband. It would have seemed absurd then to prophesy that Gilbert had taken the first step towards becoming a national hero. Claude Dansey, deputy head of the British SIS, later described this new recruit as 'the most extraordinary secret agent I ever met'. Though, heaven knew, it did not seem so at the time, after half a lifetime of backing losers Renault was now placing a huge stake – his own life – on one of the longest-priced outsiders of the twentieth century, who was to become one of its most remarkable winners – Charles de Gaulle.

Dewavrin soon recalled Renault to his office. The embryo spymaster told the visitor that he was to get his wish. He was to return through Spain to France, charged with creating networks capable of securing military intelligence. Renault was instructed immediately to seek from their respective London embassies Spanish and Portuguese visas, which were granted. Then the embryo agent-runner was given air tickets and money – a great deal of money, much more than his own wallet had held since he won the lottery.

Before Renault departed, he had a chance encounter with de Gaulle, his hero, on the stairs at Carlton Gardens, new headquarters of Free France: '*Mon général*,' Renault introduced himself with grave formality. 'I am one of your soldiers. I leave tomorrow on a mission to France, and seek the honour of shaking your hand.' De Gaulle invited the stranger into his office, asked his name and personal history, finally stood up and took his hand. He smiled and addressed his disciple by the codename he had just been allocated: '*Au revoir* [*Rémy*].* I'm counting on you.'

When Renault, seven weeks after his arrival in London, departed by flying-boat from Bournemouth for Lisbon and

---

* For much of Renault's first mission to France, his codename was Raymond. However, in this narrative to avoid confusion I adopt throughout the codename Rémy, by which he later became famous.

thence Madrid, he had received instruction in ciphering messages, but nothing else – no lessons in the techniques and practices of espionage. He was not the first agent to be dispatched – that was Sergeant Jacques Mansion, who had landed in Brittany a month earlier – but he was to be among the pioneers, most of them doomed men. His departure had been delayed by twenty-four hours after he failed to satisfy British customs at Croydon airport of his right to quit the country with a large quantity of francs. He had been ordered to cross the Spanish border into France as swiftly as possible. After arriving in Madrid on 20 August, however, he lingered for three months, his sojourn punctuated by increasingly insistent demands from Dewavrin that he expedite his mission – for instance on 6 September 'ABSOLUTELY INDISPENSABLE THAT YOU FIND WAYS TO GET INTO FRANCE STOP VERY URGENT TO CREATE RÉSEAU ABOVE ALL IN COASTAL ZONES'. In response, Renault pleaded logistical difficulties. He demanded more resources, including US dollars, local access to petrol and Philip Morris cigarettes. He sought to justify his protracted stay at Madrid's eye-wateringly expensive Palace Hotel by submitting reports, mostly misinformed, on conditions in France gathered from fellow guests recently in the country, who claimed a German invasion of Britain was imminent. Each of Rémy's message exchanges with 'Passy' was delayed in transit by a fortnight for passage through the British embassy in Madrid to Lisbon, and thence to London by diplomatic mail.

He forged one critical relationship in the Spanish capital: with the forty-two-year-old French diplomat Jacques Pigeonneau, who was to prove a pivotal figure in the communications of Resistance. His office – in Rémy's grandiloquent words – 'became a magnificent turntable between France and England'. Confident of Pigeonneau's commitment to de Gaulle,

Renault confided to him his own mission and even his ciphers. The diplomat did not betray him. Through the years that followed, Pigeonneau played an important role in assisting Resisters to pass between France and Spain, and in relaying agents' dispatches.

Renault's initial cover story held that he had been caught in London by an accident of war, and was now seeking reunion with his family. In Spain, this was modified for the ears of some acquaintances, to suggest that he proposed to resurrect his tenuous pre-war film-producing role, by making a biopic on Christopher Columbus. His exchanges with Dewavrin turned ever more irritable, even acrimonious. In his memoirs, Renault frankly admitted that apprehension, outright fear, caused him to hesitate about leaving the safety of Spain. Lack of training, of psychological hardening such as professional intelligence agents receive, helps to explain this prevarication.

His biographer Philippe Kerrand is almost contemptuous of such weakness, suggesting that no other wartime spies were guilty of it. This is untrue. Even some of the greatest agents took time-outs – SOE's wireless-operator Denis Rake pursued gay relationships at considerable risk to his mission, and several agents paid with their freedom or lives for being distracted into love affairs. The great Richard Sorge's lifestyle in Tokyo was famously louche. Renault was only one among many spies who showed themselves erratic personalities, to the exasperation of their handlers. Would any 'normal' man or woman have taken such work?

When Rémy belatedly crossed the frontier into Unoccupied Vichy France, he made contact with friends and sympathizers whose identities had been disclosed to him by London. He was soon announcing the creation of new networks which, in truth, pre-dated his arrival. Louis de La Bardonnie gave him critical assistance, especially towards passing into Occupied France by wading a stream and some energetic bicycling. De La Bardonnie was the real originator of a group Rémy later claimed as his own. As the latter gained confidence, however, he began to travel extensively around the country and meet many people, some of whom he had known before the war, others not.

His messages to London, in the absence of access to a wireless, had to be transmitted through couriers. The reports were still heavy on verbiage, light on accurate information: Dewavrin repeatedly demanded his agent should cite sources for unattributed assertions. His reports about, for instance, the effects of RAF bombing of German submarine bases in French ports, notably Bordeaux and Brest, were absurdly optimistic – claiming the attacks were '*très efficaces*' – and flatly wrong. He suggested that German soldiers had been seen weeping in public places at the prospect of participating in the impending invasion of Britain. In March 1941, he stated that this operation would be spearheaded by 150,000 paratroops allegedly already training in the Ardennes. He constantly urged on London exotic schemes, for a landing on the Belle-Île-en-Mer, or bombing of German installations. Dewavrin felt constrained to warn his man that 'a certain number of the reports you have sent us are manifestly false or exaggerated'. One of Rémy's agents, naval officer Jean Philippon, much later acknowledged: 'My informants were whispers, which I was obliged to accept as such. What was I myself, save a shadow?'

Nevertheless Renault and his networks then represented the principal intelligence sources of Free France. De Gaulle's BCRA, like all espionage organizations, was compelled to cherish passionate hopes that its geese were swans, for lack of any other birds. Carlton Gardens became increasingly impressed, fascinated, awed by the sheer weight of Rémy's reports – on the defences of Brest, petrol stocks at La Roche-Maurice, German works in progress at Bordeaux and Brest, and much else. Historians know that much of this data was wrong. Yet in those days when news from Occupied Europe was as trickles of muddy water from wells in the desert, Renault gave ever-growing comfort to Dewavrin and his comrades in London who in their almost pathetic gratitude conferred upon him superlatives – *'magnifique'*, *'superbe'*.

He was entrusted with ever larger sums of cash, for which he accounted sketchily, if at all. Some of the money was plainly spent on his family and lifestyle. All this was characteristic of many spies throughout history, and during the Second World War in particular. Their trade requires an addiction to deceits, so that even today it remains uncertain which side some agents were on. One among many reasons that the Allied high command so highly valued Ultra intelligence – the decrypts of messages dispatched by the German, Italian and Japanese high commands – was that these possessed an inherent credibility that could be matched by no 'humint' report from an agent in the field.

Renault was a remarkable man. His commitment to the cause was wholly authentic, his courage indisputable. His luck proved extraordinary, in surviving for so long in enemy territory when so many of his kin were caught. For instance, the *Réseau* Saint-Jacques, run by Maurice Duclos and covering the north coast of France between Brest and Dunkirk, was infiltrated and systematically destroyed by the Gestapo in the autumn of 1941. Rémy's relative longevity is especially noteworthy, when he lacked all tradecraft. He was fantastically indiscreet, not least in frequenting the best hotels and black market restaurants, which Dewavrin urged agents to avoid because they were the haunts of Germans and collaborators.

'The network inspired by [Rémy] was several times decimated by stupid blunders,' wrote one of its veterans later. Kerrand marvels that 'given the considerable risks he took, not always considered, it is extraordinary that [Rémy] had totally escaped the clutches of the Gestapo. It is yet more remarkable, that they did not establish even his true identity until April 1942.'

Renault's several volumes of memoirs dwell euphorically on the glorious meals he contrived to eat, especially at Prunier in Paris. Thanks to British gold, his personal standard of living in Occupied France was much higher than he had enjoyed before the war. He committed acts of reckless insecurity, such as passing some messages through an intermediary known to copy them to the Vichy authorities. He exploited monarchist and Catholic connections, but later also opened a dialogue with communists whom most Gaullists shunned. Renault used his Francoist connections – friends of Hitler – to facilitate his frequent passages in and out of Spain.

His personal freedom, indeed his life, was at stake every time he met a new contact, which meant almost daily. Each held power to dispatch him towards Fresnes or Buchenwald from the moment he revealed his attachment to de Gaulle. Resistance was obliged to advertise, in order to secure the services of volunteers and people with access to information. But advertisement was mortally perilous for any man or woman who exposed themselves. Henri Michel, an early chronicler of France under the Occupation, observed wearily that 'every network had its quota of traitors ... Treachery was the daily fare of the Resistance.' Jacques Lecompte-Boinet wrote later of the 'avalanche of contagious illnesses' to which he likened the chain of betrayals and arrests that broke up so many networks. Moreover, in 1941–42, and especially before US entry into the war, it seemed likely Hitler would win. After such an outcome the Führer's enemies in France and elsewhere across Europe would be doomed. It deserves emphasis that while most of those who joined the Resistance in the years of Allied success, 1943–44, survived the war, many of the men and women who enlisted earlier perished.

Renault's family life was extraordinary even by the standards of the time and place. Soon after entering France, with German authorization he contrived to convey his wife and children from Vannes to Spain. There, Édith lived in loneliness for some months before concluding, following the death of her youngest son as a toddler, that exile was unendurable. She returned to France and, in the autumn of 1941, to Brittany. In November, Rémy took the almost insane risk of travelling home to visit his loved ones. Soon afterwards, he moved the family to Nantes where – again, in defiance of rudimentary security – he visited them. His domestic existence lunged between pathos, tragedy and farce, as when he returned from one of many journeys to the hotel at Sainte-Foy in which Édith and his tribe of children were installed, to be met by three of them, Catherine, Cecile and Jean-Claude, who chorused: 'We did as you asked us!'

'What was that?'

'To keep an eye on *maman*, of course!'

'True enough. Was she good?'

'Very!' said Cecile.

'Why "very"?'

'She did not sleep with anybody,' asserted this six-year-old.

Emmanuel d'Astier de La Vigerie described Resistance as 'a game at the same time both childish and mortally dangerous'. In the winter of 1941, Rémy and Édith decided their oldest children, twelve-year-old Catherine and eleven-year-old Jean-Claude, must be entrusted with the secret of their father's work. He described how their eyes bulged as he spoke to them, and as he swore them to secrecy, tears ran down Jean-Claude's cheeks. His father demanded:

'Why are you crying?'

'Because I am frightened.'

'Frightened of what?'

'Frightened of talking.'

And so those children might well be, shuttled around France from alleged safe house to safe house, in an atmosphere of relentless stress and yes, fear, which could not be dispelled by parental play-acting of Happy Families at Christmas and in leisure moments.

Yet Renault survived. He travelled hither and thither across Occupied and Unoccupied France; fostered networks of genuine sympathizers over a large area of the west and north-west. He belatedly secured access to a wireless-operator who set up shop in Saumur, on the Loire, with the usual cumbersome set of that period, weighing sixty pounds. Dewavrin and Free French headquarters in London had by now cast aside earlier doubts. They believed 'Rémy' was energetic, lucky and above all successful. Renault acknowledged in his own notably unreliable memoirs: 'I was surprised to discover how good I was at lying.' Some days, his copious messages to London contained valuable intelligence; more often, they did not. But in the country of the blind – and information reaching Britain about France remained very scanty in January 1942 – the one-eyed man was king. 'Rémy' had become almost a monarch.

He conferred on his networks the name the *Confrérie Nôtre Dame* – the 'Brotherhood of Our Lady', known in London as the CND – following a visit he paid to the church of Nôtre-Dame-des-Victoires. Jacques Soustelle, another leading light in Gaullist intelligence, wrote in 1984 that Rémy was 'the foundation stone of our secret operations in France ... one of the principal sources of our information – and thus of those at the disposal of the Allies – on the resources and movements of Nazi forces ... Gilbert Renault passed from amateur status to that of a master.'

In the first year of his assignment, he travelled repeatedly to and from Spain; from Clermont-Ferrand to Toulouse; from Lorient to Pau; also to Lyons, Bordeaux, Vannes and most often to Nantes, where he rented an apartment. It was extraordinary that so many of Rémy's reports reached Carlton Gardens safely, if slowly, when their transmission required passage through some fifteen hands before reaching Madrid via the French controller of customs at the frontier, thence to Jacques Pigeonneau, to the British embassy and thereafter Lisbon and the flying-boat shuttle to England.

Even when a radio set became available, transmitting initially from the home of Louis de La Bardonnie in May 1941 and later from Saumur, long dispatches, maps and sketches had to be transported physically to London, though from August of that year they were first microfilmed in Lyons. By early 1942, the Germans deployed twenty-four fixed stations and 143 interception vehicles in France in quest of unauthorized transmissions. For Renault and other directors of Resistance, only personal contact, often across many miles, could gather information, precipitate action.

Before leaving London, Rémy had selected two books as the basis of his personal coding process. The first was a novel he had picked up in the Charing Cross Road in July 1940, *Le parfum des îles Borromées*, a tale of adultery published in 1898, and also the more readily available *Petit Larousse illustré*, of both of which London retained their own copies. At the end of July 1941, the Saumur operator Bernard Anquetil – '*L'Hermite*' – was caught by the Gestapo as a result of careless coding, for which Rémy was responsible. Anquetil was shot in October. After that Renault's own codename was changed to Rémy from Raymond, since the Germans had accessed some earlier messages in which Raymond was mentioned.

De Gaulle's Carlton Gardens mission perceived itself to be in competition not merely with the German enemy, but also with the representatives of Britain's own secret organizations, whose very engagement in French affairs the general regarded as an insult to himself and the dignity of *La Patrie*. Foremost among these was SOE – the Special Operations Executive – charged by Churchill since 1940 with 'setting Europe ablaze' and thus addressing sabotage and preparations for guerrilla warfare, rather than intelligence-gathering. As for MI6, Britain's professional Secret Intelligence Service in Broadway had almost no sources of its own in France, and depended overwhelmingly upon those of de Gaulle, hence its appeal to the BCRA about Bruneval. An often childish struggle persisted between SIS, SOE and Dewavrin, who ran agents in France but was dependent on British resources to fund, transport and communicate with them. As late as 2010, an official history of SIS maintained the legend – even perhaps the fiction – that Broadway ran such men as Gilbert Renault, a claim he, Dewavrin and indeed de Gaulle would have furiously contested from their graves. Meanwhile MI9's personnel, both English and French, sought to aid escaping PoWs and especially expensively-trained airmen to return to England along secret 'ratlines'.

In the autumn of 1941, not only did the range of Rémy's networks increase incrementally, but the quality of their information improved. They were learning. Moreover, Rémy possessed the power that relatively generous funding from London provided, together with an authority derived from his ability to prove to doubters – sometimes through *messages personnels* broadcast by the French Service of the BBC – that he was an authentic emissary of de Gaulle. The BCRA judged that of its eleven networks operating in France, Rémy's was the most important and best-organized, purveying information now garnered from the entire north-west coast between Normandy and Bordeaux.

Despite strictures about Renault expressed above, his shrewdness was manifest, and demonstrated in a long report on the general condition of France, submitted to de Gaulle and Dewavrin when he later reached London. 'The overwhelming majority of the population,' he wrote, 'is passive, and has no intention of sacrificing its comfort or its ease.' He wrote contemptuously of the 'stupidity and selfishness' of the bourgeoisie, 'which is already responsible for so many misfortunes', but excepted from his criticisms 'the liberal professions – in particular doctors and teachers – who display much courage and among which I have personally formed bonds of inestimable worth. We should concentrate propaganda on workers, on the *petit bourgeoisie*, on coastal communities and peasants.' He suggested the French Service of the BBC should name and shame collaborators. In the event this was done only seldom.

Early in December 1941, Renault met in Paris and recruited a new agent, forty-four-year-old former tank officer François Faure, to whom he gave the codename Paco, because of the man's enthusiasm for all things Spanish. They held several long conversations, seated on a chilly, lonely bench in the Avenue d'Observatoire, at which the new recruit won Renault's confidence by his calm maturity. Paco, in turn, introduced Rémy to several kindred spirits, almost all of whom had served in the armed forces. These included forty-three-year-old Roger Dumont, a doctor's son who had been a 1917–18 fighter pilot. Before the war, this keen sportsman worked as director of

France's National Tennis School. In the course of a first meeting by the Porte Maillot, Dumont impressed Renault by his directness and enthusiasm. He had acquired some earlier Resistance experience with the so-called Kléber network, now defunct. Codenamed Pol, this new sub-agent was appointed the group's specialist on aviation matters.

The spymaster was delighted to recruit such ex-officers, who had a knowledge of military affairs that he knew himself to lack. Nonetheless the risks were, of course, immense, of adding to the CND so many new names and faces, about which their chief perforce knew little. Most of those whom Renault met on this Paris visit were later caught by the Germans, deported or shot. On hearing of so-and-so's arrest, wrote Renault, he himself often mused: 'If he talks, there is likely to be a massacre.' Yet some, before they met a fate which their inexperience of secret war made all too likely, rendered significant service to the cause of freedom.

Pol began painstakingly to compile order-of-battle charts for every Luftwaffe base in France, material that was confided to a suitcase stored at an alleged safe house in Paris, pending the next departure of a courier for Spain. Here was an example of the difficulty of providing 'real time' intelligence for London, when complex material could not be transmitted in radio messages that must be brief, to have any hope of escaping German detection. Renault devised a series of questionnaires to be passed to his regional agents, about the strengths and routines of their local German forces. Characteristically, he evoked the spirit of the Testament: 'Ask, and it shall be given; seek, and ye shall find; knock, and it will be opened to you.' Material was now reaching him in such quantity he enlisted the services of his sister May, '*Maisie*', as his secretary, a role she embraced enthusiastically.

He was much addicted to wearing a Basque beret, common enough in France, but he also affected a knitted sweater of a distinctive hue, which he had bought in London's Lillywhites store in August 1940. He abandoned this latter with reluctance only in the winter of 1941, when he was warned the Bordeaux Gestapo had marked him out by his obviously English *veston*. Later in the war, London handlers for both the BCRA and SOE took pains to ensure their agents wore only French clothing.

At New Year 1942 Renault and his family sat down to lunch in the home of hosts near Nantes, whose cook triumphantly placed on the table a huge cake adorned with the Cross of Lorraine and the inscription '*Vive De Gaulle!*' On 24 January, his Paris-based wireless-operator Robert Delattre received two important messages from London, addressed to Renault, requesting utmost detail on the Bruneval site.

This had already come to the CND's attention. Two months earlier Roger Hérissé – agent Dutertre – had reported the presence of a new German installation, some fifty feet high, near Cap d'Antifer. His information was passed to Roger Dumont, who in turned mentioned it via his chief to London. As we have seen, aerial photography had already revealed this Freya array to Reg Jones and Scientific Intelligence. But Hérissé's familiarity with the Freya's erection at Bruneval meant that it came as no surprise when Dewavrin demanded further information.

In late January 1942 Gilbert Renault was under orders from the BCRA to return to London, taking with him scores of maps, reports and other intelligence material too weighty to be wirelessed or even couriered. He spent days in a rural safe house, awaiting the BBC message that would prompt him to seek a remote field near Rouen from which he would be picked up by RAF Lysander light aircraft. The rendezvous was repeatedly postponed, however, not least by poor winter weather.

Moreover there had been a wave of German arrests of CND agents in Brittany, causing alarm throughout the network. At last it became obvious that it would not be possible to retrieve Renault during the January moon period; his passage to London must wait upon late February – entirely coincidentally, the appointed window for Operation Biting. Emotionally exhausted, he thus returned his family to Paris, where they shivered amid icy weather, lacking fuel for heating, spending their days perpetually clad in overcoats, lightened only by family meals at Prunier.

2 BRUNEVAL

The Bruneval interrogative messages from Dewavrin demanded information within an impossibly tight timescale – a mere forty-eight hours. Pierre Julitte, another BCRA agent serving in France since May 1941, once rebuked Passy for failing to grasp harsh facts of secret war on the ground, above all that the swift execution of orders was often rendered impossible by agents' inability to use telephones or even the postal service, which were subject to German and Vichy interception.

Now, Renault was instructed not to risk his personal safety to visit upper Normandy. Whoever carried out the mission must, in the event of capture, tell the Germans he had been reconnoitring several coastal sites – '*trois ou quatre emplacements sur côte*'. The second signal from London requested specific details of machine-guns and strongpoints between the Bruneval cliff and the radar sites; number, age and alertness of German troops stationed in the area; together with pinpoints of their quarters.

Rémy studied the map of the area, and also his own agent's report on the big new Freya array between Étretat and Octeville.

He then discussed London's signals at a meeting with Roger Dumont. He later claimed in his memoirs that the nature of the questions made plain that the British were considering a *coup de main* by commandos rather than a mere air attack on the installations, though this seems more likely to have been a product of after-knowledge. Dumont, the former airman, read London's 'shopping list' in silence, then demanded quizzically: '*Alors?*' The best way to be discreet, responded his chief, was not to appear to understand too much: 'How much time do we need?'

Pol said: ask them for fifteen days.

'Perfect. Tell me, who was the source of the original report [on the installation]?'

'Roger Hérissé, a comrade. We call him Dutertre. He is a pilot, like me.'

Pol then departed, to seek out a friend named Charles Chauveau, codenamed Charlemagne, who chanced to be visiting Paris on business. Chauveau was yet another World War I air force veteran, a former instructor in navigation, who now owned a successful Le Havre garage and car dealership. His calling entitled him to an *ausweis*, a German pass permitting him to travel within the Channel coastal region – *la zone interdite* – to which access was forbidden for ordinary citizens. Now, Dumont told Chauveau he needed a lift to Normandy, and his friend proved happy to oblige. The two men set forth on a wintry 120-mile journey, a serious undertaking within the constraints of the Occupation. Le Havre's Gestapo, commanded by Friedrich Maitz and staffed by functionaries named Ackermann, Krieger and Maille, whose names had become local bywords for terror, was intensely active. It was already responsible for a grim roll-call of executions of local patriots. Every traveller, with or without an *ausweis*, faced the constant hazard of being stopped by German checkpoints or patrols. Chauveau, forty-six, was driving a car which he had fitted with false number-plates such as allowed him to travel in the capital. As they headed out of Paris, he stopped at the city limits to replace his Havre plates, of which the number matched his *ausweis*. Only then did Dumont confide to his friend their exact destination. He asked if the *garagiste* was confident of getting them to Bruneval. 'Easy,' said Chauveau. 'I know that area like the back of my hand.'

Reaching Le Havre, twelve miles south of Bruneval, the two men checked into a seedy hotel where no questions were asked about their identities, then shivered through the night fully clothed. In the morning, Chauveau went out to borrow snow-chains for the tyres of his Simca 5, because he knew they must traverse country lanes clogged by several inches of icy whiteness. Then they set forth for Bruneval, a hamlet nestling deep in a wooded valley – a cul-de-sac, from which its single street descended only to the beach, a half-mile below. They stopped at one of the village's first habitations, its little hotel-restaurant, the characteristically Norman timber-beamed Beau-Minet. 'I've known the owners for years,' said Chauveau. 'They are good people. Madame Vennier came from Switzerland, but they belong here now. They'll tell us what we need to know.' The Venniers fully justified his hopes, displaying astonishing courage considering that a German infantry platoon was billeted in their own hotel. Inside a quarter of an hour, Pol was fully briefed on the Luftwaffe radar technicians occupying the Gosset farm, on the plateau northwards, just inland from the 'radio station', together with details of the numbers of Germans manning nearby strongpoints. At that period of the war the atmosphere was relaxed, with local inhabitants moving relatively freely around the area on foot or bicycles, and indeed continuing to occupy cottages and houses within close proximity to German positions. The post commanding the immediate beach approach was a former villa named Stella Maris, now faced with sandbags as a machine-gun position. Dumont, with a courage bordering on recklessness, insisted he must view this for himself: 'We must look at the sea.'

'Consider!' exclaimed M. Vennier. 'Access is forbidden! There are mines everywhere!' Dumont persisted. The two men walked boldly down the unmetalled track towards the blockhouse at the foot of the cliff, five hundred yards below the hotel. A sentry appeared at a knife-rest gate in its protective wire entanglements, and halted them. Chauveau disarmed the man's wariness by addressing him in fluent German. 'We're only taking a stroll. I belong around here, but my friend is Parisian and having got this far he doesn't want to go home without seeing the sea' – invisible just around the corner of the deep defile in which they stood. The German hesitated, surprisingly unsurprised by these two middle-aged men 'enjoying the view' on an icy winter day, trudging through the snow. Chauveau continued: 'We know we're lucky to have got this far. Anyway, I wouldn't dare to go any further. They tell us there are mines?'

'*Ja, ja! Minen!*'

'Would you maybe be so kind as to come on with us?'

'*Jawohl*,' said the good-natured, obviously bored sentry, making the biggest mistake of his career as a guardian of Nazism. He became their guide through the last yards of this perilous odyssey, showing them the way through the wire and supposed minefield. Dumont winked at Chauveau, who took the cue and offered the soldier a cigarette, causing him to turn his back on the sea to light it. The *garagiste* enthused, again in German: 'This place was so pretty before the war … Ah! If you could have seen it then! Isn't it a shame that you have to pass your days in this forgotten corner?'

The confused German responded: '*Ja! Nein! Ja!*', while Chauveau's companion sought to memorize every detail of the view before and below him. The sentry confided the vital information that there were, in reality, no mines on the cliff descent or beach below. The two Frenchmen departed amid mutual professions of goodwill. Back up at the Beau-Minet, Chauveau was delighted to encounter some of his own relatives, who could provide an alibi for his presence in the hamlet. The spies, justifiably exulting in the success of their morning's work, drove a few miles to Gonneville where they stopped for a self-indulgent lunch at the Hôtel des Vieux Plats. Dumont's bravado caused him to note the names of German officers listed in its visitors' book. They then planned to inspect the German airfield at Bléville, but found the approach road closed by a barrier. The Parisian decided to remain a second night in Le Havre. Then Chauveau drove Dumont uneventfully back to the capital, where he reported to Renault. The CND's chief recognized at once that the novice agent – for the airman had joined the network less than two months earlier – had done a superb job. They spent several hours transforming the information gathered at Bruneval into messages brief enough to be wirelessed to London by Robert Delattre, tapping at a morse key in his garret.

'9-2-42 De Rémy (code A) no. 81 – *Affaire Theuville* – Stop – The path rises between high cliffs from a beach 22 metres wide [between the villa and the sea] and continues through Bruneval to the village of La Poterie stop 1. Beach and coast are not mined. 2. Two machine-guns in the first house above the beach [Stella Maris]. 3. Wired strongpoints 10 metres out from this house, covering the entrance to the road. At 100 metres then again 100 metres down the road are two wired positions two metres deep. 4. There are two machine-gun posts on each side [atop the heights] of the cliff defile. 5. 30 defenders, aged 35–40, under the orders of a senior NCO, serve three-week rotations.'

A second signal stated that these men had no special training; that a further five Germans occupied a second house, while twenty-five worked during the day on defences related to the batteries at Cap d'Antifer, sleeping overnight in the Beau-Minet. At nearby La Poterie a further sixty men of the same kind as those described above – given their average age, presumably second-line troops – were quartered in the school and *mairie*; '*aucune méfiance*' signified that there was no sense of mistrust or apprehension among these German detachments.

Both these signals were received safely in London. They represented one of the more notable 'humint' intelligence successes of the war, a tiny operation perfectly executed by all those involved, and accompanied by almost incredible good fortune. There was the luck that Pol and Charlemagne carried out their journey without check or arrest. The two men then showed courage and ingenuity to seek out precisely the information COHQ needed, in order to mount its raid. The Germans displayed an insouciance and laxity most uncommon among Hitler's forces, and of which more would be seen before the curtain fell on the Bruneval saga. Finally, Bob Delattre was able to dispatch the agents' reports without a terrifying eruption of Germans bursting into the room where he transmitted, as happened to Resistance operators so often, and would soon befall him.

The wireless-operator was a twenty-seven-year-old teacher's son from Boulogne. He had worked as a chemist's assistant, been mobilized with the French Army in 1939, then escaped German captivity to join de Gaulle's BCRA in London, by way of West Africa. He wrote to his parents before he embarked upon his mission to France: 'What am I going to do? To fight. Not with machine-guns or cannon. But with my eyes, my ears, and a little of my brain. I set forth upon an existence in an environment polluted by the Aryan race. If I must die, dry your tears. Tell yourselves that my death has not been in vain. To fight for my country, for my family, for the freedom of peoples, is my only thought.' He messaged the BCRA a month before he was betrayed and captured by the Gestapo in May 1942, dying under torture in Fresnes a year later: 'I love the work that I do and hope we shall succeed in our tasks, which I perform in the hope that success will one day bring us liberty and peace.' Which, indeed, they did, over the graves of Delattre and other men and women like him. As for Rémy, Gilbert Renault, if, in earlier days, there had been much about him that might be deemed absurd, there proved in France's supreme time of trial to be much that was fine and good. It is unlikely Operation Biting could have been brought to success without him.

5

Johnny

1 C COMPANY

And so to those who were to do the business, the young soldiers who – ignorant of their objective until the final days of training – were to steal Hitler's radar; to form the point of the needle which Britain was to thrust into an exposed finger of Nazi-occupied Europe. The men of C Company 2nd Parachute Battalion were overwhelmingly Scots, most former civilians, enlisted 'for the duration'. There were three Flemings, a Burns, a Finnie, a Campbell and a Craw, together with many Macs – McCausland, McIntyre, McKenzie, McLennan. Pte. Tom Laughland was a Glaswegian who served with the Argylls as a physical training instructor before in 1941 volunteering with his mate Cpl. Tom Hill to become paratroopers. One platoon included a commercial artist, Glasgow shipyard and factory workers, together with a furniture upholsterer. Many of them were physically smallish men, a legacy of the slums from which their families came, but they were also iron hard. Among the officers was a twenty-two-year-old English lieutenant who, in 'civvy street', was a Fleet Street cub reporter.

One of the few experienced NCOs, who would become a stalwart of Biting, was thirty-five-year-old Aberdonian bachelor

Gerry Strachan of the Black Watch, a veteran of almost two decades of service. Strachan, now the company's sergeant-major, looked, and was, a tough proposition with his thrusting chin and steely grin, a former coach of the regimental boxing team. At Hardwick Hall, men who slackened pace on marches grew accustomed to hearing his whiplash tones, demanding contemptuously: 'Are ye tired, laddy?' John Frost described Strachan as 'a man who knew just exactly how a company should be run'. The CSM repeatedly proved himself a fine warrior in a fight.

By the end of the war, Britain's forces accepted the services of any man and most women possessed of arms and legs. Earlier in the conflict, however, many eager and patriotic volunteers found themselves rejected because weapons were lacking to arm them, and personnel to train them. Lt. John 'Tim' Timothy, born in 1914, worked as a shoe salesman for Lilley & Skinner, then became a management trainee at Marks & Spencer, while enthusiastically playing sports in his leisure hours. He was rejected for military service in 1939 and again the following year, because of an old rugby injury. He was told that with his 'B' medical grading, he would be lucky to be accepted for the Service Corps.

Then recruiters appeared at a pub which he frequented in Eltham, and he secured the A1 health rating he coveted. He wanted to join the RAF or Royal Navy, but both had long waiting lists. Instead he briefly served with the Grenadiers before attending Sandhurst and securing a commission. In September 1941 he volunteered for the new 'Special Air Service' battalion, only to be rejected yet again, because of varicose veins. This desperately eager young officer appealed through a medical specialist, who passed him fit. Thus, now, he found himself a platoon commander in C Company, playing rugby for the Parachute Brigade.

Lt. Peter Young was a skinny seventeen-year-old apprenticed to a Fleet Street newspaper when, in 1939, he joined an East Surreys Territorial Army unit near his home in the London suburbs, and thereafter advanced to a commission, and entry to the Airborne, before he was twenty. Young, now just twenty-two, owed his Christian name to *Peter Pan*, in which his mother, an actress known as Carmen Wood, had once starred. His father had been a fighter pilot, killed in a post-World War I air crash.

Lt. Euan Charteris was the twenty-year-old offspring of a notorious figure of the earlier world war. His father, Brigadier John Charteris, had been Field-Marshal Earl Haig's chief of intelligence on the 1914–18 Western Front, highly influential and disastrously wrong. His son, who would make a critical contribution to Operation Biting, was youngest of three brothers. Brash and ebullient, at Wellington College he was a star of rugby and other sports, captain of his house, a sergeant-major in the Officers' Training Corps and pillar of the debating society. Charteris seconded a 1938 motion that 'a woman's place is by the fireside'; on another evening attacked democracy in favour of aristocracy in a speech described as 'a magnificent display of pure bombast'. He once blacked up to impersonate Mahatma Gandhi – a performance unlikely to win applause if reprised in the following century – and won an annual school prize for a best essay on the Duke of Wellington.

In 1937 he was a member of a Schools' Exploring Society expedition to Newfoundland. In the autumn of 1939 he went up to Christ's College Cambridge as an exhibitioner, but soon left to join the King's Own Scottish Borderers – he had been raised in Dumfriesshire. Charteris was full of energy, bumptiousness and ambition – he hoped eventually to enter politics. He was superbly fit, sometimes impatient of lesser young bloods – Wellington College remarked sardonically on his 'powerful, if rugged, intelligence'. He became celebrated in C Company for an adolescent appetite – at every meal, he ate for two. Such young men often distinguish themselves at the sharp end of war; and equally often perish.

The formidably big, burly John Frost had been serving as adjutant of 2 Para until, just weeks before the assault on Bruneval, he was appointed to the command of C Company, with promotion to major. This was apparently because though not an authentic Scot, Frost wore the tartan of a Scottish regiment. It was deemed sensible that such a band of warriors should be led by one of their own kind. Also, perhaps, higher powers saw in Frost a forceful officer, well-suited to lead the most significant wartime operation thus far by Britain's paratroops. He was born in Poona in 1912, son of an Indian Army general, educated partly at Wellington a few years before Charteris. He then passed through Sandhurst before being commissioned into the Cameronians. Seeking adventure, he applied for secondment to the Iraq Levies, an imperial buccaneer unit, with which he spent two years guarding RAF bases, while also acting as master of the Royal Exodus Hounds, which pursued jackals when its mounts were not required on the polo pitch.

Frost wrote later that he never forgot the arrival at his remote desert camp of the September 1939 signal announcing succinctly: 'War has broken out with Germany only'. The first person he told was a captain who exulted: 'Marvellous, marvellous! I was terrified that old Chamberbottom would settle up once again!' Frost recalled: 'My own first thought was that it might perhaps mean promotion.' Ever the man of action, and still a bachelor, he began agitating to escape from Iraq and return home to his regiment, an outcome he achieved only in the autumn of 1940. He sailed home bearing a parting present from followers of the Royal Exodus – a copper hunting horn which thereafter he carried into action through four years and many battles.

Frost spent the later months of 1941 defending Norfolk with a Cameronian territorial battalion against an increasingly unlikely German invasion, but mostly shooting duck with a hospitable landowner. He was unhappily conscious that after two years of war he, an ardent professional soldier, had yet to see action. He shared the unease that was widespread throughout the country about the general ethos of Britain's soldiers, after so many humiliating defeats in Norway, France and around the Mediterranean littoral. Those were days when, amid shrunken respect for the army, officers sometimes found themselves refused salutes by other ranks, and by members of the other services.

Then a circular letter reached his unit from the War Office, soliciting volunteers for 'special air service' battalions, and especially captains qualified to command companies: 'I had not very much idea of what special air service was, but presumed it would be something in the Commando line, and just what the doctor ordered.' He was less confident about the airborne aspect, though: 'My knowledge of parachutes and parachuting consisted solely of what the Germans had achieved by this method of moving into action. The press had rather scoffed at the effectiveness of the new arm.'

He had never taken seriously the threat of Germans airlanding behind the British front – 'most of us felt that the Home Guard would be more than a match for them'. He supposed the spirits of enemies who descended from the skies would be severely dampened by the number killed in jump failures. His colonel agreed, telling him scornfully: 'I can't imagine any sensible person choosing you to be a parachutist. You ought to keep your feet firmly on the ground.' The soldier persisted with his application, nonetheless, and was eventually summoned to an interview at the War Office.

A few mornings later, he stood among a throng of fellow captains and majors, addressed by a brigadier who told them: 'Gentlemen, from amongst you we are going to select the company commanders, second-in-commands and adjutants of the 1st Parachute Brigade. We have a tremendous task ahead of us and very little time.' During the ensuing week back with his old battalion, Frost reflected gloomily on his poor showing at the subsequent interviews, and thus slender prospects of acceptance. His medical record was impaired by partial deafness, caused by a fall while riding in an amateur horse race. At the War Office, he thought he had been rash to respond to a question about discipline by saying that too much of it cramped initiative.

Here, however, he had hit the right spot. Brigadier Richard 'Windy' Gale, 1st Parachute Brigade's appointed chieftain, quizzed all his aspiring officers: what do you do if, immediately after landing by parachute in action, you are faced by an enemy tank? Too often, said Gale, a nervous subaltern answered: call his superior. The brigadier instead sought men such as Frost, willing to grapple challenges on their own: 'It was action that was wanted.' The young officer, passionately committed to the army, shared in its 1941 sense of professional shame, and was bent upon playing a personal part in restoring its lustre.

He was astonished and delighted when, ten days after his visit to the War Office, he received orders to report to 1st Parachute Brigade's Hardwick Hall camp near Chesterfield in Derbyshire. In October 1941 he found himself in grim, muddy, dispiriting parkland, set between mining works and slag heaps.

He and his fellow new arrivals were to officer the 2nd Battalion, following in the bootsteps of 1 Para, which had been created almost a year earlier. Their uncertainty about what they had let themselves in for was intensified when drafts of rankers began to arrive. Some of these men, far from being aspiring heroes, were hopeless cases of whom cynical unit commanding officers had sought to rid themselves: 'A good few were hardened criminals.' They were short of experienced NCOs, backbone of every military organization.

As an officer of a doughty Caledonian regiment, Frost was pleased to find the men of the Scottish company were in better shape than others. Yet he acknowledged they were 'a wild crew'. Volunteers for special operations, whether commandos, SOE, SAS or parachutists, were seldom the sort of people to make docile household pets. More than a few of Frost's Scottish soldiers were instinctively violent products of the roughest, harshest of upbringings and early lives. But they were men who wanted to fight, and Britain in those days badly needed such eager warriors.

He observed about the experience of watching his first parachute demonstration: 'What struck me so forcibly was how completely dependent we were on the skill of the pilots.' Ignorant of all things pertaining to the RAF save the beauty of Spitfires in flight, he had taken for granted the ability of aircrew to find their way to an appointed point, by day or night. Experiences during the next three years cured him of this delusion. Again and again, airborne operations would be compromised or fail because men were dropped in the wrong places. If the green light mounted above the exit of every troop-carrying aircraft was illuminated late – even by a matter of seconds – men overshot their landing zones often by miles. Conversely, the drop signal was frequently given too early – an episode of this kind in bad weather over Scotland caused an entire stick of heavily-laden jumpers to be precipitated into the Clyde, never to be seen again. In 1943, scores of men on their way to fight in Sicily splashed fatally into the Mediterranean. More will be seen of this problem later in our own tale.

At night at Hardwick, the old professional army's prohibition on talking 'shop' in the mess was discarded: officers debated keenly and fiercely the proper employment of parachute troops. Their role in Germany's 1940 sweep across Europe had been wildly exaggerated by rumour, which especially seized the mind of Britain's prime minister. The May 1941 invasion of Crete was spearheaded by *fallschirmjäger* who achieved their objectives only at the cost of prohibitive casualties. From Russia, BBC bulletins reported incidents of lightly-armed Luftwaffe airborne attackers being 'mopped up'. Colossus, British paratroopers' inaugural venture in Italy, had been a failure as an operation of war, even if it showed that the British Army was not entirely inactive. The one unquestioned success of airborne operations was the Germans' May 1940 *coup de main*, the gliderborne descent on the Belgian fortress of Eben Emael.

Even in those very early days in the history of parachute warfare, it was obvious that its selling point was the capability to spring surprises – suddenly to deploy fighting men where the enemy least expected them; to create a new battlefield of the sponsor's choice, far behind any supposed front line. It was equally apparent, however, that for paratroopers to prevail against ground defenders they must secure their objectives quickly. If they became engaged in a protracted clash, lack of heavy weapons, vehicles and ammunition replenishment must prove a handicap, probably fatal. When Frost's aunt's chauffeur heard that young Johnny had signed up to serve as a parachutist, the old man observed disgustedly and by no means foolishly,

'Why, that's the surest way of becoming a prisoner that's ever been invented!'

In those days, embryo paratroopers did not undertake rigorously structured month-long courses such as would be standard for later trainees. Instead, men were dispatched severally from their units to the school at Ringway. John Frost arrived there with his colonel, Edwin Flavell, aiming to complete their two balloon jumps and five aircraft descents in record time. Neither had either fulfilled a proper programme of ground training – 'parachute rolls' on landing, for instance – nor worked to get themselves fully fit. On the first morning they were winched to six hundred feet above Tatton Park in a gently swaying balloon cage: 'We smiled at each other the learner parachutist's smile, which has no joy or humour in it. One merely uncovers one's teeth for a second or two, then hides them again quickly lest they should start chattering.'

Most people find unnerving the silence of the sky beneath a huge gasbag, contrasted with the deafening engine roar that suffuses a transport aircraft and its passengers. There is a cold-bloodedness about the requirement to leap from a balloon into the blue vacancy which chills even the doughtiest novices until they have braved the experience. Frost wrote: 'The first sensation of falling drew the breath from my lungs till a cracking sound from above and a sudden pull on my harness told me that the parachute was open, and the rest of it was heavenly.' On the ground, the jubilant, gleeful adjutant and colonel congratulated each other: many private soldiers proclaimed exultantly: 'Gor, it's better than sex!' but some young officers, in those relatively virginal times especially for the middle classes, lacked experience from which to make a comparison.

Flavell and Frost insisted on embarking immediately upon their second jump. The former landed safely, but the latter made the classic error of hitting the ground with his legs slightly parted, which proved as painful for himself as it does for most Airborne trainees. He spent that night in a local hospital, after being operated on to remove fluid from his knee. He returned limping to Hardwick Hall, obliged to delay completion of the course until he regained fitness.

On 14 January 1942, before the chiefs of staff had signed off their authorization for Biting, Browning's staff dispatched an order to the Parachute Brigade, requiring 2 Para's C Company to be detached to Tilshead, in 'army country' on Salisbury Plain in Wiltshire, for 'experimental training for a raid'. They should expect to be administratively independent for six weeks. Arrangements for cash to pay the men were being made with Lloyd's Bank in Amesbury. The ORs – other ranks – would mess separately from the glider pilot trainees with whom they would share a camp. Officers and men alike were to be briefed that their task was to rehearse a demonstration airborne attack on an enemy facility, for an audience of the War Cabinet, which would take place probably on the Isle of Wight.

First, though, Frost the company's commander needed to complete his interrupted parachute course. He surrendered his men to the custody of Major Philip Teichman, who fervently hoped his own elevation would prove permanent. Frost then hastened back across the Pennines to Ringway. The first intimation that he might be destined for something important was the discovery that the RAF had been told to make his qualifying jumps a priority, and he was scheduled to perform two on the first morning. To his frustration, however, winter fog closed in, and persisted. Next day, only late in the afternoon did the weather clear sufficiently to make a jump from a Whitley possible, which he completed in safety, then persuaded a passing motorist to drive him the few miles back to Ringway from the landing zone at Tatton Park, just in time to make another descent before the light failed. He achieved a further jump the following evening, and on the next day completed the course in perfect weather. He was richer by four shillings a day in pay: other ranks received half that amount – essentially danger money. A WAAF batwoman sewed the cherished winged badge on the arm of his tunic before he set forth for Tilshead, to resume command of his company.

2 TILSHEAD AND INVERARAY

In January 1942 Frost had yet to see action, but in the years that followed he was to prove himself an outstanding fighting leader – cool, tough, brave, quick-thinking. Only after the war was done did he marry and have children. Not in the least cerebral, he never seemed destined for the highest ranks, and indeed did not attain them. But he was ideally suited to lead such an operation as that to which he was now pledged, though still unknowing about its nature. In character Frost had more than a little in common with his American counterpart Dick Winters, of Easy Company 101st Airborne Division, later famous as the 'band of brothers'.

It seems nonetheless surprising that this unknown and untested major, rather than an officer with battle experience, was now to be entrusted with command of a raid upon which depended a significant fragment of Britain's battered national prestige. The most credible explanation is that the senior officers who made the choice had not reflected much on the issues at stake – the personal burden that Frost would have to shoulder through his hours on the ground in France. Only the prime minister, together with R.V. Jones and his 'boffin' colleagues, knew enough fully to grasp this. It is noteworthy that Gen. Sir Alan Brooke, head of the British Army, made no mention of Biting in his voluminous contemporary diaries, either before or after the event, though he knew it was taking place, and indeed signed off authorization. For the CIGS, preoccupied with grand strategy and – like most senior soldiers – sceptical about 'sideshows', a company-strength raid on the coast of Normandy seemed below his threshold of attention. Nevertheless he might have done well to consider the embarrassment – the crowing from Radio Berlin – that would accompany its failure.

On his arrival at Tilshead on 22 January, Frost displaced C Company's acting commander, to Philip Teichman's disappointment. The latter had been arranging accommodation and training facilities for the main body of paratroopers, who arrived two days later, after a journey delayed by snow. Teichman told his successor that while everything was secret, it appeared the unit was merely to stage a demonstration for the politicians: no 'party' – characteristic British military vernacular for an operation of war – was in the offing. Something serious might follow, Teichman had been led to believe, only if the initial exercise proved successful.

The camp at Tilshead was one among hundreds of desolate wartime clusters of hutments, set behind concertina wire on a low, barren hill above the village with views across miles of unlovely training grounds and army facilities. The day after C Company arrived from Hardwick, its men were paraded for inspection by Browning, their divisional commander, whom few of them had yet seen. Frost felt disconsolate as he mustered his hundred-odd scruffy, muddy, travel-soiled soldiers for scrutiny by the spotless 'Boy'. The general, who almost alone among those present knew what Frost's men were to train to do, took the inspection seriously. After talking at length and one by one to many of the paratroopers, he concluded that their enthusiasm and high spirits did much to compensate for their appearance. Finally Browning said to Frost: 'I think you've got a good lot of men, but I have never seen such a dirty company in all my life!' On the general's return to his headquarters amid the Georgian splendours of nearby Syrencot House, he gave orders immediately to issue C Company with new clothing.

Frost was not consulted about a reorganization of his command, which was abruptly imposed by Divisional HQ. Combined Ops had produced the overall tri-service scheme, but Browning's staff devised the tactical plan for the drop and ground attack. The major was dismayed, and indeed enduringly angered, by what he was told to do. Like all British Army infantry companies, his own was organized in platoons and sections, with an HQ that included runners to carry messages. Browning's officers instead decreed the force should be divided into disparate groups which would drop at different times, with varied assignments. He himself would lose his headquarters team: 'I didn't like this at all … I should have four bodies, all different in size and firepower, which would be difficult to control if things went wrong. Previous military experience had shown me that manoeuvres or operations which went strictly according to plan were very rare indeed.' In those days wirelesses played almost no part in actions below battalion level, while voice radios were both scarce and unreliable. The major was told that he would be getting a lot of sets, and indeed duly received these; on The Night, however, they failed comprehensively.

Orders for the paratroopers' stay at Tilshead were conveyed to Frost by Browning's appointed liaison officer, a somewhat pompous, mustachioed Grenadier of thirty-nine named Major Peter Bromley-Martin. The latter's explanation of their mission

– to stage a mock raid on an 'enemy' outpost on the Isle of Wight – did not impress C Company, nor indeed Frost and his officers. Beset by rain, icy winds and mud, they hated their temporary quarters, and likewise the glider pilots already stationed there. They disliked Bromley-Martin and other Airborne Division staff whom they met, together with everything they heard about the silly apparent purpose of their training – to impress a clutch of politicians. They wanted to go back to 2nd Battalion, and to Hardwick Hall.

Frost drove over to Syrencot House to remonstrate, only to find Browning absent. Instead he argued with the division's senior staff officer, Lt. Col. Arthur Walsh, but returned to camp having got nowhere. The company commander and Browning's people never achieved much rapport – it seems noteworthy that the general's later report on Biting pays no personal tribute to the man who led it, though some lesser participants are mentioned favourably. Next day Bromley-Martin returned to Tilshead to see Frost. For the company commander's ears alone, he confided the true nature of the operation for which he and his men were to train – a raid on a German radar installation in France. Then he put the major in his place. His job, this newly-minted paratroop officer was informed crisply, was to do what he was told; to execute the plan he would be given. If he continued to baulk about accepting this, 'someone else would be found who did'.

The company commander's enthusiasm was not much increased by their conversation. Bromley-Martin concluded, with Grenadier affectation: 'I must say I find the whole thing fascinating.' He, however, was not being invited to jump into Occupied France. Frost, who was, did not share this view. His dislike and distrust of the liaison officer persisted. If Bromley-Martin was responsible for planning Biting, as appeared to be the case, the Cameronian was thoroughly unhappy about it. In particular, he was infuriated – and remained so during and after the assault – that he, as its commander in the field, was to have no say in its organization.

Yet the planners had a case. As well as Frost's anxiety about dispersal of his little force, each of the RAF's aircraft could carry only a single 'stick' of ten men. Thus it would anyway have been hard to maintain the usual infantry company organization, even had the divisional staff not decreed otherwise. Moreover Frost, as a mere novice major who had never seen action, could scarcely be surprised that his superiors were unwilling to concede him a free hand in executing an operation of such complexity, involving all three services and commanding the keen interest of the prime minister. The ex-master of the Exodus Hounds would exercise tactical leadership on the ground which, heaven knows, represented responsibility enough. He would not, however, be granted licence to organize the 'party' nor to invite the guests. Bromley-Martin told him: 'You'll be taking your company over to France before February is out. Now it's up to you to see that everything works properly and that your Jocks are so fit they're jumping out of their skins, or you won't have a hope of bringing them out alive.'

Inevitably, Frost acceded. As his company commenced training, he reorganized the men in groups, each of which was given the codename of a naval celebrity, in deference to the amphibious nature of their task – Drake, Rodney, Nelson, Jellicoe and Hardy: 'This was to be a combined operation *par excellence*, and we hoped the Senior Service would appreciate the gesture.' Frost was impressed by twenty-year-old Lt. John Ross, a Black Watch officer from Dundee whose severity made him admirably unflappable. Somebody would have to be in charge if the major 'bought it', as might easily happen in France. He appointed Ross his second-in-command, promoting him to acting unpaid captain.

Browning decreed that, within reason, C Company were to have whatever arms and *matériel* they requested. Frost, accustomed to the army's parsimony with resources, especially in those lean times, was astonished to find himself supplied with every kind of equipment and weapon, including some he had never heard of. C Company was given its own transport and a prodigious issue of ammunition for training. Some staff officers, not in the secret, baulked at fulfilling extravagant Airborne Division requisitions for stores and clothing – for instance forty-two pistols, thirty wrist-watches, thirty wrist-compasses, fifty torches, six Hawkins anti-tank grenades, six morphia syrettes apiece for each officer, escape kits, together with 120 white oversuits to be worn if Bruneval proved snowbound on The Night. Much of this equipment did not reach Tilshead until the last stages of the company's preparations.

New faces joined its ranks – an officer and eight sappers from the recently-created parachute squadron of Royal Engineers, equipped with mine-detectors and other tools of their trade. An additional forty-odd men, almost all from 2 Para's B Company, were dispatched from Hardwick to Wiltshire as reinforcements, prospective reserves and substitutes: in all arduous training and especially airborne exercises, casualties and drop-outs were inevitable.

GHQ Home Forces breached the elaborate security precautions, by referring in circulated documents to the real purpose of Biting, provoking the fury of Browning when he got to hear of it. Several of the weapons and much of the equipment to be employed were very new, still in the experimental stage, especially the 9mm Sten sub-machine carbines which thirty of the raiding force were to carry. Stens were light, handy and could make a formidable racket, important virtues in a butcher-and-bolt raid such as this, but they were also prone to jam or self-trigger, and inaccurate beyond the shortest ranges. Components of early versions were created at the Liverpool factory which in peacetime produced Meccano children's construction kits. Rumour had it that some of these cheap-and-cheerful weapons, of which most parts were mere stampings, were assembled in garages with five man-hours' labour, at a cost of just £2 apiece. The planners were untroubled by the little guns' limitations. In darkness neither side's small arms were likely to hit much. Four million Stens were ultimately made, and supplied to Resistance groups in occupied territories around the world – they cost one-sixth the price of American tommy guns.

C Company was to exercise on Golden Ball Hill, a stretch of high downland north-east of Alton Priors, near Devizes, which descended steeply onto flatland that would pass muster as the sea. This, they were told, represented a plateau onto which they would land – in Wiltshire, from trucks rather than aircraft – assemble, and march to their objective, followed by a descent to the evacuation beach such as they would encounter on their demonstration for the War Cabinet. Some individuals were given fragments of information about their personal roles – Euan Charteris, for instance, knew that he and his section would be responsible for storming a fortified house at the foot of the hill – though not that this lay on the coast of Normandy. A company of field engineers moved hedges (yes), planted token trees and marked out roads, wire entanglements and other landmarks. The scale of resources committed to Biting was becoming remarkable, but a cynic might observe that most of Britain's Home Forces, at that period, had little else useful to do.

Given the shortage of time before the operation, it might have been better to utilize a training area on Salisbury Plain, close to Tilshead, rather than expend hours each evening winding through the Wiltshire lanes to reach and later return from Alton Priors. Though the latter location was hilly, sure enough, its topography otherwise bore only a limited relationship to that on which C Company must fight in France. Browning afterwards made the point that distances marked out at Alton proved to have been very different from those at Bruneval, and this mattered in enabling the disparate elements of C Company to master routes and timings in darkness.

They began to practise night attacks on the hill above Alton Priors, though the weather – extreme cold and heavy snowfalls – severely restricted activity. The enthusiasm of both officers and men was impressive, indeed moving, and seemed to go far to compensate for their lack of experience. Each night they returned exhausted and filthy to Tilshead, where they astonished the resident glider pilots and their cooks by the quantities of food they consumed.

Yet training schedules were repeatedly interrupted by the wintry conditions, and a company parachute drop had to be cancelled. There were wearisome delays before some kit could be issued, and much time-wasting in achieving telephone contact with higher headquarters, including the War Office to which frequent appeals were needed, to secure authorizations denied by service bureaucracies that were not privy to the Biting secret. The force lacked access to ready money to pay local bills for essentials 'extremely small in relation to the cost of the operation'. Meanwhile Frost knew he was working his men hard: whenever they were stood down he arranged transport to Salisbury or Devizes for some serious pub crawls. One night some of his men returned to camp heralded by a raucous din from a local British Legion band's instruments which they had liberated. Thereafter, observed Frost drily, 'the guardroom door yawned more widely', as did the threat of being left behind when they staged their big drop. Browning chafed that, mostly thanks to the weather, thus far 'very little satisfactory ground training' for the mission had taken place. But the wheels were now turning relentlessly, towards the dates set for a landing in France.

Even as the paratroopers prepared, elsewhere hundreds of other men – soldiers, sailors and airmen – were being mobilized to participate in Biting. Lt. Cdr. Fred Cook was summoned from HMS *Tormentor* to a conference in London with some of Combined Ops' senior naval officers – John 'Jock' Hughes-Hallett, David Luce and Peter Norton. There, he was admitted to the secret of the Bruneval plan, in which his landing-craft would play a critical part. Halfway through the subsequent discussion, Luce interrupted Hughes-Hallett – known to his critics as Hughes-Hitler, in deference to his imperious manner – to say: 'Sir, shouldn't we tell Cook he is to be naval CO of the operation?' The Australian officer returned to Portsmouth somewhat awed by the responsibility that was being thrust upon him and his half-trained flotilla.

So much emphasis was being placed on secrecy that Cook was appalled, listening to one of 'Lord Haw-Haw's' regular evening propaganda broadcasts from Berlin, to hear Goebbels' mouthpiece boast: '*Tormentor*, we know where you are at the mouth of the Hamble river. You are going to be bombed next Friday night!' Cook said: 'And by Jove we were.' The Luftwaffe killed only a few cows, but for some days afterwards a shower of German magnetic mines laid in the estuary prevented the landing-craft from putting out. Then, one morning, these little vessels were hoisted aboard the 'mother ship' HMS *Prins Albert*, which sailed north to Gourock, west of Glasgow, where a rendezvous had been fixed with Frost's paratroopers, for the next round of rehearsals.

With so many cooks stirring the Biting broth, senior officers introduced added ingredients. It was decided the landing-craft should be armed, to provide supporting fire if Frost's men were being pressed by the Germans as they quit the beach. Each ALC was to be equipped with four Bren light machine-guns and 500 rounds apiece; they would also carry Boyes anti-tank rifles, though back in 1940 these had been exposed as useless weapons, allegedly to engage enemy small craft which sought to intervene against the evacuation. The six ALCs would be accompanied by two LSCs – landing support craft fitted with 20mm Oerlikon cannon. Gerald Templer, the fiery local army chief of staff in Hampshire, fought for a detachment of his troops to man the weapons in the ALCs, to emphasize his disdain for commandos and their kin. He wished to show that line infantrymen could well undertake the raiding role. Browning resisted – wanting his own men in the boats – but was overruled. Instead forty men of the Royal Fusiliers and Monmouth Regiment were assigned to man the Brens and Boyes afloat, and boarded *Prins Albert* before it sailed for Scotland.

On 9 February, with their attached engineers and thirty-odd members of B Company who were, effectively, reserves for the raid, Frost and his men boarded a train to Scotland for four days of training with the navy. In the interests of security, they removed all Airborne insignia before heading northwards. On arrival at the ship, the soldiers enthused: their quarters and rations afloat proved a great improvement on those at Tilshead. When they began to exercise on and offshore, despite freezing conditions there was almost a holiday mood among the exuberant adventurers. All this seemed a bit of a lark.

'Even the subalterns had enough to eat,' wrote Frost, 'and there was no shortage of the civilized things in life. We were lucky with the weather, and all of us greatly enjoyed splashing about in the landing-craft, even if it meant long hours and frequent wetting in the icy waters of Loch Fyne.' Their activities were exhaustively recorded by an army photographer named Lt. Puttman, who was to accompany both C Company's training and subsequent return from France: propaganda was intended to be a significant element in the raid's purposes, assuming its success.

The worst aspect of their days and nights around Inveraray, however, were that the coastal exercises laid bare the limitations of the landing-craft and their officers. Amateur seamen and navigators all, they experienced chronic difficulty in locating a rendezvous in darkness; distinguishing light signals; retrieving Frost's men from appointed beaches. The major nursed a dry, understated reflection: 'The possibility of being left stranded on the coast of France after we had done our job was unpleasant.'

One night aboard *Prins Albert*, Frost and his men were told that next day, they should disappear ashore, because Commodore Mountbatten was on his way to inspect the ship. In the event, even as the company tramped the surrounding hills it was recalled by frantic hooting on the ferry's siren. Dickie wanted to see 'his' soldiers, as well as the sailors. Back on board, they were mustered with the naval personnel, to be addressed by the star of Combined Ops, who worked his usual cheerleading magic. He spoke with a blithe, unconsidered indiscretion which drove a coach and horses through security. Only Frost, among the paratroopers, was thus far privy to the secret of their mission, and the planners had intended to keep it that way until the last moment. Now, though, the commodore harangued them about the importance of the raid on enemy territory which they were about to undertake. He amazed and excited every man who still supposed they were merely training for an amphibious exercise, although even Mountbatten was not careless enough to disclose the objective. The major wrote: 'We were left in no doubt by his Lordship that cooperation [between the three services] had to be the thing.'

The commodore asked Frost privately if he had any concerns, to which the major responded: yes, he had. A certain Private Peter Walker – obviously a German – had suddenly been attached to the company as an interpreter. Frost did not like him, did not want him: 'So many things could go wrong with our little party, and we had been taught to fear the enemy's Intelligence. With all the talk in England then and previously about the Fifth Column, I could not help thinking that the enemy probably knew all about us, and what we were training for. There was a distinctly eerie feel to having a Hun on the strength.' 'Walker' himself was equally uncomfortable, to know himself to be the object of such mistrust.

Mountbatten immediately sent for this mysterious private soldier, and quizzed him in fluent German. The slightly-built 'Hun's' real name was Peter Nagel. He was born in Berlin in 1916, youngest of three children. At school he excelled at history and sport, but one day the principal told this Jewish teenager icily: 'People like you are not wanted in Germany.' The Nagel family reacted prudently: they fled. The boy and his mother lived for a while in Paris, then in 1936 moved to Britain, where Peter worked at Morna Fabrics, a business his father established in Leicester, having achieved a feat unusual in those days

– transferring his savings out of Nazi Germany through a phoney business deal with Wolsey, a British textile firm. Morna achieved increasing success.

In March 1940 young Peter enlisted in the Pioneer Corps, where his language skills attracted the attention of the secret world. Despite some shamelessly antisemitic criticisms that he encountered, an August 1941 report from SOE's Special School reported Nagel to be 'well-educated, extremely intelligent, and if not for his youthful appearance and inexperience ... might be a good leader ... very keen all round, extremely reliable and very courageous'. An instructor asserted in January 1942 that the cocky, streetwise Nagel was 'by conviction a European, ideologically an anarchist ... an inveterate and successful womanizer'. He was posted to No. 2 Commando, now 1 Para, from which he was seconded to C Company, wearing identity discs that declared him to be Peter Walker,* Religion C of E. Mountbatten, after completing his catechism, turned to Frost: 'I judge him to be brave and intelligent. After all, he risks far more than you do.' The major withdrew his objections. He later concluded that Mountbatten had been right. Walker was a remarkable man, who would prove invaluable to Biting.

It deserves notice that, through those middle days of February 1942 when Frost and his men were training, their country suffered yet another round of defeats. Though the paratroopers' enthusiasm for their task remained undiminished, they prepared for battle amid what seemed a national culture of failure. On 12 February, the German battlecruisers *Scharnhorst* and *Gneisenau*, together with the cruiser *Prinz*

---

* Some earlier books, including that of John Frost, refer to Peter Nagel as 'Newman', but Nicolas Bucourt highlights the fact that on post-raid memorial documents signed by participants, there is no Peter Newman, always Peter Walker. I accept the latter version.

Eugen, sailed east from Brest to Wilhelmshaven at first undetected by the Royal Navy or RAF, then undamaged by repeated air attacks, though belatedly mined. The 'Channel Dash' prompted blazing headlines in the press, and was billed as a humiliation, of a kind unknown to England since the Spanish Armada in 1588. Four days later, on the 16th, the surrender of Singapore was announced, largest imperial capitulation in history, to a much smaller Japanese army. Churchill was devastated. He was desperate for good news. If great successes were not attainable, small ones must for a season suffice. Biting might be one such.

6
Charlie

The day after Mountbatten's inspection, *Prins Albert* sailed round the Scottish west coast to Gourock and disembarked the paratroopers. They boarded a train back to southern England where on 15 February, in icy weather, they resumed training for the attack. A new face joined the company – an airman named Charles Cox. Reg Jones and his colleagues agreed that it was essential to dispatch to Bruneval an expert familiar with radar. It would be quite an undertaking for a mechanic – a fitter, in air force terminology – who was untrained for battle, coolly to address the Würzburg set, probably under German fire, and facing drastic time pressure. Derek Garrard, one of Jones's assistants, immediately volunteered for the role, but his participation was vetoed by Sir Charles Portal, chief of air staff: Garrard knew too much to be allowed to risk capture. Jones heaved a private sigh of relief, because the same constraint applied to himself: he would otherwise have felt obliged to raise his own hand to accompany Biting.

An uneasy compromise was decided upon: a TRE specialist – the sunny, bespectacled Donald Priest – would sail with Fred Cook's evacuation flotilla, tasked to meet the paratroopers and granted a temporary commission as an RAF flight-lieutenant. If Frost's men held a secure perimeter Preist, an enthusiast for living dangerously especially in fast cars, would land, climb the cliff and inspect the Würzburg himself. This scenario was wildly implausible, but in any event Preist could make a rapid examination of the radar equipment when it was loaded aboard the landing-craft, to check the raiders had secured what they were being sent for.

But somebody technically literate must drop with C Company, follow up its assault, then address the Bruneval installation with a tool kit. On 30 January Sgt. Charles Cox was at his usual duty post, as one of the crew of an RAF Chain Home Low radar station at Hartland Point on the North Devon coast. In peacetime, the twenty-eight-year-old had been a cinema projectionist and radio ham, living in Wisbech, Cambridgeshire. His mother had been on the stage, playing roles unspecified, and his father was a postman. He himself was a lively, bright young man, already married with a small baby. He was a little baffled suddenly to be handed a railway warrant to London and told to report to an office in the Air Ministry. Next morning, 1 February, he found himself, along with a second airman radar specialist named Corporal Smith, standing at attention before the desk of Canadian-born Air Commodore Victor Tait, the RAF's director of radar. Much later, the technician was asked if he had volunteered for Biting. He responded: 'Sort of.' The conversation which took place at the Air Ministry explains his equivocal choice of words.

Tait, an exotic character who had spent most of the 1930s creating a pocket air force for Egypt's King Farouk, said to the two men gravely: 'You've volunteered for a dangerous job.' Cox hastened to correct this misstatement, saying that he had never volunteered for anything. Tait, perhaps disingenuously, claimed to have been told that Cox and Smith had been identified as among the very few qualified personnel for a certain task, and to have put their hands up for it. Whether or not they were in reality press-ganged, the air commodore said: 'Now you're here, will you volunteer?' Cox answered: 'Exactly what would I be letting myself in for, sir?'

'I'm not at liberty to tell you ... I honestly think the job offers a reasonable chance of survival. It's of great importance to the Royal Air Force. And if you're half the chaps I think you are, you'll jump at it.'

Both men volunteered. This version of the story is Cox's, but it is the only one we have, and there seems no reason to doubt it, save that in his written narrative he made no mention of Corporal Smith. The two were among a relatively small number of skilled radar mechanics who were physically fit enough to qualify as parachutists and drop into France. Cox had hitherto neither taken to the sky in a plane nor put to sea in a ship. Indeed, the young man's life had been remarkably humdrum. From that morning, however, the things which befell him in the ensuing month would more than make up for any earlier lack of incident. Before Cox and Smith left the Air Ministry they were given a step in rank, in the former's case to flight-sergeant, and two days later issued with new railway warrants, this time to Manchester. Thus did they discover that they would be expected to jump into enemy territory.

Once in the north, they fulfilled instructions to report to the adjutant of No.1 Parachute Training School at Ringway. Smith wrenched a muscle on his second balloon jump, and so could not continue with the course right away. Cox, meanwhile, completed without accident an abbreviated version, and indeed found the experience exhilarating. A few days later, with wings sewn onto his tunic, he was dispatched onwards to Tilshead, now alone. He received a civil welcome from C Company, though he struggled to understand some of its Jocks through their heavy accents.

He was introduced to Dennis Vernon, who commanded the Royal Engineers section that he would accompany into action. The lieutenant, some months younger than himself, came from Cambridge, where he had attended the Leys School, then the university's Emmanuel College. Vernon was plainly clever, and also notably cool under pressure. His superiors had chosen well when they dispatched him to join Biting. Air Commodore Tait was obliged to inform Cox that his RAF comrade Smith had now fallen ill, and was unfit to complete the Ringway course. The little flight-sergeant said he was sure Vernon could do anything in France that his mate in blue would have been asked to accomplish. It was anyway too late to jump-qualify then train another RAF technician.

Vernon was commissioned to photograph the Würzburg from all angles with a flashlight Leica camera. A senior radar specialist, Col. Basil Schonland, visited Tilshead to brief Cox's engineer comrades on the technology. A mobile gun-laying radar was driven into the camp and parked by their quarters, so that they could practise disassembling it. All this was a revelation to the sappers, but they needed to understand the exact purpose of Biting, in case Cox and Vernon became casualties during the raid.

The 'Demounting party', as the planners somewhat clumsily christened Vernon's team, was instructed to secure the central portion of the Würzburg aerial, protruding from the centre of the bowl or 'great mussel', as the Germans knew it. They were told that most of the essential electronic equipment was located in a metal cabinet mounted right behind the pedestal supporting the aerial dish. Beyond discovering how Würzburg worked, Reg Jones added laconically that it seemed desirable 'to find out whether there was anything to be learned from the enemy' which might improve British radar construction. The planners budgeted for the engineers to have thirty minutes' access to the enemy installation, before a withdrawal to the beach became essential. This was optimistic. In such a relatively lengthy time span, once the defenders were alerted and shooting started, Germans from the surrounding area would have time to concentrate in force against Frost's 120 thieves. This made it all the more important that the attackers should be dropped with absolute precision, within quick reach of the Bruneval radar site.

In the days that followed the 15 February jump at Syrencot, C Company rehearsed, or attempted to do so, with *Prins Albert*'s landing-craft, now back at their base on the Hamble. The navy identified three beaches between Weymouth and Swanage that were suitable for realistic exercises, but Royal Engineers had to remove anti-invasion mines and obstacles before they could be used. The need to travel by road each day to the coast in a convoy of five lorries wasted precious hours of the short winter days, and the subsequent trials were less than successful. On 17 February, yet another surge of bad weather forced cancellation of a scheduled full-scale rehearsal with the navy. The frozen ground also made it impossibly rash to stage another parachute jump, in which a crop of injuries would be inevitable. Frost's men instead practised their roles in the ground attack: only a week remained before the first date when moon and tide made Biting feasible.

Cox and Vernon were suddenly granted two days' alleged compassionate leave in London. In truth, Reg Jones wanted to meet them. Single-mindedly focused upon every operation that pertained to his work and to the war effort, he considered Bruneval his baby. Cox managed to fit in a hasty rail journey home to Wisbech 'for one precious night' with his wife Violet. We can speculate that Charlie may have confided to her some hints of the almost unimaginably dramatic experience that lay ahead for him. Then he and Vernon met by appointment in a waiting room at the Air Ministry. They were shown into an office where three men sat behind a table, two of them obviously English and wearing civilian clothes; the third French, clad in battledress. 'The Englishman in the middle' – Jones – 'powerfully built, sure of himself ... did the talking, while the third man spoke occasionally when what you would call the technical side of matters was under discussion' – this last was most likely Derek Garrard.

Cox's account of the interview at the Air Ministry bears rehearsal at length. 'Both the Englishmen,' he wrote, 'evidently knew more about radar than we did. Without raising his voice or saying anything dramatic, [Jones] made us feel that our job was something really worth doing, and that we were lucky to find ourselves doing it.' The scientist's blend of confidence and natural authority, which had already carried him close to the heart of the war effort before he was thirty, imbued the flight-sergeant with conviction, even though the theme of their conversation was hair-raising. Jones had applied to the War Office to grant Cox temporary military status and uniform, for the duration of the operation. In 1942, however, inter-service collaboration was at a low ebb. Jones wrote much later: 'It seems incredible, even at this distance of time, but the War Office adamantly refused to co-operate.'

Thus, when Cox met Jones, the scientist said that it seemed only fair to emphasize the special danger he would face, as the uniquely blue-clad member of the raiding force. The airman responded: 'I've been thinking about that, sir.' He proposed, if captured, to tell the Germans he had been dispatcher in one of the dropping aircraft, and had made an impulsive decision to jump with his charges. Jones replied frankly that he thought it unlikely such a thin cover story would wash. Instead, he told Cox he should say, 'if caught on the job, that we were simply a demolition squad out to do mischief to a valuable bit of enemy equipment. We would both come in for special questioning, since I was the only airman in the parachuting party, and Vernon was the only engineer officer.'

Jones warned that the Germans often planted an 'English' stool pigeon in a new prisoner's cell. He said: 'Don't be worried too much about physical torture, because I don't think they are using it. What you have to be tremendously careful about is being thrown into solitary confinement in a cold, damp cell, with nothing but bread and water for a few days. Then a new German officer will come round on a tour of inspection, and will himself protest about the way you are being treated. He will take you out of your cell and explain that he will try to make amends for your bad treatment, giving you cigarettes, a decent meal, a warm fire and something to drink. After a while you will feel such a glow and so grateful to this very decent officer that when he starts asking you questions you will hardly be able to resist telling him anything he wants to know. So for God's sake, Cox, be on your guard against any German officer who is kind to you.' Reg Jones delighted in the airman's response. He stiffened smartly to attention before the scientist's desk and said: 'I can stand a lot of kindness, sir!'

Cox went on to recount: 'We were given advice on how to escape capture if things went badly wrong with the raid. With the French people in the locality we would be among friends. Granted half a chance, any of the farmers or villagers would hide us and risk their lives ... just as they were doing for all our boys shot down over France. It might well be, the big man said, that even if things went wrong, we would be smuggled, Dennis and me, fairly quickly back to England, either by boat or in a small pick-up aircraft. But in case we were completely on our own over there, we were given French money, maps printed on fine silk and collar studs with miniature compasses hidden in the bases. We had to memorize three addresses, two in France and one in Switzerland. If we got to any of the three, we had a code password. The people in the houses would do the rest. We would simply be packages in their care.'

Much of the above was absurdly optimistic, of course. In early 1942 most French people were understandably wary of lending active assistance to evaders or escapers, which made all the more impressive the courage of those who did so. But Jones's business, that morning at the Air Ministry, was to fill these two bright, thoroughly decent but green young men with the confidence that would be indispensable to fulfil their roles in an extraordinarily hazardous mission. Cox was not an eager warrior such as were most of C Company, impatient to grapple the enemy. He was a very ordinary chap, more than happy to do his duty, but somewhat awe-struck by this melodrama in which he found himself plucked from among the war's extras to play a starring role. If he and Vernon failed, Biting failed. Jones and Priest patiently explained to the airman and the engineer exactly what components of the Würzburg were most coveted. Then, accompanied by earnest expressions of good luck, the two visitors were ushered to a staff car outside the Air Ministry which bore them to Waterloo Station, where they boarded a train for Salisbury, to be once again met and driven back to their spartan quarters at Tilshead. Cox said: 'We were beginning to feel quite important people, but we were soon cut down to size.'

7

'Party' Planning

1 'PICK'

So there was to be a 'party', a 'show', in officers' mess parlance – a real operation of war – and not a mere exercise! One of the most thoughtful spectators of Biting, granted a dress circle view as the raid unfolded, was a soldier named Charles Carrington. Raised in New Zealand where his father was dean of Christchurch Cathedral, he saw much front-line service in the First World War, later became a writer and academic. Recalled to the colours in 1939, aged forty-two, he was posted to serve as the army's liaison officer at RAF Bomber Command, in the rank of colonel. Carrington knew everybody; was respected and trusted, as a soldier seldom was by airmen.

When 'Boy' Browning arrived at Bomber Command headquarters near High Wycombe to evangelize to an audience of its senior personnel about the dawning age of parachute assault, wrote Carrington, 'it mightily impressed the enthusiastic young officers, I thought, but quite failed to convince the seniors. Browning decried the German airborne effort in Crete as ill-organised, and painted a fanciful picture of a [future British] Channel crossing led by a gigantic airborne invasion with highly trained, strictly disciplined troops, partly parachutists and partly glider-borne, in daylight under fighter cover, a tight mass of bomber aircraft, using airborne smoke clouds as cover.'

As for the immediate issue of Bruneval, Air Vice-Marshal Jack Slessor, forceful AOC of Bomber Command's elite 5 Group, opposed fleabite Combined Operations in general and Biting in particular. In Carrington's words, 'He disliked publicity stunts which were then in vogue among army officers who followed the rising star of [Lt. Gen. Sir Bernard] Montgomery.' The colonel thought that 'Boy' Browning overcalled his hand, by demanding the creation of an armada of troop-dropping aircraft at a moment when Britain was desperately short of planes of every kind, 'perhaps doing the cause of Army/Air requirements more harm than good'.

The best the RAF seemed willing to offer airborne forces were its Armstrong Whitworth Albemarles, known to be a design failure, unfit for front-line service. A new air transport unit, 38 Wing, had recently been created to work with Browning's formation under the command of Sir Nigel Norman, but this then lacked its own aircraft and pilots capable of playing a central role in Biting. Maj. Gen. John Kennedy, director of military operations at the War Office, wrote of the period: 'Our chief complaints against the Air Staff were, first, that they would never submit their general bombing policy to the Chiefs of Staff for discussion; and second that they were violently opposed to the provision of proper air support for the Army, which they regarded as a diversion of effort from winning the war.'

Yet if Biting was to be launched with a prospect of success, Browning needed to borrow some planes. At that date, in January 1942, an interregnum prevailed at Bomber Command headquarters. Following the sacking as its C-in-C of the ineffectual Sir Richard Peirse, High Wycombe awaited the arrival of his successor the famous, or notorious, Sir Arthur Harris. Harris was an obsessive, committed to the progressive supposedly war-winning destruction of Germany's urban and industrial centres, to the exclusion of all diversions. Carrington believed that if the principal exponent of 'area bombing' had already been at his post in January, Mountbatten and Browning would never have secured the aircraft that made Bruneval possible, heedless of the prime minister's enthusiasm. As it was, however, a month before the new bomber baron's arrival Carrington was surprised to see Browning deep in conversation in the High Wycombe mess with the deputy C-in-C, Air Vice-Marshal Robert Saundby. They appeared to be getting on famously, even though the latter was almost as passionate an opponent of diversions from the bombing of Germany as Harris would show himself.

Saundby's personal influence was probably decisive, in authorizing the commitment of 51 Squadron, part of 4 Group based in Yorkshire, to carry C Company to France. For the superstitious this represented an ill-omened choice, because 51 had carried out the botched Tragino aqueduct drop more than a year earlier. But the aircrew who participated in Operation Colossus were long gone, and needs must – few Bomber Command units were still equipped with the Whitleys least unsuited to dropping paratroopers. A squadron-leader from Army Co-Operation Command at Andover, who was thought to understand parachuting, was dispatched to Yorkshire to instruct the fliers. Those young men were somewhat bemused by their new assignment, but mostly grateful for a reprieve from bomber 'ops'. Exit holes had to be cut in the floors of sixteen planes – four would become reserves on The Night. Wires were fitted to the roofs of the fuselages for static lines, which snatched open jumpers' parachute packs a second after each man precipitated himself into the void. Once the modifications to the planes were made – on 25 January, only four days after the 'Go' authorization was issued by the chiefs of staff – crews began to practise dropping man-sized dummies and weapons containers.

A trip to a target just inside the continent – which, in the interests of security, was then unspecified – held few terrors for pilots who had for months been flying, and seeing their comrades die, deep inside Germany. But they were acutely conscious of the responsibility imposed by carrying live cargoes, men whose mission would fail if they were dropped in the wrong place, and who would perish if their departures from the bombers were bungled. Thus, they addressed very seriously the training sorties in Yorkshire. Attention was given to marking the paratroopers' containers for quick identification on the ground in darkness: those carrying weapons would have a red light; Dennis Vernon's sapper stores a purple one; the three holding folding trolleys for carrying away the Würzburg components were yellow-lit. All were additionally marked with varied numbers of white stripes.

The mission was to be led by 51 Squadron's commander, Wing-Commander Charles Pickard. 'Pick' was among the more remarkable British airmen of the war, yet another of the outsize personalities who became committed to Biting. He was born in 1915, youngest of five children of a Sheffield businessman who moved to London. He was educated at Framlingham College, where he was much liked, but struggled to read or write anything longer than a team list. He left school still affectionately known at home as 'Boy', baby of the family, though he had grown to a gangling six foot four. A keen sportsman who especially excelled in the saddle of a horse, when a friend whose family owned an African farm offered to take him down to

Kenya for a protracted adventure, he accepted at once. The experience proved an idyll. Handsome, genial, clubbable and a natural enthusiast, young Pickard developed into a star polo player and loved long rides through the bush. A fine shot, he enlisted as a reservist officer in the King's Own African Rifles.

After four years, however, in 1936 it became plain to him and most of his contemporaries that war was looming in Europe; that Happy Valley offered no role in this save for those of Kenya's adventurers and adulterers content to spend such a conflict on safari or in bed. It was time to go home. None of them had money to fund an ocean passage. Pickard was among four kindred spirits who together bought an old car, crammed themselves into it, and drove north through Somaliland, Sudan and Egypt. He survived a bad bout of malaria to catch a boat for the last stage of the journey home, where he attempted to become an army officer. Lacking respectable school certificates, he was rejected. Instead, in January 1937 he was granted a short service commission in the RAF, and qualified as a pilot with an 'above average' rating.

Shortly before the outbreak of war, a pretty girl named Dorothy Hodgkin defied the strong objections of her parents, a colonel and his wife, and married the impecunious airman at Caxton Hall. They set up home with a huge Old English sheepdog named Ming, and Pickard began a rapid ascent up the ranks of the expanding air force. Everybody liked him, and he was a first-class pilot. He served a spell as personal aide to an air marshal, then in the first months of the war flew successively Hampden and Wellington bombers on leaflet-dropping sorties over Germany. Like his near-contemporary Guy Gibson, he would be recognized as a 'press-on type', never deterred from completing an 'op' by technical or weather difficulties. He forged a partnership with a navigator, Alan Broadley, a fellow

Yorkshireman who subsequently flew with Pickard on almost every trip.

Like all that first generation of wartime bomber crews, the pair recognized that death was actuarially the likeliest conclusion of their careers, long before the coming of victory – they entertained no thought of defeat. Given that Bomber Command's losses over Germany were often above 5 per cent and seldom less than 2 per cent, it needed no mathematical genius to recognize that any man who flew a tour of thirty operations, never mind two or three tours, was more likely to perish than to endure. Moreover, luck played at least as large a role as proficiency and courage in determining who survived.

On the ground, Pick sustained the enthusiasms of his first youth. While living in married quarters on an airfield near Newmarket, he acquired two redundant racehorses and rode out most mornings with Dorothy and Ming. In every such relationship between pilot and wife there was no refuge from the oppressive stress of knowing that pleasures must be snatched like passing clouds, because the man in the marriage might well be dead before the next dawn. Many of those who perished left behind widows who thereafter either subsisted on fading memories, or sought to erase the record of a dream that had been forfeited, and to build another life. Neither course was easy for very young women, especially one such as Dorothy, now nursing a baby son.

Off duty, when not in the saddle Pickard stunted the station's Tiger Moth biplane, for the sheer joy of being airborne. And at night over Germany, again and again his aircraft was mauled by flak. Once, he was obliged to ditch in the North Sea on the way home. Pickard and his crew spent fourteen hours pitching in their dinghy – an unspeakable ordeal in peace or war – before being rescued by an RAF launch. Yet he never flinched from those assaults on Germany: when posted to train Czech pilots, he accompanied each novice in turn on their first mission, himself flying as a 'second dickey', occupying the co-pilot's seat.

In March 1941 Pick embarked upon a role that made him a celebrity. He was persuaded, somewhat against his inclinations, to star in a documentary made by the Crown Film Unit for propaganda purposes: *Target for Tonight* portrayed the experience of a bomber pilot and his aircraft 'F-for Freddie'. Pickard was personable, good-looking, and beyond peradventure the real thing. The film became a huge box office hit. All RAF pilots were glamorous figures in the eyes of the wartime public, but *Target for Tonight* made Pickard a standard-bearer for his doomed tribe.

In the summer of 1941 he flew another thirty-three operational sorties over Europe, bringing his total to sixty-four not including those completed as a second pilot with the Czechs. He was then 'screened', transferred to non-operational duties which he detested, including ferrying senior officers. He agitated for a return to the war, and eventually got it. In November he was appointed CO of 51 Squadron based at Dishforth in his native county, flying Whitleys that were mostly employed on photo-reconnaissance tasks. Although still only twenty-seven, he had earned enormous respect both for his personality and his record – he had been awarded both the DSO and DFC. He was liked because he displayed no 'side', that adolescent conceit which afflicted some other RAF stars such as the prickly, assertive little Gibson and the boorish legless fighter pilot Douglas Bader. Pickard's lanky form – he was too tall ever to be really comfortable through six or seven hours in a cockpit – and imperturbable pipe-smoking serenity impressed all those who encountered him.

Thus Combined Operations, when it secured 51 Squadron, recognized that it was being loaned the services of an 'A' team, of which brave, skilful, tousled and somehow cuddly Pickard was captain. Like so many contemporary heroes, however, he could have passed for ten years older than his real age. Daphne du Maurier wrote to Grace Browning, the general's sister, about Tommy's equally endemic exhaustion under the strain of his responsibilities: 'When this war is over, all the men will look 200.'

Early in February the Whitleys flew down from Yorkshire to Thruxton, a half-built Wiltshire airfield near Andover, followed in trucks by their ground crews. On the 7th, before C Company travelled to Scotland, its officers and men were borne fifteen miles east from Tilshead to 51 Squadron's temporary residence, to meet for the first time Pickard and his pilots, who would fly them into action. Because Thruxton still lacked living quarters, the crews were obliged to doss down in some discomfort at nearby RAF Andover. The soldiers, almost none of whom had heard a shot fired in earnest, were impressed by the calm professionalism of their chauffeurs, who had heard many. On the night of 12 February, while C Company was still in Scotland, Pick flew across the Channel, carrying Biting's appointed air supremo Group-Captain Sir Nigel Norman as a passenger, to 'stooge around' offshore for a few minutes. They were delighted by the ease with which they picked out French coastal landmarks. Before the month was out, they would need to pinpoint these in earnest.

After returning to Wiltshire from Inveraray, Frost and his men began their new round of training with a demonstration jump before 'Boy' Browning. On 15 February Pickard's Whitleys, having taken off from Thruxton, dropped the paratroopers ten miles away, on a landing zone that later became familiar to most of British airborne forces, north-east of Larkhill around Browning's headquarters at Syrencot House. This was the first flight on which 51 Squadron carried live parachutists. Frost fumed at the confusion which attended the aircraft loading and every other aspect of the exercise. They left the field very late, and were borne through failing afternoon light to the drop zone, where they landed on iron-frozen ground. The greatest fear suffusing the company was that of suffering a jump injury, so common in airborne operations, which might render a man unfit to fly to France. In the event, there were no casualties worse than a few bruises and sprains. Browning applauded. Frost, however, did not. He castigated the whole exercise as 'a shambles ... disorder and confusion and a mighty waste of time ... The general said he was satisfied – more than I was.' Only one stick, that of the Seaforths led by the big, formidable Glaswegian Sgt. David Grieve, quit their plane in the quick succession that was vital to achieve a concentrated landing.

Yet now, for all those committed to Biting, ready or unready, it was almost time to go. Browning fretted, and rightly so, that too much of C Company's training time had been expended upon hanging around with the navy, attempting to practise the evacuation phase of the operation. Insufficient hours were made available to address the tactical challenges of storming enemy positions in darkness – the disciplines of fire and movement, of supporting each other in advances by bounds. This was partly because so many of the short winter hours had been wasted travelling between Tilshead and first Alton Priors, then the south coast. Now it was too late to remedy that. Between beach exercises, C Company practised packing and loading containers, fitting them into Whitley bomb bays; boarding the aircraft. During off-duty nights, the paratroopers relaxed in

A/30. 1 PRU. 5·12·41. F/8

The image that started it all: Tony Hill's shot of a Würzburg *gerät*, located beside the Manoir de la Falaise at La Poterie-Cap d'Antifer in Normandy.

The eager adventurers: men of C Company, 2nd Parachute Battalion, during rehearsals for Biting at Inveraray. Note their smocks, copied from those worn by German *fallschirmjäger*.

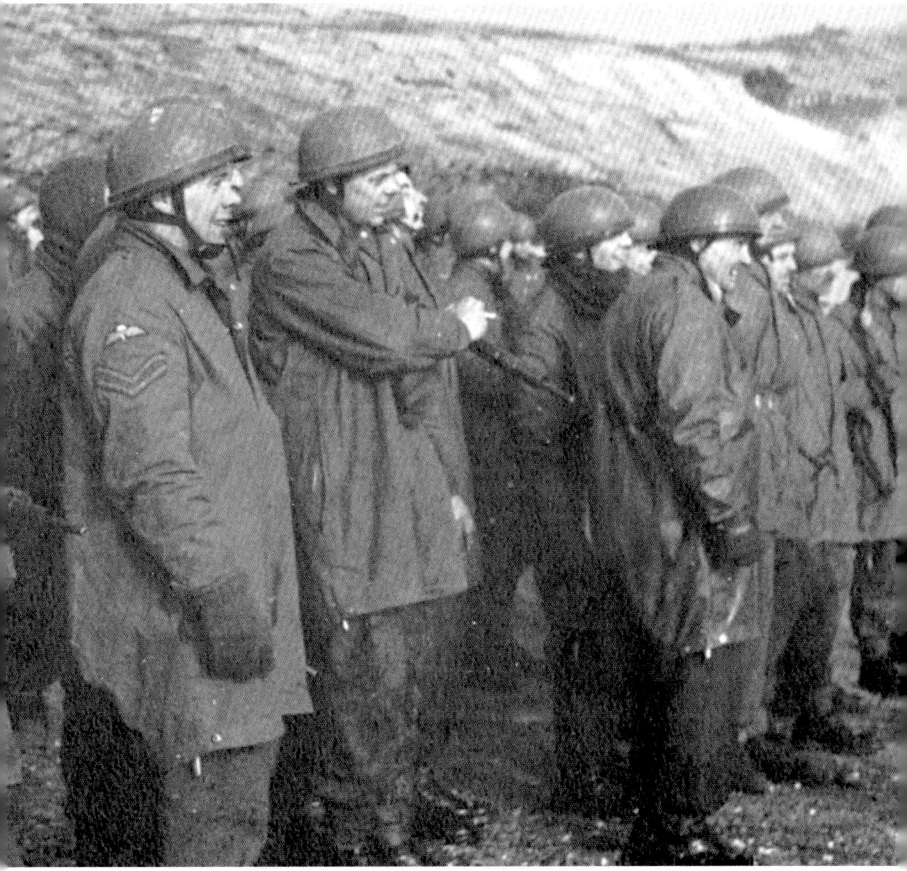

The men who found things out: (top left) PRU pilot Tony Hill; Dr Reg Jones before the war; (below) in his accustomed Basque beret 'Rémy', escaping from France in 1942.

(Above) 'Pol' Roger Dumont and (right) 'Charlemagne' Charles Chauveau. (Below) Daphne du Maurier with her husband, the commander of Britain's nascent airborne forces Maj. Gen. Frederick Browning in off-duty 'mufti'.

Sainte-Marie-au-B

To Etretat

La Poterie - Cap d'Antifer

Le Presbytère

Drop Zone

Assembl Poir

'Rectangle'

'Lone House'

< To Freya radar scanners

'Henry'

Route nationale 40

To Le Havre

'Redoubt'

Bruneval

'Beach Fort'

Another early 1942 RAF aerial view of what became the battlefield of Operation Biting, showing key landmarks. The image does not reveal how steep and rough was the descent from the radar station to the beach, and how exposed to fire from defenders entrenched on the western or opposite side of the defile, above 'Beach Fort'. German wire entanglements on the hillside above the latter are not visible.

(Above) 'Dickie' Commodore Lord Louis Mountbatten inspects ratings of HMS *Prins Albert* during the exercises at Inveraray and (below) Frost's men practise their exit by landing-craft.

(Above) 'Bobby' Marquis de Casa Maury, Mountbatten's polo-playing friend, implausibly translated into Combined Ops' intelligence chief for Biting, at his 1937 wedding to Freda Dudley Ward, former mistress of Edward Prince of Wales; and (below) Lt. Col. Johnny Goschen, one of Browning's staff officers, in earnest conversation with Major John Frost.

SAINT-JOUIN-BRUNEVAL. — La Descente.

Vital landmarks for Biting: (above left) an Edwardian image of the almost sheer defile leading down from Bruneval hamlet to the sea: the attackers had to descend the right-hand hill, under fire from Germans entrenched on the left face. (Below left) 'Lone House', stormed by Frost and his men. Opposite (above) 'Beach Fort', chief impediment to C Company's escape. German trenches ran above it, from which the defenders fired on C Company; and (below) a modern view of the beach from the sea, somewhat changed from 1942, but showing the topography as the navy saw it.

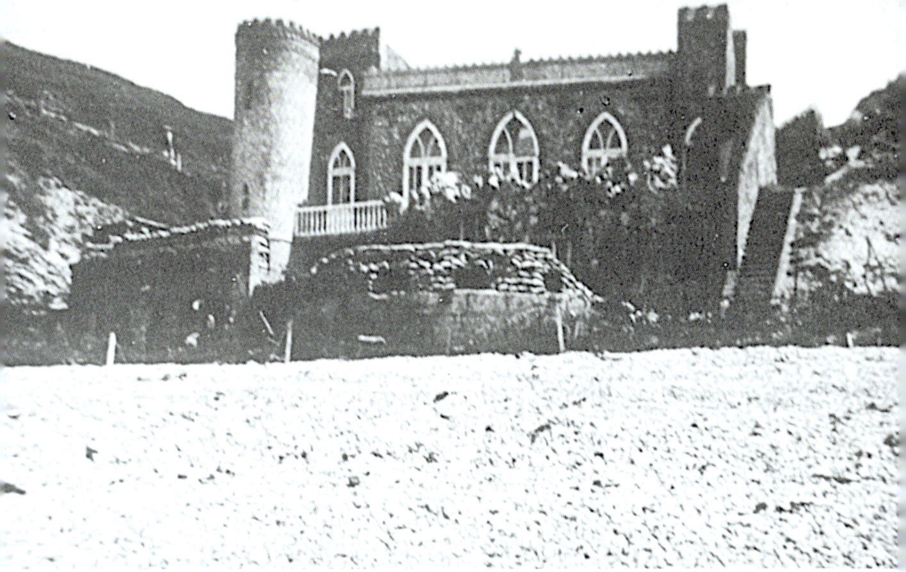

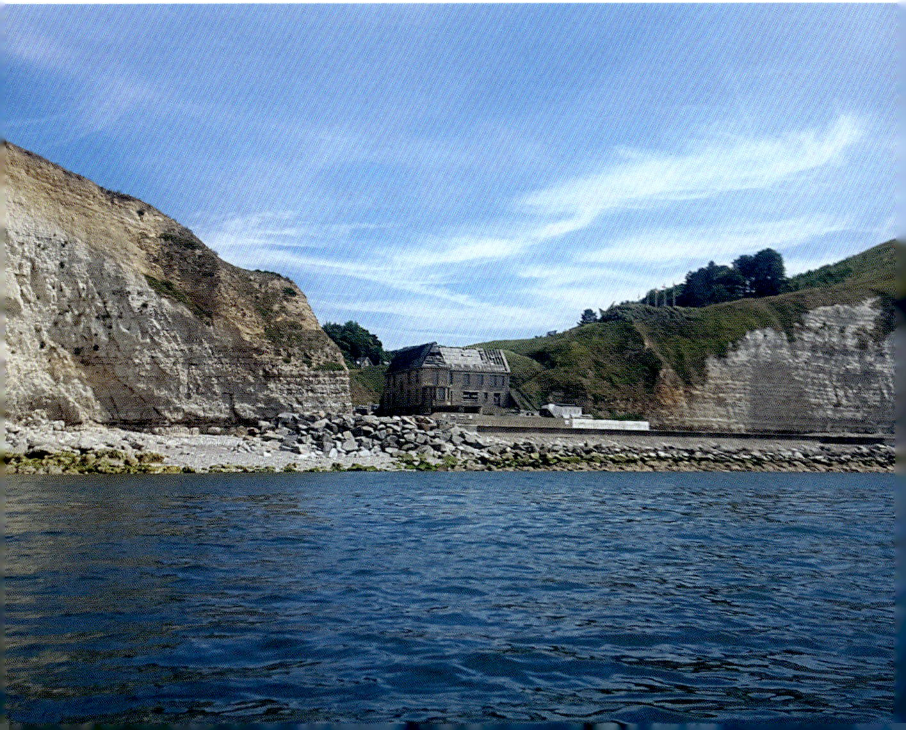

MGBs – motor gunboats – of the flotilla which played a key role in the naval dimension of Biting.

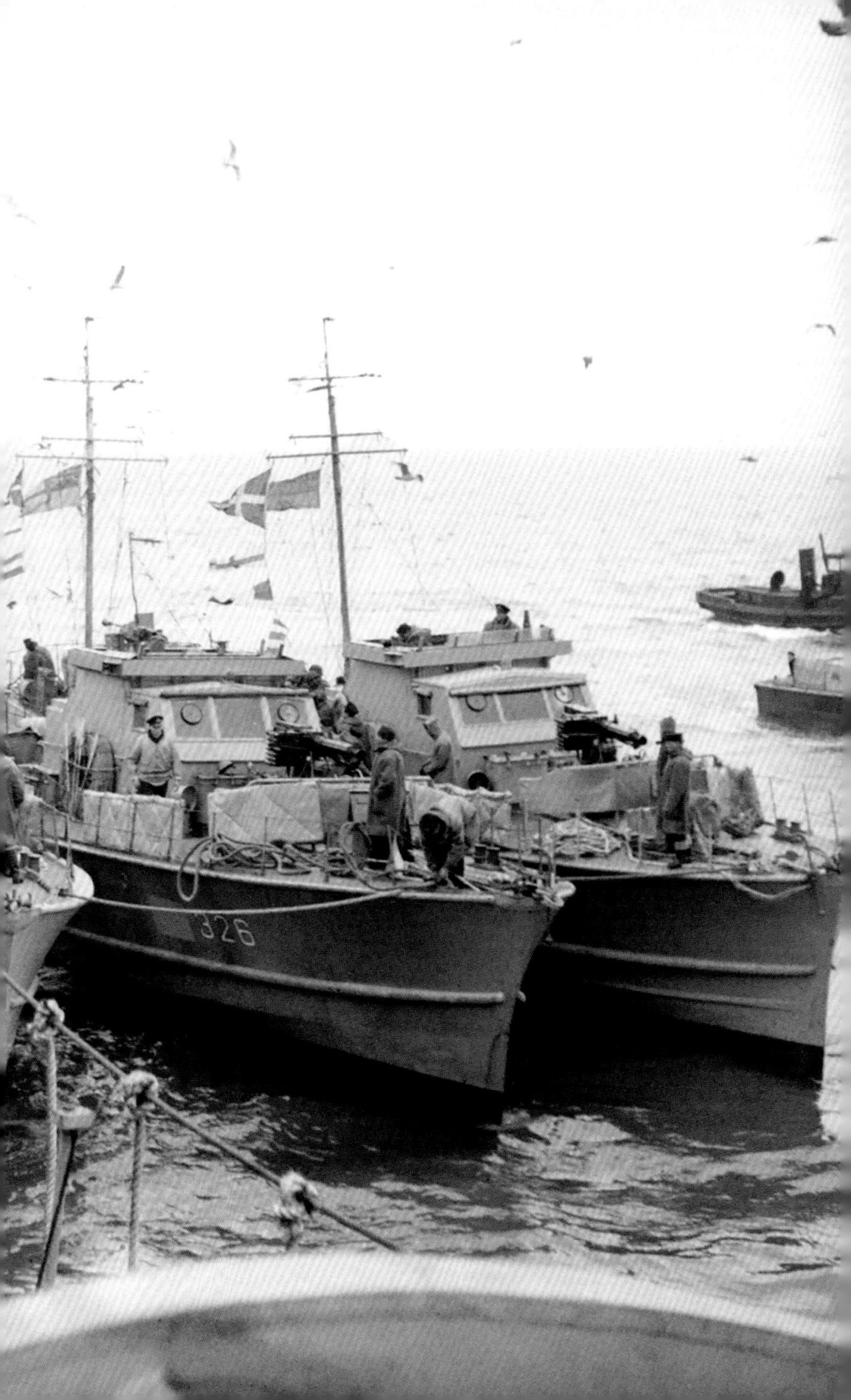
326

'Carry out Operation Biting Tonight': Admiral Sir William James in the great cabin of HMS *Victory*, from which he gave the 'go' order, and (below left) the admiral as he is best known to posterity. (Below right) Wing-Commander Charles Pickard, who led 51 Squadron to drop C Company.

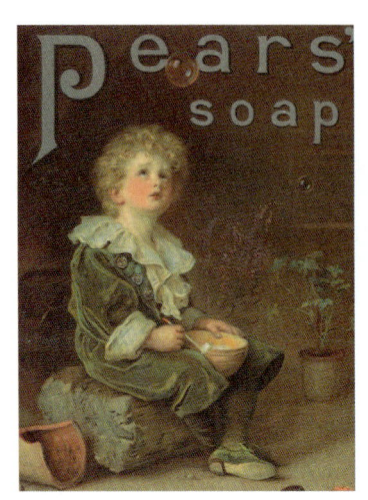

Defenders: Luftwaffe personnel off-duty in the local brothel at Étretat and (below) German troops parade through the town's streets.

An RAF Whitley dropping paratroopers under training. Notice its lowered undercarriage, to reduce the aircraft's speed, and how scattered is the 'stick' of men approaching the ground.

Tilshead's quaint old flint-and-brick pub, the Rose & Crown, a mile below the camp. Some of those who became as drunk and noisy as thin wartime beer allowed were foolish enough to boast that they were about to go into battle. Hearing of this, Frost vented his wrath on the big talkers. If there was any repetition, he threatened them with the worst sanction he could impose: to be left behind on The Night.

The major would have been enraged had he glimpsed a letter home written on the 21st by one of his men, Private Hugh McIntyre, to a brother in Ayrshire: 'Just a wee note to you Geordie I hope this scribble finds you in the pink. This leaves me in the pink and keeping fine … I am going to tell you something now Geordie I am going on a raid this week and don't tell anybody not even Mother or Father or your best friends and I shouldn't be writing this it's a great secret and I'll be home next Saturday on leave and I will send you a telegram when I arrive back.' Suffice it now to say that such a message was never dispatched.

2 THE ENEMY

At last Frost was permitted to brief his officers and men about the exact purpose of Biting. NCOs were given an outline of their task on 17 February, and next day all ranks received details of their allocation to sections – 'sticks' – in the twelve aircraft that would carry 120 of them into action. On the 19th, Frost briefed them from aerial photos. 'Gentlemen,' he announced, 'the demonstration' – the now-discarded cover story – 'is over. The operation starts here.' Next day first the subalterns, then the NCOs and other ranks, assembled to study the details of their respective roles before a painted plaster-of-Paris model of the Bruneval radar site. This had been constructed in the cellars of RAF Danesfield, working from Tony Hill's aerial photographs, by men and women directed by F/Lt. Geoffrey Deeley, who in civil life had been director of sculpture at a London art college.

In the course of the war it was found that those who had previously made their livings constructing fancy wedding cakes were especially suited to Medmenham's variety of arts and crafts. The Bruneval models – two were eventually made – proved invaluable, familiarizing Frost's men with the terrain on which they would fight for the radar site in a way that maps and photos could not, though a subsequent post-mortem urged that briefings and maps for future operations should be extended to cover the ground for three miles around the drop zone, instead of the single square mile of the Bruneval model. Moreover the model did not – importantly – show the south side of the deep defile and German beach defences which were to prove critical factors on The Night. And Frost's men were still not told exactly where on the coast of France their objective lay. This detail was withheld from most until the day of the drop.

It was a curiosity of the British royal family's intimate German connections that even as Lord Louis Mountbatten presided over Biting, the Nazi trophy which it was designed to seize rested in the unworthy custody of one of his own cousins. Twenty-nine-year-old Captain Prince Alexander-Ferdinand von Preussen commanded the Luftwaffe's 23 *Flugmelde*, the signals company responsible for the radar installations at Bruneval and Sainte-Adresse. The prince was a great-great-grandson of Queen Victoria. He was also a grandson of the last kaiser, and his father was a friend of Hermann Goering.

This last relationship almost certainly explains von Preussen's appointment to a 'cushy billet' in France, where his function was ornamental rather than technical. He seemed to know little about radar, but much about partying, mostly with his aristocratic peers – subordinates found him chilly and aloof. Shortly before Biting was staged, von Preussen, who had joined the National Socialist Party as far back as 1932, transferred his headquarters from cosy Étretat to a spacious villa on the seafront at Sainte-Adresse, some twelve miles south. From there von Preussen's officers paid bi-weekly visits to the radar sites under their command, but left the daily operational stuff to their local NCOs. The most senior Luftwaffe functionary in the Bruneval area during late February 1942 was a Lt. Schleich, billeted at La Poterie, but he played no part in the events about to unfold.

The radar installations had suffered technical glitches and delays before becoming fully operational. Telephone communication between the sites and the regional Luftwaffe control centre at Rouen remained unsatisfactory. Local flak guns were still linked to sound-locators, rather than to radar. Von Preussen's unit now boasted two Freya arrays at Bruneval, the second an improved model, together with a Würzburg designated W110 at that site and a second, W120, at Sainte-Adresse. These were manned by something over a hundred personnel, quartered nearby and serving in shifts.

The German occupiers had a phrase in those heady days of victory, idyllic for themselves: 'living like gods in France'. Hitler had fixed an exchange rate for the franc against the Reichsmark which strongly favoured the latter, so that his soldiers, sailors and airmen enjoyed the best of French food and wines very cheaply. The technicians at Bruneval, who found their labours not especially taxing, also had access to the local brothel in Étretat. The only violent incident to have troubled them was an RAF harassing raid on 27 August 1941, in the course of which a bundle of air-dropped incendiaries smashed through the roof of the château beside the Würzburg site to set fire to their NCO's bed on the upper floor. Next morning the sergeant was obliged to indent to the unit quartermaster in La Poterie for replacement clothing – his own had been incinerated before the fire was put out.

The British could see on their photographs the German-occupied buildings, but did not always correctly deduce their significance. The structure that seemed to them of most importance was the aforementioned château just east of the radar. This was rightfully named the Manoir de la Falaise, property of a famous Paris surgeon named Professor Antonin Gosset. The panzer spearheads which reached Bruneval on 22 June 1940 occupied the Gosset château, and successor units had retained it ever since. Most of its contents had long since been removed to Germany excepting the family silver, which the Gossets' cook successfully abstracted for safe-keeping.

After the incendiary episode, the radar site personnel decided the château was too conspicuous to remain a comfortable dormitory. Instead the Luftwaffe men excavated a deep dugout forty yards from the installation, in which during their watches the nine-man crew snatched rest in rotation. The British, however, assumed the château was still occupied. It was marked on their model and maps as LONE HOUSE.

Three hundred yards northwards, screened by trees on all four sides, lay the château's attached farm, a big cluster of buildings centred upon a pretty farmhouse. This housed the Luftwaffe communications centre for the three radars, together with vehicle garages and sleeping quarters. The British called it Le Presbytère, though in truth that was the name of a hamlet several hundred yards further inland. Local French people knew the place as the Gosset farm. On the British model the complex became simply RECTANGLE, in keeping with its shape. Its personnel were all issued with pistols or rifles, but they were technicians rather than fighting soldiers, and lacked heavy weapons. On several occasions during the war when ground fighting erupted in the vicinity of RAF overseas bases, their personnel declined to participate, asserting that this was soldiers' business. A similar spirit prevailed in much of the Luftwaffe.

The deployments and capabilities of the nearby army units, especially of those soldiers posted between the radar site and the sea, were a serious preoccupation of the British planners. Even if C Company and the engineers secured the radar components, the raid would fail, humiliatingly, if they could not fight a way to the beach with their spoils. The ground defence of the area, as distinct from the radar technology, was in the hands of the 336th Infantry Division. A shadow overhung the comfortable routines of the men of this formation: since mid-February, they had been under warning orders to prepare for a move to the Eastern Front. Their French idyll was to be harshly terminated. Meanwhile, they were enjoying their last weeks of defending *Festung Europa* amid relatively generous access to food, wine and women.

The formation's 685th Regiment, a thousand strong, was commanded by fifty-one-year-old Col. Ernst-Georg von Eisenhart-Rothe, whose headquarters was situated in a handsome mansion near Étretat. The picturesque little coastal town, set on a steep hillside six miles north of Bruneval, had been a fashionable *belle époque* watering place, attracting such artistic giants as the composer Jacques Offenbach, the painters Claude Monet, Gustave Courbet and Eugène Boudin, the novelist Alexandre Dumas. Von Eisenhart-Rothe's troops were deployed and dispersed over a considerable area between

Étretat and the hamlets south of Bruneval, where its neighbouring 687th Regiment took over responsibility.

Fifteen members of the 685th's 1st Company were quartered in the village of La Poterie, less than two miles east of Bruneval. The defences below the latter, which Frost's men must overcome, had been created to check invaders landing from the sea. High on the cliff, between the radar site and the beach, were new pillboxes labelled by the British as REDOUBT. Covering the deep defile beyond and below, leading down to the sea, there appeared to be linked trenches and dense wire entanglements. Most formidable, and right above the beach, was the big, fancifully castellated villa, built in 1860 and for a time a casino, once named the Villa Stella Maris, which the Germans had now concreted into a strongpoint. They had also created sandbagged emplacements in front of the villa, facing the sea. The British named Stella Maris and its linked network of trenches, overlaid with camouflage nets, BEACH FORT. Inland of this was a house on the north side of the defile, believed to be another strongpoint which they dubbed GUARDROOM.*

The 685th's officers had recently been making an effort to improve the army's distant relationship with their comrades of the Luftwaffe. At meetings between the two services, a system of joint patrols was agreed, not least to watch for saboteurs: there were periodic outbreaks of telephone-line cutting, for which several French suspects or hostages had been shot. From the British viewpoint, an important and encouraging factor was

---

* A puzzle surrounds the location of Guardroom, which Frost in his briefing to the company described as 'further inland' from Beach Fort. We know that while German soldiers occupied the Villa Stella Maris, all the significant defensive fire came from the trenches above it. This suggests that the house named on C Company's maps and photos as Guardroom proved to be unoccupied, or at least undefended.

that none of the small bodies of von Eisenhart-Rothe's soldiers posted in the immediate vicinity of Bruneval possessed their own transport. They were in contact with each other by field telephone, but could move against any threat only at the pace of their own feet, like Frost's paratroopers.

The briefing issued to C Company by Airborne Division headquarters on 21 February stated: 'A small enemy force, probably not more than 10 all ranks, will be operating a 53cm RDF from [Lone] House, dugouts, hut and square pit situated on the edge of the cliff some 800 yds NW of the village of Bruneval.' Though the hundred-odd personnel at Rectangle were air force signallers, not soldiers, 'it is highly likely that prepared defences are concealed on the edge of the trees [on the south side of the farm complex] ... There is a very considerable strongpoint [Beach Fort] on the tongue of land south of the road from the [beach] exit. This contains four M.G. [machine-gun] posts and possibly more, facing outwards. There are two M.G.s in the first house nearest cliff and this house is surrounded by barbed wire ten metres thick, which prevents entry from the road.'

The British planners could be almost certain their retreat to the beach would be opposed by Germans thoroughly awakened by the inescapable shoot-out around the radar site. They could not divine, however, exactly what resistance they might encounter at different locations. In truth, there were only nine soldiers in and around Stella Maris, together with another eighteen in Bruneval, and a similar number of infantrymen in the village of La Poterie. C Company should thus comfortably outnumber the defenders. The Combined Operations planners were nonetheless taking a mighty risk, by discounting the strength of German forces – an entire regiment, if not also other elements of the 336th Division – which might be mobilized against the raiders from the surrounding area, within the two hours that Frost's men were scheduled to be in France.

The British christened the Würzburg set HENRY, for no reason that anybody could discover. C Company's objectives, as stated in Frost's orders, were 'to capture various parts of HENRY and bring them down to the boats. To capture prisoners who have been in charge of HENRY. And to obtain all possible information about HENRY, and any documents referring to him which may be in LONE HOUSE.'

The designated parachute landing zone lay more than half a mile inland, a similar distance from the radar site. On 27 January Combined Ops had quizzed SOE about whether it might be possible for an agent to plant a beacon to mark the LZ for 51 Squadron, but was told that this was impossible within the appointed time frame. The entire C Company – perforce scattered along a landing path of six hundred yards – would drop east of the objective, retrieve weapons and equipment from the containers, then assemble in a wooded and scrubby cleft west of the LZ. From there Frost's sections would disperse to carry out their various tasks, of which the foremost was the assault on Lone House and the radar site, some four hundred yards north-west of the appointed rendezvous, up rising ground.

There was an issue here, which would dog the planning of airborne operations for the rest of the war and beyond. Was it preferable to drop attackers directly onto their objectives, accepting inevitable confusion and casualties in order to achieve absolute surprise? This had been the course adopted by the Germans in May 1940, when they landed seventy-eight gliderborne paratroopers atop the Belgian fortress of Eben Emael on the Albert Canal near Liège, securing its much larger garrison's prompt surrender. The British, however, at Bruneval as later in the war at Arnhem, preferred to sacrifice speed and propinquity, to use a drop zone where the attackers could land undisturbed on easy terrain, then organize before joining battle. The planners of Biting took a big gamble by committing C Company to a scheduled interval of at least thirty minutes, and probably longer, between leaving the aircraft and reaching the radar site. If the defenders were on their toes, they could mobilize to formidable effect within such a time frame.

Forty men of 'Nelson', many of them former Seaforth Highlanders, would land first, since they faced the longest march to their objectives. These were to be led by John Ross, Frost's second-in-command, supported by Euan Charteris, known to his comrades as 'Junior', because he was their youngest officer, and looked it. The Nelsons were tasked to overrun German positions on both sides of the defile leading to the beach below Bruneval, cut a path through the wire blocking access to the sea, then secure the radar thieves' withdrawal. They must successively storm German pillboxes at Redoubt, together with the presumed strongpoints at Guardroom and Beach Fort. Their three 'light assault' sections would be commanded by Charteris. A fourth 'heavy' section, including some sappers armed with anti-tank mines to be laid on the Bruneval road, would be personally led by Ross, who was also thereafter to be responsible as beachmaster for marking a route through a possible German minefield, and supervising the evacuation by landing-craft. The Nelsons were allocated much of C Company's firepower, because they and the Rodneys were expected to face a large share of the night's fighting, up against enemy soldiers rather than mere technicians.

Frost's own party, fourteen strong, was to secure Lone House. The entire company was warned not to fire a shot until they heard the major blow four whistle blasts when his own group was ready to attack. Any German encountered before this signal was, if possible, to be dispatched silently. Simultaneous with Frost's assault ten Jellicoes, led by Peter Young, would dash directly for the radar site. The moment it was secure, the Hardys of the technical team, commanded by Dennis Vernon, would be called forward from their holding position, to tackle the Würzburg. Until the paratroopers were in control, however, it was vital to keep the specialists out of the line of fire. If Cox and the engineers were disabled or killed before they could do their business, Biting would be set at naught. This was not a raid designed to shoot up German coastal defenders. Frost wrote in his orders to the company: 'It is emphasized that the whole operation fails unless HENRY is effectively dealt with and the parts required are captured. All ranks must be fully aware of this.'

And while Frost's and Young's sections made the main assault, a group of ten Drakes, led by Lt. Peter Naoumoff, would take up a blocking, or at least screening, position to the north-east, between the radar site and the Gosset farmhouse complex, where most of the local Germans were thought to be stationed or billeted. Hitherto Naoumoff had merely been attached to the company as a spare officer. Twenty-two-year-old 'Popoff', as his fellow subalterns called him, was an unusual character – son of a White Russian émigré, brought up in west London and educated at Reigate Grammar School. Before joining Frost's band, he had been serving as battalion intelligence officer. Now that C Company was going into action, the major declined to break the young man's heart by leaving him behind.

John Timothy's forty Rodneys would protect the eastern flank – block the road from the hamlet of La Poterie – from which it was most likely that any motorized German interference would come; elements of an infantry company were known to be billeted there. Once Vernon's and Cox's Hardys had fulfilled their task, Timothy's men would form the reserve and rearguard, as Frost led his own groups ahead of them to the beach.

By the standards of those days C Company was lavishly equipped with tactical wirelesses: five No. 38 sets with a notional one-mile range, for the parties to talk to each other; two heavier No. 18 sets, with a nominal ten-mile range, to communicate with the navy. In the event, none of this technology played any useful role: messages had to be carried to and from Frost by runners; C Company's signallers might as well have stayed at home. The British Army's infantry voice radios contributed little to small unit manoeuvres in any battle of the Second World War.

The longer Frost studied the plan imposed on him by Browning's staff, the less happy he felt about his own meagre ration of discretion, and likely lack of control on the night: he was wise enough to anticipate the wireless failures. When questions were invited following the briefing, one man asked how they could hope to achieve surprise when the RAF's camera planes had been diving over the Germans' heads for days, to secure Tony Hill's oblique images. Frost flannelled: 'Oh, telephoto lens, you know. Taken from miles away.' Somebody asked if the company would blacken faces. Absolutely not, said the major: 'I want to be able to recognize you in the moonlight.'

Another decision – almost certainly a good one – was made not to use tracer ammunition, albeit with an inevitable loss of accuracy for the company's fifteen Bren-gunners. Tracer streaking across the night sky assisted accurate shooting, but at the cost of giving away the firers' positions and strength. Another questioner demanded: when the whistle blasts are sounded outside Lone House, what if the door is locked?

Somebody said facetiously: 'Ring the bell!' Frost expressed admiration for the 'almost incredible detail' of the intelligence brief, largely provided by Roger Dumont, through Rémy, though Bobby Casa Maury at Combined Ops received the credit: 'The strengths, the billets, the weapons, morale and even the names of some Germans were known.'

The perils of the operation were many and various. However, the British soldiers, none of them yet thirty save CSM Strachan, were in exuberant mood as they chattered around the model of their objective. We must think of those briefing sessions as taking place in rooms wreathed in smoke, because in those days almost every man was addicted to cigarettes, from Frost downwards. Peter Young said, 'Excitement and enthusiasm reached fever pitch. Here, in the dreary, depressing days of early 1942, was actually a chance to hit back. A new vigour was apparent.' They speculated on the likely lassitude of Germans drinking in the Venniers' cramped little bar at the Beau-Minet hotel in Bruneval.

Such was the spirit among that first, unblooded generation of British paratroopers that they shared serene confidence in their ability to overcome whatever enemies they met. Later in the war, after fearsome attrition by battlefield losses, the ranks of the airborne divisions were filled up with many men posted from line units. In North Africa, Frost was once asked if he would accept some anti-aircraft gunners, to fill the depleted ranks of 2 Para. He assented at once, saying: 'As long as they can shoot and dig!' and never regretted it. In February 1942, however, every man of C Company was there because he had coolly chosen a conspicuously dangerous role in the war.

It was plain to everyone from Mountbatten and Browning to the humblest Scottish soldier that surprise, and only surprise, could confer success. If the Germans were expecting them, the

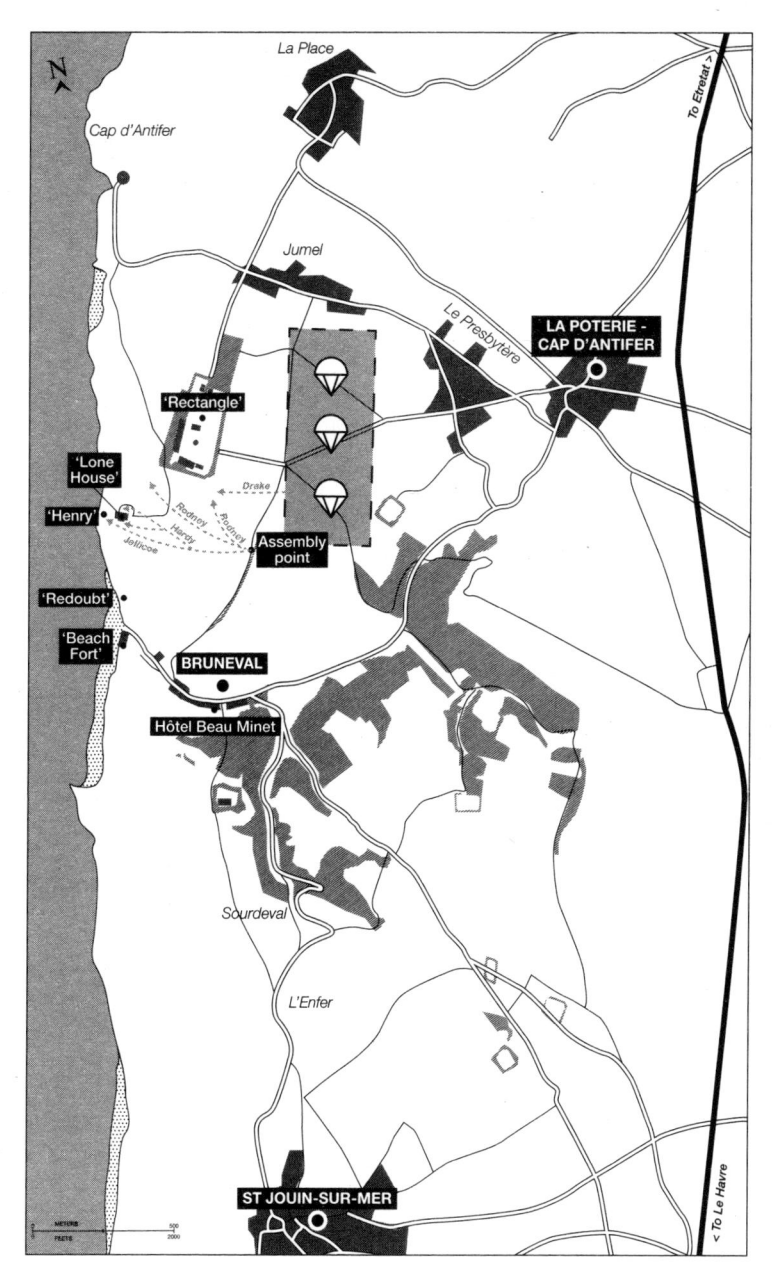

C Company's Normandy battlefield

little force was doomed. But surprise was what airborne warfare was conceived to deliver; what the German *fallschirmjäger* had triumphantly achieved on the Dutch-Belgian border in 1940. The plan reflected extreme optimism about the feebleness of the enemy response to the airborne landing. But it might just work.

Frost emphasized the importance of sustaining silence until he blew his whistle. Only German signals personnel were to be taken prisoner – ordinary soldiers possessed no intelligence value. In the exercises in Dorset, four men dragged and heaved across country each of the two-wheeled trolleys which they would take to France, loaded with boulders to simulate the Würzburg components which they hoped to carry on The Night. Lt. Vernon's engineers, their foremost responsibility to dismantle and remove the radar, also studied the infantry tasks, in case circumstances of battle obliged them to fight alongside the paratroopers. They practised clearing German mines using two Polish-model detectors, and laying their own anti-tank mines on the road towards the beach, to check any German vehicles arriving from elsewhere. The engineers were issued with bulging bags of tools and even white tape for marking paths through minefields. The RAF gave Vernon and his NCO Corporal Sid Jones perfunctory lessons in flashlight photography, to snatch images of the Würzburg on its mounting. When the photos from France later proved useless, everybody admitted this tuition had been too rushed.

On 19 February, officers from MI9 lectured the company on escape techniques, if any of the raiders were so unfortunate as to find themselves left behind in France. There had been a vexed debate in secret circles about whether C Company should be given addresses of French people in Normandy known to be sympathetic to the Allies, and who indeed had helped British escapers back in 1940. Such disclosure was vetoed by Col. Claude Dansey, the deputy chief of MI6 who, in the words of MI9's historians, had an even lower opinion than his colleagues 'of the security-mindedness of junior officers and other ranks ... and [thought] that the chance of a successful evasion from the beach was too small to justify the risk'. Nonetheless Combined Ops defied Dansey to disclose such addresses to Charles Cox and Vernon, together with Charles Pickard, all of whom memorized them. This security breach infuriated MI9 when one of its officers, Jimmy Langley, learned of it two years later, at his own wedding where Pickard served as best man.

On 20 February C Company received a visit from a troop of 3 Commando, which demonstrated techniques for breaking through or surmounting wire entanglements, such as they must expect to meet. A succession of exercises with the navy on the south coast proved chaotic. During one such, on a Dorset beach, the men were dropped at their objective in lorries. The Whitleys of 51 Squadron were scheduled then to overfly them, dropping weapons containers: these, however, all landed wide. When the paratroopers assembled on the sands for evacuation, they discovered the navy was looking for them elsewhere: C Company awaited its deliverers in a British minefield, ten miles from the landing-craft. They were now just two days short of the first possible 'D-Day' for Biting, so this fiasco was serious. Sir Nigel Norman, responsible for the RAF's role, admitted that Lulworth was 'a very bad show' but added in mitigation: 'I think it taught us a lot.' The navy insisted there must be a successful rehearsal of the evacuation before Frost's men jumped. This was scheduled for Friday 20th, in Southampton Water, but poor weather forced a postponement until Sunday 22nd.

The prime minister was kept informed about these delays and setbacks, and about Biting's perceived windows of opportunity. Ismay wrote on 22 February: 'It will be a great pity if the weather breaks during these 48 hours, but [Mountbatten] is in complete agreement with C-in-C Portsmouth and General Browning that so hazardous an enterprise must not be undertaken without the most complete and thorough rehearsal.' Monday 23rd had been designated as the first possible 'D-Day', when moon and tide were suitable for the descent on Bruneval. That night, the weather was perfect: the paratroopers cursed the loss of an opportunity to launch their mission in earnest. Instead, they carried out an exercise with the landing-craft which degenerated into another farce. Frost said: 'The last rehearsal could not have been a more dismal failure.'

The navy had miscalculated the tides. Several ALCs became stranded sixty yards offshore, immovable until the next flood. They were unable to embark troops and could not be floated off even by the combined efforts of scores of muscular paratroopers, heaving against the hulls, thigh-deep in icy Southampton Water. Vernon and Cox had rejoined C Company in time to participate in its succession of waterlogged rehearsals. As the diminutive flight-sergeant shivered in his sea-soaked jump smock, he was stabbed by the sudden thought: 'Supposing either Dennis Vernon or I had caught pneumonia, and hadn't been able to go on the raid?' Neither of these two did succumb, fortunately, but it was increasingly evident that the ALCs, indispensable to withdrawal of Frost's men and their intended booty, were difficult craft to manage, especially on an enemy shore. Their 'hostilities only' skippers and ratings, who included a former wine merchant, a Lloyd's insurance underwriter and a repertory actor, lacked ship-handling skills. Four precious training days had now been wasted, on abortive rehearsals with the navy for the evacuation phase, when C Company might more usefully have been practising assaults on pillboxes. Come to that, it remains a mystery why Combined Operations ordered *Prins Albert*'s voyage to Scotland, and C Company's lengthy train journeys, a further expenditure of precious time, instead of confining exercises to the south coast.

There were now thought to be only three nights left when moon and tides at Bruneval fitted the operational schedule. Despite the chaos of the exercises, it was decided that 51 Squadron's pilots, Frost's paratroopers and the navy's inshore skippers were sufficiently practised to risk giving the 'go' order. If the weather worked, Biting would be launched. It is hard to doubt that the impatience and even impetuousness of the prime minister, Mountbatten and Browning must have contributed to this decision: all manner of great men would be distressed and even angered if, after so much sweat, toil and tears, there was to be no blood, hopefully German. On Tuesday 24 February, C Company cleaned and oiled weapons, filled magazines, packed the bulky arms and equipment containers which were then dispatched by truck to the airfield. The men carrying Sten guns and pistols would jump with these holstered or tucked beneath their harnesses, while rifles and Brens travelled separately. Each jumper wore a brown gabardine smock reaching down to the knee, explicitly copied from those used by the Luftwaffe's airborne warriors, together with silk gloves against the pervasive cold.

They ate lunch, then were urged to rest for an hour or two before boarding the transport to Thruxton. At teatime, however, Frost received an anti-climactic telephone call from divisional headquarters: 'Owing to adverse weather conditions', there would have to be a twenty-four-hour postponement. They could accept only the lightest of winds – 15 mph or less – to achieve a concentrated parachute drop, such as was vital to success. Next day, Wednesday, was a repeat. Each evening the weapons containers had to be hauled back from Thruxton; unpacked. 'We are all thoroughly miserable,' Frost wrote in his diary. 'Each morning we brace ourselves for the venture, and each night ... we have time to think of all the things that can go wrong, and to reflect that if we don't go on Thursday ... we shall have to wait for a whole month to pass before conditions may be suitable.' They did not go on Thursday. They prepared, instead, to be sent on leave.

8

The Jump

On Friday 27 February, conditions on the coast of northern France were deemed marginal for a beach evacuation in the early hours of next morning, following a flight to Bruneval that night. Low tide would fall at 0340. The landing-craft sought a reasonable depth of water inshore, to avoid the risk of stranding. Now, instead, they faced making a rendezvous when the ebb was far advanced: the three previous nights had been more suitable. Yet if they did not launch Biting now, another moon-cycle must come around before conditions were once more acceptable, and who knew how the war, and enemy defences, might evolve meanwhile? Frost, attuned to disappointment, assumed he would receive another order to stand down. Sir William James, C-in-C Portsmouth, had been appointed Biting's supreme commander, a grandiose title for the arbiter of a modest operation. The admiral had been bombed out of his rightful headquarters in the dockyard, and instead directed naval movements from Nelson's old flagship HMS *Victory*, forever berthed alongside the quay, set in a steel cradle weakened by the Luftwaffe's battering. At 0900 on the 27th, Fred Cook mounted the gangway; was shown into the admiral's Great Cabin. He pleaded for a twenty-four-hour extension of the window originally agreed, to allow his flotilla to sail that night. The Australian officer asserted confidently: Biting can still be done.

James's claim upon fame had been established not at sea, but back in 1885, when at the age of four he modelled for one of the most famous portraits ever painted by Sir John Everett Millais, who was his grandfather. James, poor man, remained for the rest of his life indelibly associated with Pears soap, and familiarly known afloat and ashore as 'Bubbles'. He was nonetheless something of an intellectual, a rare distinction for a sailor, and a respected naval historian. Now, a critical decision was thrust upon him. If Cook believed his landing-craft could get in to the beach, weather conditions for the airborne assault appeared good enough to risk setting the raid in motion. At Tilshead, however, Frost's men had become inured to anti-climax. Once again, they packed the parachute containers, loaded and dispatched them on the lorries for the drive to Thruxton, 'but this time listlessly and without enthusiasm', in the major's words. Gerry Strachan was the only man who refused to be downcast: the sergeant-major was convinced they would go that night, and broadcast his enthusiasm through the company. He was right. At 1507 Admiral James messaged tersely to the warships, army and RAF units assigned to the Bruneval mission: 'CARRY OUT OPERATION BITING TONIGHT'. Mountbatten signalled, 'To all hands: good luck. Bite-em-hard!'

An hour later Browning arrived at Tilshead, to confirm that the assault would definitely go ahead. For the general, prime mover of the fledgling airborne forces, this was a vitally important moment. Only if paratroopers proved able successfully to mount a small operation, to jump into a miniature battle and prevail, might Britain's warlords endorse a commitment to much bigger things during the years ahead – the creation of a skyborne army.

Even as the general chatted to his soldiers, Cook's flotilla was putting to sea, headed for a rendezvous off the coast of France. The 'mother ship' *Prins Albert* carried the eight landing-craft which constituted the key seagoing element of Biting. At sunset, 1700, she sailed from Portsmouth for the eighty-five-mile passage to Bruneval. Outside the harbour's East Boom, the big ferry rendezvoused with its escort of the destroyer *Blencathra* and five MGBs – motor gunboats, each armed with a 40mm Bofors, 20mm Oerlikons, .5 machine-guns and assorted lesser weapons. The craft carried crews of sixteen, and their 2,700-horsepower engines made them capable of twenty-seven knots. They were well accustomed to duelling with German warships, especially E-boats, in the Channel by night, although the outcome of such clashes was not always to the advantage of the Royal Navy.

Fred Cook and Lt. Cdr. Henry Peate, commanding the ferry, were the only 'proper' naval officers afloat in the flotilla that night, as distinct from civilians who had merely donned deep blue uniforms for war service. None of the smaller craft carried radar, and they could contrive only erratic voice communication. Their complement now included an army doctor and twenty medics, tasked to care for casualties evacuated from Bruneval, or caused by action at sea – Frost's company, 'lean and mean', had no medics of its own. Once the ALCs had been lowered a few miles offshore, Peate would hasten *Prins Albert* home to Portsmouth, while Cook exercised local command from an MGB. The two LSCs – landing-craft modified to become fire-support vessels, armed with Lewis guns and a 20mm Oerlikon apiece – would also move inshore, taking station to port and starboard of the ALCs.

All manner of important people had taken an interest in what was unfolding. At Bomber Command headquarters, High

Wycombe, Wing-Commander Sam Elworthy, a much-respected officer who was a future chief of defence staff, said to Charles Carrington, like himself reared in New Zealand: 'I suppose you know there's to be a commando raid on France tonight. Shall we go and see the take-off?' They drove across blacked-out southern England to RAF Andover, where they paused for dinner in the mess. Then they travelled ten miles further west to Thruxton, and the makeshift operations room that had been established in a hangar, brilliantly lit in contrast to the darkness shrouding the runway. A cluster of 'brass' was already assembled, including Air Marshal Arthur 'Ugly' Barratt, chief of the RAF's Army Co-Operation Command.

At Tilshead Frost delivered a few final words to his men, urging them that night to uphold the great names of their regiments – remember that as yet the maroon beret, and their explicitly Airborne identity, still lay in the future. Then he watched his company, now including ten men from other elements of 2 Para, board their chilly trucks and leave for the airfield. Of the 149 soldiers of the battalion who had trained for the raid, some forty, most of them bitterly disappointed, were not to fly to France, either because there was no place for them in the Whitleys, or in a few cases because they were deemed unsuitable or unfit – one, for instance, was in acute pain after losing three teeth in unarmed combat training. The RAF would carry 120 men, including seven officers – three more than a company would customarily muster – nine engineers, Peter 'Walker' the interpreter and Flight-Sergeant Cox, all of whom now set forth for Thruxton.

Frost himself lingered to eat in the Tilshead mess, among glider pilots who knew nothing about his mission: 'It was hard to keep silent and yet hard to talk. The next few hours would mean so much. One could look at each munching face and say to oneself: "Aha! You have no idea. In two or three hours I'll be flying off to France. I have a rather exciting appointment!"' Instead they exchanged the usual gossip about nothings, though he admitted later that 'fleetingly, during pauses in the conversation, a twinge of fear would grip one's heart'. Then the major left the table to don fighting kit and webbing; fill pockets with tools for the night's work. His final appearance in the officers' mess, sparing a departing glance at the somnolent figures gathered around the anteroom fire, caused no surprise: he and his paratroopers had often gone forth at such an hour, dressed for night exercises.

A staff car with the usual masked headlights bore the major and his batman Corporal Sam Taylor to Thruxton, where the company was now dispersed in three Nissen huts around the field, near the aircraft they were respectively to board. He visited each group in turn, revelling in the clear, brilliant moonlight overhead, and sharing mugs of tea with his men. An occasional vehicle dashed around the perimeter and sometimes an aircraft engine started up. One of Frost's 'sticks' was singing enthusiastically, albeit wildly off-key. From Admiral James's headquarters in Portsmouth, on the secure telephone Group-Captain Norman came through to Charles Pickard in the operations room to wish them luck. He warned of a fresh snowfall across the Channel and said, 'I'm afraid the flak seems lively.'

Frost entered just as the airman put down the phone. Pick reported the conversation; told the major there was now snow on the ground in France. 'Damn,' said Frost. 'We could have worn our whites!' Coveralls had been issued for just this eventuality, but they had been left behind at the barracks. The soldier was irritated to learn – from Norman's words about the flak – that British aircraft had already flown near Bruneval. He was almost certainly wrong to be dismayed: if the enemy grew accustomed to hostile aircraft – two diversionary nuisance missions had been carried out earlier in the night by twin-engined Douglas Havocs of 23 Squadron, which plied circuitous courses around northern Normandy, while earlier in February 4 Group had conducted successive attacks south of Le Havre – they might be slower to discern anything special about the arrival of Pickard's Whitleys.

Then it was time to fit parachutes. The raiders in their respective huts addressed the bulky packs laid out in neat rows on the floors. Each man picked one hoping, in Charlie Cox's characteristically chirpy words, 'that the dear girl who'd packed it had had her mind on the job'. They had made all their training jumps beneath white canopies, but the silk of these operational ones was tinted in camouflage shades, by planners who had not anticipated the night's snow. Having fastened their harnesses, 'we wandered about wide-legged, like Michelin men' in the bitter cold.

Frost observed a contrast between the rough, tough exuberance of his soldiers and the sobriety of the Whitley crews: the success and indeed lives of their passengers depended upon the skill and exactitude of the fliers. The major said wryly: 'We paraded as a strange new bombload.' More than a few of 51 Squadron's crews feared they were flying the paratroopers to their deaths. Pickard drew Frost aside and said apologetically, also unhelpfully: 'I feel like a bloody murderer!' The soldier's waterbottle was filled with tea heavily infused with rum, which he now passed around.

Then it was time to go. As each stick in turn mustered and marched out to their aircraft, the company's piper Archie Ewing took the lead and played successively the marches of their various regiments – Black Watch, Argylls, Seaforths and so on. The skirl of the pipes evoked exultant cheers from the men, who were in tearing spirits. The airmen were impressed by the soldiers' discipline as they set forth for the Whitleys, each man carrying a shouldered 'fleabag' – sleeping bag – provided by their RAF hosts. 'They marched past like Guardsmen,' said Pickard.

It is justly said that 'you fight best when you don't know where it hurts'. Almost all these young men were setting forth to do or die for the first time in their lives. They were bursting with confidence in themselves and the operation. Those who were afraid – which meant most – nursed such feelings in the secrecy of their hearts, once they settled in the acute discomfort of the Whitley bellies. Afterwards Frost would look back and marvel at the naivety of himself and his company: 'We knew so little ... The Germans were to us a terrible people. Their armies knew no halting, and despite reverses in front of Moscow they seemed formidable in the extreme.' The mission commander was above all fearful of the seemingly omniscient German intelligence service. If the Abwehr had somehow gained a hint that the English were coming – even the cunning Nazis were unlikely to divine that they faced a largely Caledonian invasion – the venture was doomed. For a few impulsive seconds, Frost felt a pang of yearning for a last-minute cancellation, to relieve him of the responsibility that would soon be all his own. But of course the mood passed, as did any thought of the raid being aborted. Biting was 'on'.

They took off in succession between 2215 and 2224, hurtling down the short Thruxton runway. After the last plane left, the RAF ground controller signalled succinctly to 'Bubbles' James in Portsmouth the code words 'Walnut Twelve', to indicate that the entire squadron was safely in the air. 'This was no grand armada,' wrote Frost. 'We were so very much by ourselves.' The passengers in the lead aircraft, high on adrenalin, roared out a cheer as their wheels left the ground. The bombers, devoid of seats – 'fiendishly uncomfortable', in one man's words – offered no space to sit or lie in comfort on the ribbed aluminium floor, far less to slumber. The passengers were also cold, and shrouded themselves in blankets or fleabags. The deafening engine noise defied conversation, though Junior Charteris made the shouted discovery that his neighbour was one day older than himself. Both were thus a week off their respective twenty-first birthdays, which they solemnly swore to celebrate together.

In several aircraft men bellowed in apology for song, with F/Sgt. Cox prominent among the choir in his own plane, alongside Frost: 'We sang "Lulu", "Come Sit by My Side if You Love Me", and "Annie Laurie".' Then Cox soloed with 'The Rose of Tralee' and 'Because'. 'Morale in the aircraft was terrific,' said Peter Young, who was in a Whitley close behind. 'We sang choruses and played cards.' Frost, in old age, looked back sentimentally at that night and recalled from the experience of later drops onto much further-flung battlefields: 'So have we sung many times since on long flights over other countries when the engines seemed to play the music of an unseen band.'

Had the lumbering Whitleys been steering a direct course, the flight to France would have been only a hop. Instead, however, it was protracted and complicated by the need to hold the squadron together. Night bombers and their pilots were not intended or trained to fly in formation, yet it was essential to drop C Company as a tightly-concentrated group, each stick seconds behind the last, with a scheduled five minutes between each of the three waves of four aircraft. When Pickard was admitted to the secret of Biting's target, he had discussed at length with the planners the best choice of routes. It was agreed that, after making a landfall around Fécamp, north of Bruneval, 51 Squadron should stage a timed run southwards, parallel to the coast and half a mile offshore, checking landmarks before turning through almost 180 degrees somewhat north of Le Havre, to make the final run-in to the drop. The Bruneval model, aerial photos and maps were made available for study in the squadron crewroom a week before the operation was launched.

After taking off they flew 'stepped up', at designated heights in a vertical rather than horizontal formation, with a hundred feet between each plane, towards Tangmere beacon, then on to Selsey Bill. There was considerable cloud and ground haze over England, but in the moonlight crews had little trouble keeping each other in sight. Selsey was only thirty minutes' air time from Thruxton, but Pickard had allowed an additional half-hour leeway before turning to cross the Channel, in case of mishaps. Since there were none, the pilots had to 'stooge around' – fly circular courses – until the moment appointed to turn south-west. Cold and desperately uncomfortable, men kept asking their officers how many more minutes lay ahead before the target, to which uncertain answers were offered. At 2315 Pickard fired a Very pistol from the cockpit window as a signal for his own wave to head out to sea, with the other two following at five-minute intervals. Halfway across the Channel they encountered thicker cloud. The Whitleys descended below this, so that the lowest in the formations was flying only fifty feet above the water.

In most aircraft, every few minutes one of the crew scrambled aft from the cockpit to shout a report of progress – to reassure the paratroopers that everything was on course and to plan. Some men could see below the glittering waters, seeming to move gently through the moonlight. The cold intensified, and so did a new source of discomfort: the prodigious quantities of tea which they had consumed before embarking worked increasingly painfully on their bladders. They lacked any means of relieving themselves – Browning's subsequent report on the operation included a recommendation for the German-style jump overalls to be modified to permit urination, and indeed they would be redesigned.

The raiders made their Fécamp landfall exactly as planned. Pickard circled to allow the others to close up on him. Dispatchers bellowed to their passengers over the roar of the engines 'Prepare for action!' Frost's men scrambled out of their fleabags; hooked static lines to the overhead cables; shuffled clumsily into seated queues, stretching fore and aft from the floor hatches that were now uncovered, increasing the cold. The designated first jumpers took up positions with their feet dangling down into the night sky, awaiting the signal from dispatchers now crouched behind them. Most of the paratroopers had previously completed a dozen training descents, but none by night.

Even as the bombers approached the coast, so too below them did the vessels of Commander Fred Cook's naval flotilla, which had sailed from Portsmouth six hours earlier. Their run across the Channel was tense, but uneventful. Ten miles off the French shoreline, six ALCs and the two LSCs were lowered, started their engines and cast off in record time, two and a half minutes. *Prins Albert* turned away, escorted by the little Hunt-class destroyer *Blencathra*, while Welshmen aboard the flotilla sang 'Land of My Fathers'. Unlike the paratroopers, the Bren-gunners in the boats had blackened their faces with burnt cork, earnest of their eagerness to join the fray. For the benefit of

German radar-operators, the departing ferry made a series of to-and-fro passes, such as a minelayer might have performed, then sped back to Portsmouth at twenty-two knots.

The ALCs and gunboats crept towards the coast. At 2306 the crews were cheered to see the lighthouse at Cap d'Antifer suddenly blaze forth, confirming their position. They saw flashes and heard distant explosions, probably reflecting RAF activities unconnected with Biting. The tension was relentless, the expectation heart-stopping. Cook wrote later: 'We could not believe our good luck – but not for long. The Hun didn't switch on [the Antifer light] for us, but for two German destroyers and two E-Boats moving slowly towards Le Havre.' The four southward-bound enemy warships were steaming little more than a mile on the seaward side of the British flotilla: 'We held our breaths. I ordered all twelve boats to cut engines and maintain complete silence. We just rolled and prayed. Why we were not discovered I shall never know – perhaps the background of the cliffs, or the firing on shore, or the bombing of Le Havre might have distracted the German warships.'

The destroyers and E-boats passed on, down Channel. Soon afterwards the flotilla's crews felt sufficiently distant from enemy ears to give a cheer when they heard Pickard's Whitleys pass low on their landward bows, heading south, before they turned to close on the drop zone. But that near-confrontation with German warships would influence what followed three hours later: Cook and his officers remained justly fearful that these enemies might reappear, to play havoc with the evacuation. In a shoot-out, the escorting British gunboats would not be remotely a match for the German vessels, and such a collision was all too possible in the disputed waters of the Channel. Other raiders, and later in the war rehearsal fleets for D-Day, suffered grievously from such mischances, including the disastrous clash of British assault craft with a German convoy, on their passage towards Dieppe during the night of 18/19 August 1942. It is hard to imagine why Mountbatten's planners were so sanguine about Cook's slow-motion flotilla reaching Bruneval unmolested. Yet fortune was with them. At 0130, almost exactly on schedule and undetected by the Germans, they reached the designated 'Point X', less than two miles offshore, at which they were to await a wirelessed summons from Frost. The boats wallowed uncomfortably, their occupants suffused by apprehension that a wrong move, or a return of German warships, could wreck the scheduled evacuation.

High or not-so-high above, Pickard led his squadron down the coastline for seven miles – just over three minutes' flight time. They were at 350 feet and 100 mph when cannon aboard German flak ships opened fire. Those with a view out of the planes saw tracer streaking up, appearing to accelerate viciously as it whipped past them. Then, as they turned inland, ground-based 20mm and 37mm guns began directing fire towards them. Being so close to the enemy, they could hear as well as see the guns, which to a paratrooper 'sounded as if a man were hammering a piece of tin below us'. A Whitley gunner noted with bemused respect that his plane's Scots passengers did not stop singing, even under fire. John Timothy passed around his waterbottle, filled with neat rum. Pickard said afterwards: 'The flak was damn accurate.' Three of his planes suffered hits, though none was crippled. Pickard's gunners returned the fire, probably ill-advisedly, because their own tracer made the planes more conspicuous targets, but the squadron commander applauded: 'They put up a very good show.' It was an almost universal delusion among wartime night bomber crews that their own gun turrets justified their terrific weight, as by results – damage inflicted on the enemy – they did not.

Though one German soldier below was mortally wounded by Pickard's gunners, the Whitleys might have done better to hold their fire. The pilots briefly dived to a hundred feet, also banking to evade the enemy batteries. The eight bombers of the second and third waves, seeing the flak ahead, turned inland to avoid it, though one of their planes was hit in the starboard wing. The price of such lunges was that some bomb-aimers, guiding the pilots, became disoriented and mislaid their visual marks. Most recovered them, however, before just short of Le Havre and its wavering searchlight beams, they swung north again for the final approach, pilots concentrating fiercely on holding their courses; passengers keyed up to the highest pitch of expectation and readiness.

By a notable coincidence, even as the Whitleys were airborne over the Channel 'Rémy', nursing a shocking head cold, was flying the other way. The *Résistant* whose network had contributed so much to making Biting possible had been retrieved from a field near Rouen earlier that night, along with his fellow agent Pierre Julitte, by a Lysander light aircraft of the RAF's Special Duties Squadron. At Carlton Gardens Passy, and indeed de Gaulle, wanted to confer with their agents, and also to receive the mass of paper material they had gathered, such as could only be hand-carried to London. Rémy brought with him a complete set of 1/50,000 scale maps of France; samples of Vichy identity cards and travel documents; newspapers; the first political dispatch of Rémy's important journalist connection Pierre Brossolette; the farewell message of Gabriel Péri, a communist deputy executed by the Germans in December; and a veritable tidal wave of reports expressing his own opinions which the network organizer intended for Passy and his staff. The two agents landed safely at Tempsford in Bedfordshire soon after 2300, and were already being driven to London when C Company descended upon France.

As 51 Squadron neared the drop zone Pickard sent the succinct signal to his squadron 'raid on!' The aircraft were flying just above stalling speed, a mere 90 mph, which they briefly lowered their undercarriages to achieve. The bomb-aimers, each lying prone above their aircraft's Perspex nose panels, gazed down upon the snow-covered landscape, clutching toggles in readiness to signal the jumpers at the instant they glimpsed the pinpoint, seconds short of the LZ. Dispatchers shouted for the paratroopers to take up action stations, five on each end of the open hatch. The first man in each stick was now poised, gazing down upon French fields and woods hurtling by. Junior Charteris described a sensation of unreality, common to many men at war, especially when going into action for the first time: 'I felt as though I was acting in a play.' Then, suddenly, for most paratroopers there was a green light, nearly parallel with the houses of Bruneval though eight hundred yards inland, a shouted 'Go!' from the dispatcher and a slap on the back, repeated ten times in rapid succession. Almost all the jumpers performed their drills with perfect exactitude, slipping forth from their aircraft at three- or four-second intervals without a hitch.

The lead Whitley, that of F/Lt. Coates, dropped its cargo of Nelsons on schedule at 0014, in the midst of the designated drop zone. Every aircraft had been fitted with an ingenious trigger cable device, causing the containers in the bomb bay to fall away as the fifth man of each stick jumped. These gadgets worked as intended, so that sections found their weapons and equipment hitting the ground within yards of them. Coates' passengers, Captain John Ross and his group, easily identified their own location and nearby landmarks in the moonlight during the forty-second descents. A second Whitley, piloted by F/Lt. Towsey, dropped Sgt. Jim 'Shorty' Sharp's Nelsons nearby.

The next men down – also Nelsons – were much less fortunate. Pickard's aircraft, carrying Lt. Euan Charteris and his section, together with Sgt. John Pohe's nearby Whitley bearing a second group led by Sgt. David Grieve, both received the green 'go' light when Pickard's bomb-aimer pressed his button while still two miles south-west of the drop zone. Pickard's later report blamed the local flak, and consequent evasive action, for evicting his passengers 'rather short'. Especially under snow, one stretch of Norman countryside looked bewilderingly like another, in moonlight from a height of several hundred feet and at relatively high speed. At 0015, Charteris's men plunged into the sky, and again all landed without injury. He himself said: 'There was so little wind that the rigging lines wrapped themselves round me.' But they were in the wrong place, the Val aux Chats, near a hamlet named L'Enfer.

Charteris was at first disoriented and thus shocked: 'That was a nasty moment ... I don't think there's any feeling quite so unpleasant as suddenly finding yourself in enemy territory and not knowing where you are.' A serious flaw in the briefing of C Company was that, while Frost's men were minutely informed about the immediate surroundings of the radar station, they had been told little or nothing about the wider countryside. Their instructions were founded upon the assumption, now shown to be false, that they would be deposited on the appointed drop zone. As Charteris led his stick away from their landing place, he said to the men they were in the wrong valley, but – speaking with an assurance he did not feel – 'that I thought we could get to the proper spot in the direction I was taking. My secret worry was lest we should have to turn about; that, I thought, would be poor for morale.'

They had seen another stick of paratroopers descend from a Whitley almost parallel with their own exit points, simultaneously but five hundred yards further inland. These were Grieve and his Nelsons. Their landings, however, were considerably dispersed, presumably because some men had been slow to exit. The sergeant and Corporal Vic Stewart, last out of the aircraft and so furthest north, found themselves separated from the rest of their section. After some minutes searching for the others, the two set off north-westwards, glimpsing Charteris and his men ahead. When they met the lieutenant, he urged them to join him. Grieve, though, decided it was important first to locate the rest of his own stick, then to lead them towards the battlefield. Charteris therefore pressed on with his section, leaving the two NCOs peering anxiously across the whiteness, hoping to spot their lost comrades, but seeing nothing of them.

The rest of the sergeant's group, six paratroopers and two engineers, were much dismayed by finding themselves leaderless and lost, and even more so by being almost disarmed: they were unable to spot their weapons container in the snow, and so carried only grenades and pistols. But the sappers did find the container holding their own specialist equipment. They abandoned five anti-tank mines, designed to be laid on the approach road to Bruneval, as being too heavy to lug for at least a mile across the snowclad countryside. They retained only a mine-detector, which could be vital. They lingered for some time close to where they had landed, hoping to be rejoined by their NCO and given orders. The countryside was broken and, in many places, steep and densely wooded. When Grieve failed to appear and they did at last set off northward, following the pole star, they moved with extreme caution, exploiting the cover of trees and hedges to march roughly parallel with the road, rather than on it. This slowed them, but was prudent: almost unarmed, they needed to avoid meeting Germans.

Meanwhile P/O Jeff Haydon, an Australian from Canberra, was convinced his Whitley had reached the drop zone when he saw discarded parachutes on the ground below, and so at 0024 illuminated the green light for Sgt. Alex Reid's stick of Rodneys, slightly to the west of the 'chutes, and thus nearer the sea. His passengers all descended safely, but realized at once that they, too, were in the wrong place – the canopies which Haydon had seen on the ground were those of Charteris and his stick. Probably around 0045 they met the lieutenant, who urged them to follow him. Perhaps surprisingly, Reid declined, saying he would adopt his own course. It has been suggested that this tough, experienced sergeant regarded young Charteris with the disdain NCOs often display towards recent school prefects masquerading as subalterns. The sergeant and his nine companions set off boldly, until Rob Stirling their Bren-gunner urged that they were going wrong, as indeed they were – southeast instead of north. Reid said ruefully later it was odd that while Stirling had never, before the army, quit the Glasgow of his birth, this city boy possessed an uncanny sense of direction in open country.

They corrected their course and soon glimpsed dark figures converging upon them, who proved to be Grieve and Stewart. These two now decided to abandon the quest for the rest of their own section, and joined Reid. The group advanced in single file, pursuing a route parallel with the coast and only a hundred yards inland. Fortuitously, this would lead them – much later – to a point directly above and behind the German machine-gun emplacements covering the deep defile to the beach.

The most fraught experience of the jump befell the stick of Rodneys carried by Sgt. Andy Cook, a New Zealander. He lost his bearings when making the turn northwards for the final run-in and approached west instead of east of Bruneval. His bomb-aimer illuminated the green light at 0025 perilously close to the cliff, and the sea. Five men jumped, led by Sgt. Tom Lumb. The sixth appears either to have become jammed in the hatch, his leg caught up in the static lines of earlier jumpers, or just possibly he baulked, extremely sensibly, because the plane's course would likely have caused the last five men to land in the Channel, which was plainly visible below. The plane swung out to sea, in the eyes of onlookers apparently headed back towards England. After some seconds, however, it turned again for France.

It seems reasonable to imagine a fierce argument, with much shouting over the engine noise, though it is impossible to guess whether it was the paratroopers or the pilot's own sense of duty which persuaded Cook to make a second run. This time, the crew of X-X-Ray picked up the right landmarks, approached the designated landing zone, and dropped its last five men in exactly the right place but late, at 0030 – and also unarmed; their weapons container had gone down with Sgt. Lumb. The crew report in the squadron's operational record book stated that no. 6 of the paratroopers 'hung up on the 1st run', without explaining any cause. Cook may not have given an entirely frank account of his experience. The five paratroopers who landed accurately joined Timothy's Rodneys, as planned, though without weapons their value was limited.

The half-stick of Rodneys led by Tom Lumb, atop the cliff parallel with the hamlet of Bruneval, were unhappy men. When it became apparent that their companions had dropped elsewhere, if at all, Lumb led his little group inland a short distance,

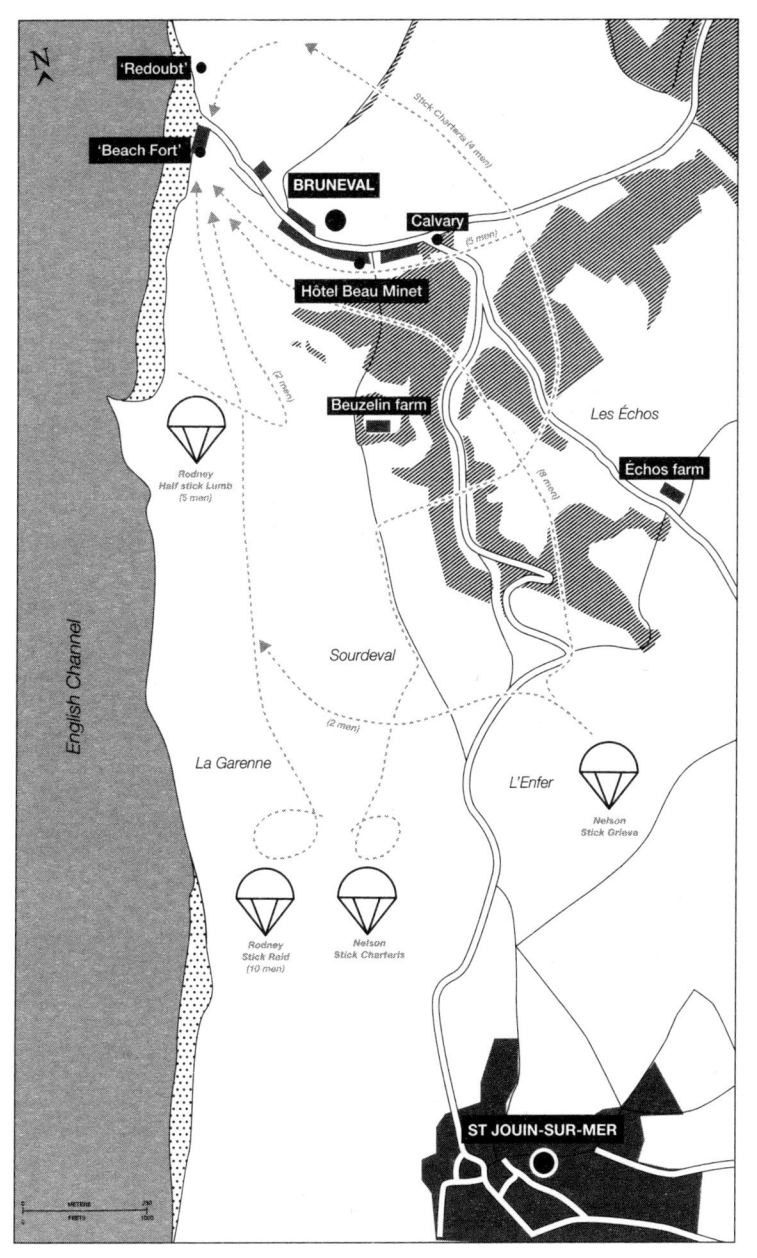

The dropping points of John Frost's missing 'sticks'

then figuratively scratched his head. He apparently ordered Bren-gunner Alan Scott and signallers George Cornell and Frank Embury to stay put with the gun and their heavy 18 wireless set, while himself and Corporal Campbell went ahead to reconnoitre. This was not a good decision – to separate in the midst of France in darkness; to divide a small party. Cornell and Embury were outsiders with C Company, late arrivals sent to reinforce Frost from 2nd Battalion's B Company.

In any event, the two were now lost lambs, along with Scott. They remained at their halting place for at least the ensuing two hours, an eternity in the context of that eventful night. It is readily understandable that they did not move while silence prevailed elsewhere. But once the shooting began, it seems odd the three paratroopers, if only in the interests of their own salvation, were so slow to attempt to reach the main body, when the back of the fortified beach emplacement Stella Maris – Beach Fort on the British model – was clearly visible from their hiding place, albeit on the further side of a wire entanglement. Among the most significant consequences of the night's misdrops was that both C Company's 18 wireless sets, needed to call in Cook's landing-craft flotilla, were now adrift south of Bruneval, and far from John Frost.

At midnight plus twenty, five or six minutes after the Nelsons, the next wave of Whitleys droned through the sky north-east of Bruneval, dropping Frost and CSM Strachan, Charles Cox, Private Nagel/Walker the interpreter, five infantrymen and one engineer. The sappers had been prudently dispersed between different sticks, to try to ensure that some, at least, were at hand to tackle the Würzburg. Frost felt a surge of relief, and indeed of exultation, to see that the topography below, clearly visible in the moonlight, was exactly as he had been briefed to expect it, though night washed colour from the landscape, which appeared only in shades of black and white. He bumped into the cushioning snow, rolled then leaped to his feet, pulling in the rigging lines before slipping off his harness. He heard distant bursts of automatic fire – probably light flak guns firing at the aircraft – but not a sound in his own vicinity or from the clearly visible château beyond which Henry, the Würzburg site, was located. Almost all the paratroopers' first action on landing was to satisfy a desperate need to relieve aching bladders which, though it used up precious seconds, Frost felt to be an appropriate gesture of defiance upon commencing their miniature invasion of Hitler's Europe.

At 0026 P/O Mair's Whitley dropped Sgt. Rob Muir and another nine of the Rodneys, while S/Ldr. Meade delivered ten more, including their commander Lt. 'Tim' Timothy. Sgt. Gray, carrying the Drakes commanded by Lt. Naoumoff, lost his bearings after Fécamp and dropped his party a quarter of an hour late, at 0039, when the airmen could see dozens of discarded canopies already lying limp on the ground below. Thus, Gray's crew were at least in no doubt that their passengers had landed in the drop zone – every plane's rear-gunner was charged with reporting forward to the cockpits that the right number of parachutes had opened behind them.

Each paratrooper in turn that night revelled in delectable moments of silence as the aircraft receded, together with the even more reassuring experience of glimpsing his overhead canopy deployed; himself drifting gently through a windless sky towards a white earth. Peter Young claimed to have had time to clip a magazine onto his Sten before hitting the ground. In the distance, they could hear and see flak still venting colourful venom against intruding aircraft, but those guns were sited miles away. 'The first thing that struck me,' said Charles Cox, 'was how quiet everything was and how lonely I felt, and then I heard some rustling and saw something outlined against the snow. It was a container.'

Dozens of shadowy figures were soon scrambling around the landing zone, pulling off their harnesses and loading weapons. Then Frost led them trotting the few hundred yards – distance varied according to where in his stick a man had jumped – to the appointed assembly place high in a wooded, scrubby cleft of ground some five hundred yards short of the radar site. The major endured some bad minutes debating the whereabouts of Naoumoff's Drakes, until these suddenly descended to the ground behind him. Then Ross reported the absence of half his Nelsons and Timothy likewise the lack of fifteen Rodneys. Parachutes had been seen in the distance, drifting down beyond Bruneval, but nobody could anticipate when or whether their wearers might join the looming battle. Frost would have to launch his attack without a third of his fighting strength, discounting the engineers and signallers.

C Company's drop was no more nor less chaotic than that of most wartime airborne operations. The first and last man of each stick were perforce separated by six hundred yards. Logic might suggest it was a mistake for the Whitleys to have approached in three waves, separated by several minutes. If all twelve aircraft of the squadron had approached together, the followers would have been in no doubt where earlier arrivals had landed. But this raises the obvious issue that if the leader had misjudged the correct drop zone, as did Pickard, Pohe, Gray and Cook, or their bomb-aimers, Biting would have been doomed.

As it was, while Frost's force was substantially weakened, by extraordinary good fortune all the vital players – especially the major himself, Vernon and Cox – were exactly where they were supposed to be, poised to assault Henry. C Company had suffered not a single jump injury, some sort of operational record, which must have owed much to the snow. Moreover, the repeated passages of low-flying bombers across several miles of northern France, a process protracted over thirty minutes, utterly confused the Germans on the ground. A soldier of the 687th Regiment, based at Saint-Jouin-sur-Mer, three miles to the south, reported Charteris's and Grieve's sticks descending. Some local French people were also awakened by the overhead bombers. A few brave souls, mostly young, dressed and went outside to see what was happening: the big, flat fields of the landing zone began only a few yards from several houses. The planes stampeded farm animals, at least one group of which burst from its shed.

Perversely, the multiple reports of air landings at different sites which now reached the Luftwaffe at Octeville, Étretat and the radar sites, together with the army in La Poterie, Étretat, Bruneval and Saint-Jouin, intensified German bewilderment. If the whole of C Company had landed as planned, the defenders could have had scant doubt about their objective. But with paratroopers also reported well south of Bruneval, what was the British game? Were they planning to strike towards the airfields around Le Havre? Did they intend to establish and hold an airhead in Normandy? For vital hours after C Company began to descend from the sky, the defenders remained uncertain about their purposes. They saw method in the wildly dispersed parachute drop, whereas in truth there were only accident and error. And this confusion well served John Frost's purposes that night.

The last of 51 Squadron's Whitleys, Q-Queenie, which had delivered Naoumoff's Drakes, did not return to Thruxton until 0255 by which time, in Col. Carrington's words, 'Pickard was showing some anxiety.' John Pohe, the New Zealand Maori pilot who had dropped Grieve and his men, was devastated by the discovery that he, like P/O Haydon, had dispatched his passengers almost two miles short of their objective, a mistake they had been obliged to recognize when they passed the landmarks of Bruneval, the radar sites and Cap d'Antifer many seconds after evicting their passengers. Pickard showed no sign of awareness that he too had badly misdropped his men, but there is no evidence about whether he was genuinely oblivious of this, or instead felt too embarrassed, as squadron CO, to admit the mistake. The air operation had proved, frankly, somewhat of a muddle, though there is no record of what was, and was not, said about this among the airmen now back at Thruxton.

It seems wrong to think harshly of the Whitley crews, taking drastic evasive action in the face of light flak – one cannon shell cracked through the fuselage of G-George, close to its paratroopers. They were trained and experienced in flying independently at high altitude over Europe, struggling to secure every foot of height to distance themselves from the ground defences. Here, by contrast, their clumsy old bombers had been compelled to approach an objective close enough to the ground to glimpse the figures of enemies below in the moonlight, and the tracer of all colours streaking towards them. It seems less remarkable that some aircraft dropped their men off-target than that eight of twelve pilots achieved accuracy.

The fliers who had carried out the drop endured hours of anxiety afterwards. They took deeply seriously their responsibility for the Biting paratroopers. This tiny force – though dispatched into action by the united wills of many men, some of them great ones in the land including the prime minister, Mountbatten, Browning, Jones, Rémy and his agents, together with 51 Squadron – was now entirely alone and arbiter of its own destinies, as its men embarked upon their mission beyond the curtain wall of Nazi-occupied Europe.

9

Henry

As the drone of the departing bombers faded, on the ground around Bruneval a silence was restored that is almost incomprehensible, given the defenders' awareness of the airborne intruders. Nearby Germans afterwards reported that their radar sites tracked the incoming British aircraft – W120 at Sainte-Adresse warned Luftwaffe Centre at Octeville, even as the Bruneval Freyas and W110 Würzburg did likewise. These alarms caused most of the local personnel not manning anti-aircraft weapons or equipment to take to their shelters, anticipating a rain of bombs, an apprehension that persisted as successive waves of British aircraft swooped low, and continued to do so at intervals through the ensuing twenty-five minutes. The lighthouse crew at Cap d'Antifer spotted overhead aircraft dropping paratroops – moonlight provided illumination to both sides, especially with the added glow from the snow carpet. A few minutes later, local army and air force personnel saw Frost's men descending, and sounded the alarm. Just after 0015 senior Luftwaffe NCO Rudy Lang hurried into the radio room at the Gosset farm and phoned his local headquarters at Étretat. In a first call he said he thought the bombers might be dropping dummies. Then he telephoned again to announce that the new arrivals were, instead, indubitably live paratroopers.

As for the elements of the Wehrmacht roused from slumber in and around Bruneval, they had been deployed on the French coast to resist British incursions from the sea and, for that matter, to meet a full-scale invasion such as was unlikely to come for years. Nobody appears to have briefed the soldiers to regard protection of the Würzburg as a vital responsibility. Rather, they treated the radar installations as Luftwaffe technical stuff – no rightful business of the army. There was no senior officer within reach, to grip the defence in its wholly unexpected predicament in the first hours of 28 February. Major Hugo Paschke, the local battalion commander, was asleep at his spacious headquarters in the Manoir de Saint-Clair, a couple of miles east of Étretat. Meanwhile the commander of the Luftwaffe's 23 *Flugmelde*, Prince Alexander-Ferdinand von Preussen, on the previous afternoon announced to his staff in Sainte-Adresse that he was off to 'make a personal tour of inspection': Mountbatten's smart cousin then departed for a night in Paris, from which he returned only next morning.

Following news of the landings, confusion overtook the German staffs in and around Étretat. Those were days when many men could not drive, and even for Hitler's legions vehicles were by no means universally accessible. The Luftwaffe's Lt. Joachim Ruben shouted for his driver, to discover that the man could not be found. Precious time was then wasted, seeking out another vehicle and somebody to drive it. But at last, and before Frost's men plunged into action, Ruben and two NCOs were guiding an Opel staff car up the steep, icy road that rose from Étretat to the plateau and thence to the Gosset farm, twenty minutes south of the town. According to the German after-action narrative, 'all Army and Luftwaffe posts in the area were at once alerted ... Scouts sent from the Freya position and the Luftwaffe Communications Station [at the Gosset farm] returned with information that the enemy was on the move south of the farm, in the direction of the Château [Lone House]. The parachutist commandos had split into several groups and were converging on the Würzburg position and on the Château.'

Yet despite all this, the Germans left it to the British to fire the first shots of the night, almost forty-five minutes after Frost and his men dropped from the Whitleys. The major knew that time was vital; also that he had only one choice – to attack with the men to hand. John Timothy and the available twenty-five of his forty Rodneys deployed in an arc between the dropping zone and the château, to block the landward side of Henry against German reinforcements. Their firing positions commanded the approaches from the Gosset farm and La Poterie, with Corporal Ralph Johnston watching their rear.

Lt. Naoumoff's last-come Drakes hastened some six hundred yards from their landing to the point directly north of the château and radar site, where they lay down in the snow with their weapons and waited for the Germans in the Rectangle – the Gosset farm – to react to the imminent assault on Henry. It then became their role to ensure that the enemy was unable to do so effectively, or at least to give warning of threats to Frost and his parties.

John Ross reported to Frost that Charteris and two sections of Nelsons were missing. The major responded: wait for them a few minutes, then go ahead with the plan anyway – head first for the pillboxes atop the cliff, between the Würzburg and the defile. He promised to reinforce the diminished Nelsons as soon as possible – Ross's role was critical: no access to the beach meant no escape from France. The young captain, facing the daunting challenge of suppressing German defensive positions with only half the force mandated for the task, waited in vain for ten minutes, then set off with two sections, weapons cocked, up the slope towards the clifftop bunkers and, beyond and below them, the defile.

Sgt. Dave Tasker and a half-stick of this force warily approached the pillboxes on the north shoulder – Redoubt on the British model. To their relief they found them untenanted, and took possession. But they could see the heavy wire entanglements beyond and below, laid out as obstacles to amphibious invaders, but also blocking the way to the beach. They knew there were Germans on the Bruneval side of the valley. In accordance with orders, Tasker and his men remained at the emplacements. This was prudent, because if Germans reoccupied them, they could sweep C Company's exit route with fire. Sgt. Jimmy Sharp and the others moved down the open hillside towards the defile, following Ross and his heavy section, which included two engineers equipped with a mine-detector to check and if necessary clear the beach, and two Bren gun pairs.

Meanwhile Frost's and Young's men trotted fast across the four hundred yards of rising ground between the assembly point and Lone House and beyond it the objective of Biting, Reg Jones's holy grail, the Würzburg radar. They were momentarily checked by farm fences before approaching the château and Henry from the south side, at every step expecting to receive a burst of fire. They spent several minutes making a cautious tactical advance, then Gerry Strachan led men scaling the wall onto the château's terrace, to ensure that this was undefended. When the others ran around the big building to its north entrance, far from needing to ring the bell they found the front door yawning open. A young Luftwaffe man posted there as a sentry, Willy Ermoneit, a farmer's son from East Prussia with two brothers on the Eastern Front, after hearing shots a few moments earlier had dashed off towards the radar site, leaving just one German occupant of the big house, though of course the British, keyed to the highest pitch of anticipation, did not know this.

Lance-Corporal Georg Schmidt, a Wehrmacht communications orderly posted in a room of the rambling first floor of Stella Maris – Beach Fort on the British photos and fancifully named by its builders eighty years earlier 'the castle of Kroumin', half a mile below Bruneval hamlet and on the cusp of its beach – was wakened by his NCO, Sgt. Treinies. Around 0025 he was ordered, no doubt roughly, to answer the insistent buzzing of the field telephone. Schmidt lifted the receiver to hear the voice of Lt. Huhne, their acting company commander, calling from the local army command post in the little *mairie* of La Poterie, two miles distant. Huhne had just come in from a night exercise with the platoon billeted in that village, now in their welcome beds. He announced that from his own window he had seen British paratroopers descending: the Stella Maris group must mobilize immediately! Schmidt, oldest man of his section, who would not see thirty-five again, held his officer in low esteem – 'in Russia he would not have lasted twenty-four hours in a command' – but for now, Huhne was the Wehrmacht officer responsible for the local defence of Bruneval.

Within minutes of the passing of the overhead Whitleys, and well before Frost's paratroopers fired their first shots, the men in Stella Maris were dragging on boots and gathering equipment, hectored by Treinies, who rebuked their sloth. Grenades were issued. A Châtellerault 7.5mm light machine-gun, once property of the French Army, was hastily carried to a firing position in the camouflage-netted trenches further uphill, from which it could cover the face opposite, open ground nearest to the drop zone where the enemy had been seen landing. A twenty-five-round magazine was slapped onto the weapon; the gunner took his place behind it. Just eight minutes after the alarm was given, according to L/Cpl. Schmidt, the Germans in the beach positions were ready to fire on the paratroopers, for whom they then faced a considerable wait.

These trenches, sited behind wire entanglements and running up the southern side of the deep defile around Beach Fort, had only recently been dug, and were unmentioned in the pre-Biting intelligence brief. They would become the pivotal obstacles to C Company's escape; the Châtellerault would cause them more grief than any other enemy weapon that night. The problem for Treinies was that he commanded just nine men, including Schmidt the telephonist, to man positions between a knife-rest gate linking the dense wire entanglements where these crossed the road higher up the defile, and Stella Maris with its sandbagged emplacements, covering the beach. He immediately decided against dividing his tiny force, by sending men clambering up the steep face to occupy the pillboxes atop the northern side, which they could almost certainly have reached before Sgt. Tasker. They would all fire from the south side of the track, from the trenches above and behind Stella Maris.

Meanwhile in La Poterie, Lt. Huhne was struggling to assemble his own platoon, summoned from their billets; then to exchange live bullets for the blank ammunition issued for their night exercise, only just concluded; to prime grenades and prepare to fight, a contingency which at the previous dusk had seemed impossibly remote from these soldiers' lives. Only after a protracted delay did the lieutenant muster fifteen armed men. Leaving behind cooks and suchlike, with these followers Huhne set off to cover the mile to the Gosset farm, advancing with extreme caution for fear of being ambushed by the British invaders.

Close at hand, what were almost certainly the first shots of the night, save for anti-aircraft fire, were unleashed by John Judge, one of Timothy's Bren-gunners, when Sgt. Muir his section leader ordered him to shoot at the lights of a vehicle headed along the open track towards the Gosset farm. This was the Opel carrying Lt. Ruben and his two Luftwaffe NCOs, approaching from Étretat. Several bursts from a range of two hundred yards did no damage to the Germans but caused them rapidly to back up and seek a safer approach to the farm, from the north.

John Frost, poised outside Lone House, heard the firing and recollected that this was the appointed moment for his whistle. He gave four long blasts, clearly heard by both paratroopers and Germans, which signalled closure, or rather an explosive breach, of the night's weirdly protracted silence. He and his men burst simultaneously through the château's front door and terrace entrance, even as Young's party started shooting around Henry. Seconds later, more gunfire was heard from the direction of the Bruneval beach defile – Ross's sections in action.

The château proved bereft of furniture, filthy dirty. Floor by floor the paratroopers ran through each room of the big house, until they reached the attic to behold a solitary German, nineteen-year-old Luftwaffe man Paul Kaffurbitz, firing out of the window towards Young's section. Though he sought refuge behind a chest of drawers, a burst of Sten fire killed the young German. Then the paratroopers clattered noisily back downstairs. Leaving just two men in the château, they followed their leader towards Henry, fifty yards westwards, from which they could hear firing and the detonation of British grenades.

* * *

John Ross and the Nelsons approached the beach defile only moments before firing erupted at Henry, around 0100, and at least thirty minutes after the nearby Germans had been alerted. The paratroopers were spotted straight away by the defenders already at readiness in the trenches above Stella Maris, where in January Pol and Charlemagne had trafficked with the rashly amiable sentry. According to the German account the strongpoints, now manned by Sgt. Treinies and his section, were so built that they were effective only against attacks through the ravine from seaward. It was true that the pillboxes high on the northern shoulder were seized by the Nelsons before defenders could be found to man them. Moreover, the house higher up the defile, dubbed Guardroom by the planners, proved to be undefended. The trenches above Stella Maris, however, enjoyed a good field of fire uphill, commanding both sides of the defile, and every movement on the opposite hillside was visible in the moonlight.

Treinies started his battle confused about whether the shadowy figures whom he glimpsed appearing from the opposite side of the valley, highlighted against the snow, might be Germans. He discharged a recognition signal, a red Very cartridge, to which he received no response. He fired a burst in the air from his MP34 machine-pistol, again to test for a reaction. When none came, he was sure the approaching figures must be enemies. He then released a white flare which hung over the hillside opposite, brilliantly illuminating Ross and his men. The Germans opened fire.

The Nelsons responded with their two Brens, eight rifles and three Stens, but to little effect. Ross yearned for a mortar, and indeed for more firepower of any kind. His heavy section had been tasked and briefed to deploy on the northern shoulder of the defile, providing fire support with the Bren guns for a direct assault to be executed by Charteris with three sections. In their absence, the Nelsons were ill-prepared and understrength to assume responsibility for the different role of clearing the defile and capturing Beach Fort themselves. For some time they exchanged fire with the enemy, while making little progress. In their immediate path lay a dense wire entanglement, forming an arc around the beach perhaps half a mile from end to end. Sgt. Bill Sunley began to address this with heavy cutters at the nearest point, striving to avoid drawing German attention and fire.

This was a moment when the white snow smocks left behind at Tilshead would have been a godsend: as it was, the dark figures stood out mortally clearly in the Germans' sights, as did the muzzle flashes of their weapons. Treinies' Châtellerault wounded Bren-gunner Les Shaw who fell hit in the knee, with a shattered tibia. His mate Jim Calderwood dragged him out of German view, then Sunley scrambled up and stabbed him with a morphia syrette. Sgt. Jim Sharp told Piper Ewing to drop his rifle and take over the Bren. Shaw eventually persuaded the others to leave him and get back to the fight, but here was an issue which dogged C Company that night: with no medics among the paratroopers, men who needed to concentrate single-mindedly on engaging the enemy instead tended mates whom they were unwilling even temporarily to abandon.

Neither side's shooting did much damage to the other, except when men moved. German fire was insistently high, and British not much better aimed. Paratroopers tossed grenades, which fell well short of the German trenches. Frost spared a moment during the night to reflect ruefully that during training, 'unfortunately we failed to spend quite as much time on the ranges as we should have done … There is no shortcut or substitute for skill at arms and, without this, fitness, discipline, enthusiasm and all the rest counted for little when there was a real enemy to contend with.' An immense amount of ammunition was expended by both sides around Bruneval – next day the Germans would collect seventy empty Bren magazines – for an astonishingly small proportion of hits. Moreover while Sten guns were impressively noisy, which counted for a lot against hesitant enemies such as were the Germans whom C Company encountered that night, their 9mm pistol rounds lacked killing power beyond the shortest ranges.

The momentum of the Nelsons' advance was lost. They would probably have fared better had they been dropped much closer to the defile at the outset, before the Germans were awakened, but nobody had thought of that. Now, instead, Ross's one and a half sections were attempting to grapple and overwhelm the occupants of the trenches, with a third of the force which had been intended to perform this dangerous and difficult fire-and-movement. Bren-gunner Bill Grant was hit in the stomach just fifty yards from the German positions on the opposite face. Bill Sunley reached him, administered another morphia syrette, then with Grant's mate Andrew Young dragged the stricken man out of German sight. Sharp took over the Bren, and when he glimpsed flame from the barrel of the German gun opposite, delivered fire so heavy that for a while the Châtellerault fell silent.

Yet they could keep shooting all night at the defenders in their trench on the opposite side of the wire and the track, with scant chance of damaging them. The Germans above Stella Maris, like those at the Gosset farm, hugged their positions and made no attempt to reach the Würzburg and thus to impede Frost and the engineers. But as long as Treinies and his handful of men continued to cover the beach approach, C Company seemed stuck. A protracted respite ensued, during which the rival combatants, facing each other across the defile, fired only intermittently.

Frost's first impression on seeing the Würzburg, in those days when radar dishes were novelties, was that it resembled 'an old-fashioned gramophone loudspeaker'. Young and his Hardys had taken possession moments earlier, almost unopposed. Only a tenuous network of crisscrossed, knee-high barbed wire encircled the radar installation, where a dense entanglement must have checked the attackers. The paratroopers picked their way through this slight obstacle without attracting notice. 'Then we were seen,' said Young, who had already eased the pin out of a grenade held in one hand. 'Groups of Germans wearing overcoats over pyjamas climbed slowly up from dugouts and stood, hands in pockets against the cold night air, just watching us. None carried arms and we discovered later they thought we were German soldiers on manoeuvres.'

It was certainly true that the Luftwaffe men had known about the noisy little night exercise Lt. Huhne and his Wehrmacht platoon completed less than an hour earlier. But Young's version, like all personal accounts of battles, is far from entirely accurate, not least because he went on to claim that he and his men 'killed a lot of Germans', which they did not. The Würzburg crew were indeed bewildered – some of them had been in France for only two days. But their NCO, Sgt. Gerhard Wenzel, was alerted many minutes before, and had since been struggling to rouse his men and chivvy them to take up their rifles. Wenzel was a jolly little figure, popular with the radar-operators who mocked him as 'the old man' – a twenty-five-year-old. His first revelation of the night had been to glimpse a big inanimate shape drifting down, which caused him to duck with his hands over his ears, because he supposed it to be a bomb, and expected an explosion. Then he saw a running man in the field eastward, and knew enemies were at hand. Meanwhile the set operator twenty-one-year-old Hans Senge – according to the German after-action report – was attempting to assemble an explosive charge to destroy the radar when Young interrupted his efforts with Sten-gun fire which killed him. Wenzel, likewise shot down, staggered or crawled away; was later found dead by the south wall of the villa, thirty yards distant. These, together with Kaffurbitz dead in the château, became the only three Luftwaffe fatalities of the night.

Young Willy Ermoneit, who had abandoned his appointed post in the château a few minutes earlier to explore outside, reached the radar site just as the British stormed it. He emptied the magazine of his Steyr sub-machine-gun towards them, without effect, before prudently taking to his heels. For this deed, in the Germans' subsequent quest for heroes, he was awarded the Iron Cross, second class. His comrades on the site fled towards the Gosset farm.

One technician was so desperate to escape he plunged over the cliff, discarding his rifle and pursued by paratroopers. Peter Walker, the interpreter, joined Sgt. Greg 'Mack the Knife' McKenzie peering down at the apparently paralysed, certainly terrified, Luftwaffe man clinging on a few feet below, who was attempting the difficult feat of retaining his position on the cliff face while also sustaining a posture of surrender. Within a few seconds, in his own language Walker cajoled the man back up – they wanted him as a prisoner, not a corpse. Young erupted into a laughter which he had not expected to experience in the midst of a battle: 'I thought I had seen nothing funnier than a German trying to scramble up the lip of a cliff with his hands up.'

Walker's first act upon literally collaring the prisoner was to tear the Luftwaffe badge from his tunic. A bemused comrade asked: 'Why have you done that?' This German Jew answered: 'For my personal satisfaction!' The captive hastily proffered his wristwatch as earnest of eagerness to placate his captors, and this was pocketed by McKenzie – it is curious that, in every twentieth-century war, soldiers of all nationalities in peril of their lives have often snatched their enemies' watches, portable trophies. Somebody urged killing the twenty-year-old, who was now sobbing and shaking in his shock and terror, but they knew they needed him in one piece. Peter Young and his men, in their enthusiasm for the assault, had been over-keen to kill Germans – his own sergeant certainly thought so – and forgetful of the priority of securing live prisoners to meet Reg Jones. Four of the latter had been able to bolt across the open ground northwards to the Gosset farm, leaving just the one radar-operator in British hands.

Silence was briefly restored around Henry, and the prisoner was hustled forward to be presented to Frost. Through Walker, the major quizzed the man, a technician named Heller who pronounced himself stunned; at this soft billet in Upper Normandy, he had not the least expectation of finding himself in the midst of a battlefield. The British officer demanded: did the men at the Gosset farm have mortars? If the enemy, who soon began shooting briskly from three directions, mortared the radar site, C Company would be in deep trouble. During the planned evacuation, they might inflict even graver carnage on the beach. Yes, answered Heller, they had access to the weapons; but had never done much with them. This was not true – the nearest mortars were at Étretat and Saint-Jouin – but the Luftwaffe man seems confusedly to have told the British whatever came into his head.

The Germans at the Gosset farm had already telephoned Étretat to demand an 81mm mortar, but this failed to arrive in time to be used that night. The British profited mightily from being pioneers, first significant raiders to assault Hitler's French coastline. Later in the war, indeed later in 1942, Churchill's armed forces would experience at bloody cost the speed and effectiveness with which German troops could respond, when confronted by intruders from the sea. That February night, however, the soldiers and Luftwaffe men who met C Company seemed capable only of firing on the British wherever they chanced to have men deployed.

A prime cause of German sluggishness in massing force remained uncertainty about the raiders' objectives. The Luftwaffe men around the two Freyas, on the cliff beyond and west of the Gosset farm, held their positions to defend the big scanners, which they expected to be attacked at any moment. Questions were asked afterwards by their superiors, about why they had not hastened to join the battle around the Würzburg. Yet they were exonerated when it was found that, amid expectations of further British landings, they received insistent orders from Étretat to ensure at all costs that a radar watch continued to be maintained, and that the Freyas were protected from assault. Meanwhile south of Bruneval, in the sector occupied by the 336th Division's 687th Regiment, its pickets who witnessed the descent of the misdropped paratroopers caused its headquarters to fear an attack in their own direction.

After Lt. Ruben and his NCOs came under Bren fire, they abandoned their vehicle and hurried on foot by a more circuitous route to the Gosset farm, where they found confusion among the Luftwaffe men. The three made a brief attempt to go further – to get to the Würzburg – but had advanced only a few yards when they bumped into Lt. Naoumoff's Drakes. Surprised German and British voices first demanded each other's surrender, then there was an exchange of fire in which neither side hit anything, before the Luftwaffe trio swiftly retreated into the night.

Back at the Gosset farm, the lieutenant sought to muster a fighting force, and found that the radar personnel had only a few rounds apiece for their rifles. Sgt. Karl Deckert volunteered to take their Opel by the north road to La Poterie and beg a machine-gun from the army. Arrived at the *mairie*, he was obliged to conduct a farcical negotiation with the NCO in charge, who declared defiantly that, airborne attack or no airborne attack, he would not surrender a single weapon to a Luftwaffe man without his company commander's order. After much pleading, the soldier gave way and Deckert returned to the Gosset farm with a machine-gun and its two-man crew. This was set up even as Frost and his men milled around the Würzburg and the château.

As soon as the shooting had temporarily stopped in the immediate vicinity of Henry, Dennis Vernon ran forward, confirmed that the site was secure, then waved and shouted, 'Come on, the RE's!' Around 0100, Cox and two engineers joined him, having cursed considerably about the difficulty of dragging their three trolleys through the snow, then heaving them over the Germans' barbed-wire trellis, only two feet high but ten feet wide. Two of the awkward load-carriers were quickly abandoned as redundant. The raiders conferred momentarily: Young reported to Vernon that he had searched the château and dugouts without finding any documents such as Reg Jones wanted. Then Cox and the others, after donning rubber gloves to avoid shocks from high-tension cables, set to work with insulated tools on the big metal radar cabinet.

They discovered the set was mounted on a turntable bolted to a flatbed four-wheeled truck, surrounded by sandbags up to platform level. Cox said: 'I found it to my surprise just like the photograph.' The flight-sergeant made hasty notes and sketches while the engineers wrestled with the steel casing, five feet high by three wide and two deep. The airman scribbled: 'Top of the compartment taken up by transmitter and what looks like first stage of receiver. Large power pack with finned metal rectifiers occupies bottom. Between the TX [transmitter] and power unit 1 the pulse gear and the receiver IF [intermediate frequency]. Everything solid and in good order.'

Cox said later: 'I thought it a beautiful job, and I've been in wireless all my life.' Each unit was mounted in an aluminium box for easy removal and exchange. He pulled aside the thick black rubber curtain across the entrance to the control cabin, then said to Peter Walker, standing with their Luftwaffe prisoner: 'Hey, Peter, this thing's still hot. Ask the Jerry if he was tracking our aircraft as we came in.' Yes, the Jerries had been, albeit not this particular Jerry.

Within seconds the Demounting party discovered that to accomplish anything they must use flashlights, which soon drew fire from Rectangle. This intensified when Vernon set about taking photographs with his Leica, each flash in the darkness provoking a new spasm of German shooting. It is unsurprising that the lieutenant's images afterwards proved useless, and that most of the thirty-six bulbs which he had optimistically borne into battle went undischarged. Frost told the lieutenant to abandon an almost suicidal activity.

The Germans' subsequent narrative stated: 'The commandos were nevertheless prevented from proceeding with their attack on the Freya position. The remainder of the Luftwaffe Communications Station unit … took part in this action', meaning that Lt. Ruben now had his men shooting towards the Würzburg site. The after-action report represented, of course, a complete misreading of events. Frost's men never intended to attack the Freya site, nor indeed to overrun the Gosset farm. Happily for C Company, however, the enemy supposed otherwise, probably because within the farm buildings was a Luftwaffe signals hub, which employed by far the largest proportion of the personnel posted on the Bruneval sites, interpreting and transmitting the information about British aircraft and shipping received by the radar plotters.

Lt. Huhne, the army's representative in La Poterie, had in the meantime led his own men through the darkness towards the Gosset farm – and met Bren and rifle fire from Timothy's Rodneys. The Germans went to ground; shot hesitantly back; but made no attempt to press on towards Frost's group. The soldiers, like the Luftwaffe, sustained their belief that the British must aspire to break through to the Freya and plotting station. Thus, instead of seeking to launch a counter-attack to save the Würzburg, the Germans contented themselves with defending the larger installations – with containing the British, not knowing the latter were entirely happy to be contained within the ground they held. The defenders sustained their delusions, and their firing positions, almost until C Company began to withdraw an hour later, while Naoumoff and his Drakes, together with the Rodneys, more or less literally kept the enemy's heads down, though without inflicting losses.

It is an interesting speculation, to which no clues survive, whether Jones and TRE ever considered requesting C Company to include the Gosset farm among its objectives, because the communications centre assuredly held technical secrets. The initial plan for Biting called for the Drakes to work around the farm buildings and open fire from their northern side, creating a diversion in the opposite direction to that in which Frost's assault groups would be deployed. This idea had been abandoned, because of the likelihood that a small British party could find itself cut off from the rest of the paratroopers. Meanwhile, to overrun the densely-populated buildings, albeit only two hundred yards from Lone House, would likely have proved beyond the powers of Frost and his men. The Gosset farm nonetheless served its turn that night, because even if the British did not endow it with any priority, the Germans did.

On the Würzburg site, while the British engineers' flashing photo-bulbs and torches provided aiming marks for the enemy, they were firing persistently high, and the sappers stuck to their work. One of Vernon's men used a hammer and chisel to remove Telefunken labels and multiple number codes from the radar set, to provide Reg Jones and his boffins with indications of German production rates. As for the electronic elements, they discovered that their tools, even the longest screwdriver, were ineffective. Instead, impelled by the mingled urgencies generated by adrenalin, fear and desperation, they began to wrench whole sections from the set by main force, thus securing the pulse units and IF amplifier. When the aerial in the 2.8-metre scanner dish defied them, Cox told a sapper to take a hacksaw to it. The vital transmitter in the cabinet resisted until, in desperation, the airman and Vernon seized its handles while a third man plied a crowbar. The set, together with its frame containing the aerial switching unit, tore free.

As the engineers laboured on Henry, from below Bruneval hamlet they could hear the stammer of a German – in truth, French – machine-gun in action, together with the matching clamour of Brens, which must be Ross's. They were also catching constant exchanges of fire from the north and north-east – Naoumoff's and Timothy's men shooting it out with Germans in the trees fronting the Rectangle, and on the approach from La Poterie. The Rodneys encountered new evidence of German pusillanimity. A stand-by section of the 685th arrived in La Poterie, and was persuaded to set forth to join Lt. Huhne's firefight with the British. These men retired, however, after letting off flares and receiving the contents of two Bren magazines, delivered by Pte. Dick Scott, although again without inflicting casualties.

Frost speculated that the missing stick of Rodneys, seen to have landed south of Bruneval, might by now have descended to support the Nelsons. Then a messenger arrived from Timothy, who reported that his fourth section remained absent, but that he and the other three groups were still at their agreed positions further inland; everything was going according to plan – they were holding the Germans at a safe distance – except that their 38 wireless was dead, and one man had been wounded. Frost sent a runner to Naoumoff, in front of Rectangle, telling him to pull back through the Würzburg site, shouting the password 'Biting!' as often as may be, to reduce the risk from friendly fire in a confused situation.

Naoumoff's retiring section soon reached the company commander, who ordered the Drakes to descend to reinforce Ross. The lieutenant passed the shoulder then headed towards the beach by a virgin route that took his men somewhat west of Ross, slipping and sliding down the hill only a few yards short of the cliff, where the defile became as deep and steep as any railway cutting. Amazingly unnoticed by the Germans, he and his men gained possession of an empty trench on the north side. From that position they began tossing grenades towards the Germans, though Treinies' section was too well sited, up the opposite face, to take any harm. The defenders still blocked the passage to the beach, but were now closely besieged, by

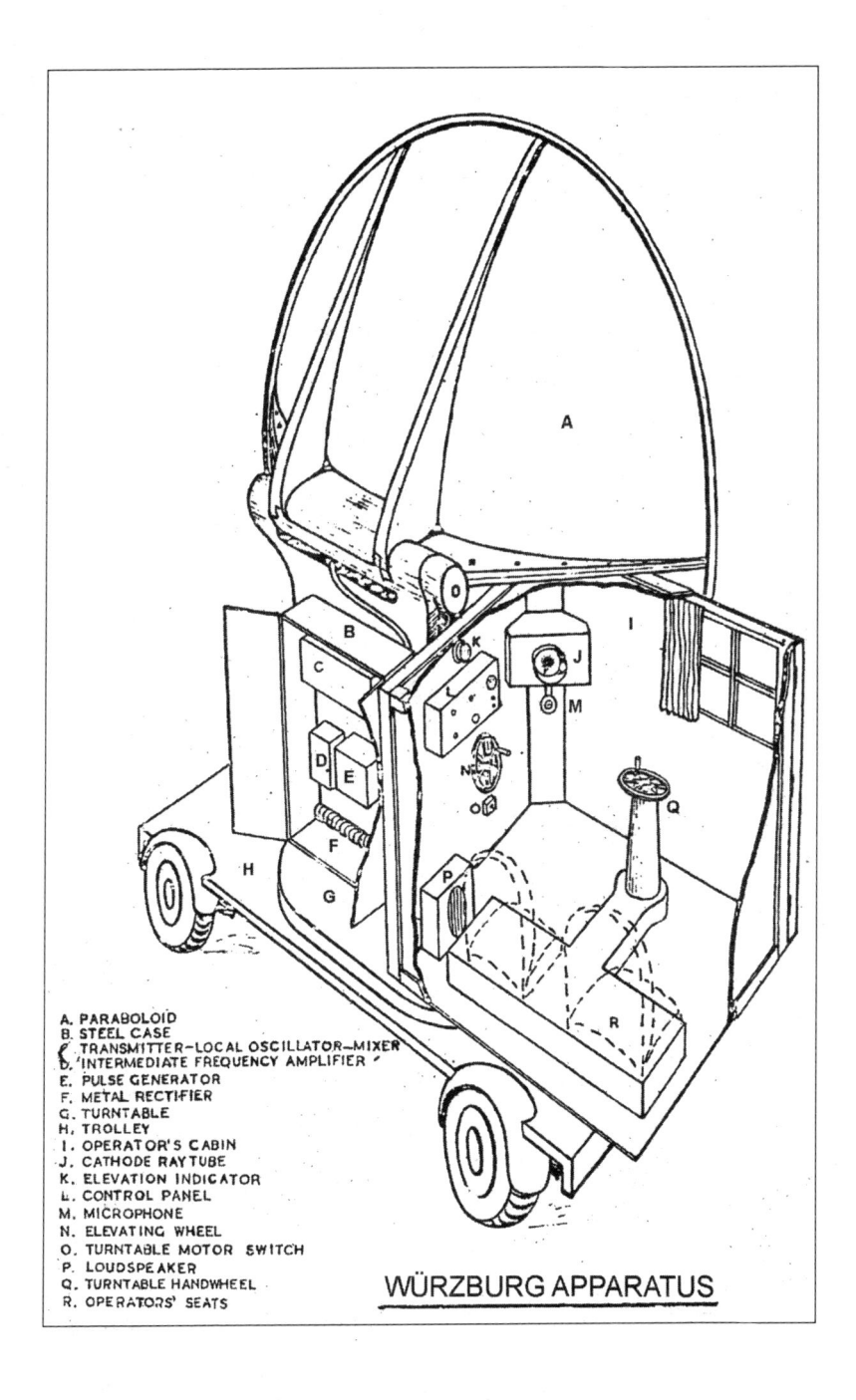

A. PARABOLOID
B. STEEL CASE
C. TRANSMITTER—LOCAL OSCILLATOR—MIXER
D. INTERMEDIATE FREQUENCY AMPLIFIER
E. PULSE GENERATOR
F. METAL RECTIFIER
G. TURNTABLE
H. TROLLEY
I. OPERATOR'S CABIN
J. CATHODE RAY TUBE
K. ELEVATION INDICATOR
L. CONTROL PANEL
M. MICROPHONE
N. ELEVATING WHEEL
O. TURNTABLE MOTOR SWITCH
P. LOUDSPEAKER
Q. TURNTABLE HANDWHEEL
R. OPERATORS' SEATS

WÜRZBURG APPARATUS

much superior numbers. Sgt. Bill Sunley crawled towards Ross and shouted that he could shift the knife-rest gate in the wire, opening a path through which the Nelsons could advance, though covering the last yards to Stella Maris under fire would still be a hazardous business. There were lulls in the little battle in the defile, but every British movement prompted renewed German fire. Ross sent a runner up to Frost, to report that he and the defenders were still deadlocked.

Around Henry, German shooting increased. Lt. Huhne's machine-guns now joined the one borrowed by Lt. Ruben, sending tracer arching two hundred yards across the night sky from the Gosset farm. In Frost's words, 'it became extremely uncomfortable in our area'. One burst of fire caught two unlucky paratroopers outside the château, killing Pte. Hugh McIntyre with a bullet in the head and wounding Corporal Jeff Heslop in the thigh. McIntyre, it may be recalled, was the twenty-eight-year-old Ayrshire man who had breached security a week earlier to write to his brother about the raid, promising he would be 'home next Saturday ... I'll be seeing you next week'. Though most of the incoming fire remained inaccurate, a couple of rounds pierced the Würzburg dish.

The major now felt the full weight of the loneliness of command in action. He had no radio contact with any other party, and so knew only what was happening within his line of sight. He mutely cursed Browning's staff, which had imposed the organization depriving him of the headquarters that customarily formed a key component of an infantry company. Sporadic gunfire was audible both north and south, and he noticed the lights of vehicles flickering behind the thick belt of trees screening the Gosset farm. As the minutes ticked by, he envisaged the Germans setting up heavy weapons: if they started to use mortars or artillery, the company would be in deep trouble. The engineers' labours seemed interminable, though the use of jemmies in lieu of screwdrivers hastened progress.

At last, Vernon reported that he and Cox had extracted most of the key components of the Würzburg, which they had loaded onto the one trolley that seemed necessary. As German fire intensified, the major made an abrupt decision: they would pull out. They had a Luftwaffe technician as their prisoner, and most of the innards of the radar set. The engineers had enjoyed just ten minutes' access to the installation, instead of the half-hour the planners intended, but the longer span had always seemed wildly optimistic. Their only significant miss was failure to seize the display on which the operator viewed incoming radar signals: they ran out of time before they could address the technology inside the little crew cabin.

Frost now faced his next big uncertainty: about what he and his treasure-hunters would face, on their half-mile descent towards the beach through the moonlight and amid erratic fire. They began trudging and trotting towards the scrubby hillside that led down into the defile which offered the only approach to the sea, paratroopers covering the trolley party who, despite the assistance of the five unarmed Rodneys, struggled with their eighty-pound load on rough turf covered with several inches of snow. Gerry Strachan, that pillar of strength who had always seemed indestructible, was moving a little behind Frost at the head of the Hardys and Jellicoes, just below the pillboxes on the crest occupied earlier by Sgt. Tasker and four Nelsons, when a burst of German fire from the south side of the defile – the trenches above Stella Maris, some two hundred yards distant – caught him. He fell with three Châtellerault bullets in the stomach. One of the engineers, Reg Heard, was also hit, in the hand.

The major dragged Strachan beneath the concrete lip of the casement approach. He jabbed a morphia syrette into the CSM's abdomen, then administered field dressings to the wounds. While firing intensified in all directions, the sergeant-major, delirious, began to shout incomprehensible orders. Frost ordered the engineer party to go to ground with their precious burdens until the enemy fire was suppressed, the path opened to the beach.

The paratroopers had triumphantly accomplished the purpose of their operation; done the job which Reg Jones had asked of them. Yet now they faced the further vital challenge: to get home. Everything thus far would have been in vain if they could not carry their booty safely to the beach, and make the rendezvous with the navy. And at that moment, the way to escape was barred by a handful of Germans who proved the only enemies that night to display determination and courage in confronting the airborne invaders.

10

Junior

Even as the night's principal drama unfolded around Henry, a mile and more southwards Frost's missing paratroopers were experiencing testing times of their own as they strove, with varied degrees of energy and effectiveness, to reach the battlefield. Five dispersed parties were stalled beyond Bruneval or moving uncertainly across rough and in many places wooded terrain, interrupted by deep valleys. Between 0015 and at least 0230, these fragments of C Company conducted a droll war dance with Germans roused from their billets in the Beau-Minet hotel.

Though it did not seem so at the time, Frost's thirty-five absentees gave important help to the success of Biting, just as on a vastly larger scale the American and British airborne landings in the early hours of 6 June 1944 assisted the D-Day amphibious assaults. On both occasions, the dispersal of the attackers confused the Germans, who felt obliged to dispatch men in all directions, pursuing elusive paratroopers. C Company enjoyed a critical advantage in the early hours of 28 February 1942: every man, even those who were lost, knew what he was in France to attempt to do.

The Germans, by contrast, remained bewildered about British purposes. Most of Bruneval's defenders passed the hours during which Frost and his men were in action hastening hither and thither, plunged in uncertainty. Sgt. Vormschlag, commander of the understrength Beau-Minet platoon of the 685th Regiment, was given a hopeless task when ordered by Lt. Huhne in La Poterie to cover the ground above the hamlet. He mustered just eighteen men to defend several square miles. Vormschlag acted intelligently: he split one section into two patrols, to seek out and engage paratroopers approaching from the south. He deployed the other section in fixed positions at Beuzelin farm, just south of Bruneval, and at Polet farm, two hundred yards north-eastwards, where their machine-guns could cover the roads up which the British were most likely to approach, or to cross. On this unnaturally clear, still night, the Germans occasionally heard Scottish curses. The paratroopers, in their turn, caught snatches of enemy conversation and exclamation. There were sustained periods of silence, during which the wary skirmishers of both sides did not dare for an instant to relax their vigilance, liable to be shattered by exchanges of fire, followed again by tense lulls.

Charteris was advancing fastest and with most conviction. The lieutenant was leading his stick in diamond formation when machine-gun bursts from the Beuzelin farm ahead caused them urgently to take cover, though not in time to spare Pte. Jim Sutherland from being hit in the arm and shoulder. Brengunner Charlie Branwhite returned fire, scarring the enemy-held buildings with pock-marks. The lieutenant jabbed morphia into the wounded man, then the section swung abruptly eastwards to escape from the German line of fire. For a few minutes Sutherland stumbled on with the others. It soon became plain, however, that a shocked and increasingly drowsy man could not sustain the pace. Charteris told Branwhite to find a farm building where the wounded paratrooper could be left in shelter. In this the twenty-year-old officer displayed impressive maturity, grasping that his duty was to reach the battlefield with utmost speed, distracted neither by enemy outposts nor by compassion.

Branwhite the Bren-gunner, a twenty-six-year-old former Glasgow shipyard worker, had suffered a tragic loss only a month earlier, when his wife Helen died while giving birth to twins. The babies, and his elder daughter, had been placed in care pending their father's return from the war. Now, Branwhite helped Sutherland's painful progress towards dimly visible dwellings. It appears the inhabitants of the first house at which they called kept their door stubbornly closed. Instead they approached the Échos farm, a nearby cluster of buildings owned by Paul Delamare. The latter, long since awakened by the planes and gunfire, assumed the shadowy figures whom he saw moving across country were airmen from a shot-down bomber, and he was not disabused of this idea until daybreak.

Throughout the night's events scores of local people stayed locked in their homes, in some cases within a few yards of the rival combatants exchanging fire. Most, like Delamare, lay sensibly mute, nursing their terrors and uncertainty, until dawn revealed realities both good and ill. Branwhite supported Sutherland into a shed, made him as comfortable as he could contrive and wished him luck, then left the paratrooper alone while he himself hastened after Charteris and the section's footprints in the snow, 'as if the devil was after me'.

A bleakly comic incident next interrupted their progress when a strange voice sought to open a conversation with Peter McCormack, rear man of the section, who was electrified by this new acquaintance's choice of language. 'My God, it's a bloody German!' exclaimed the astonished Scot to his mate

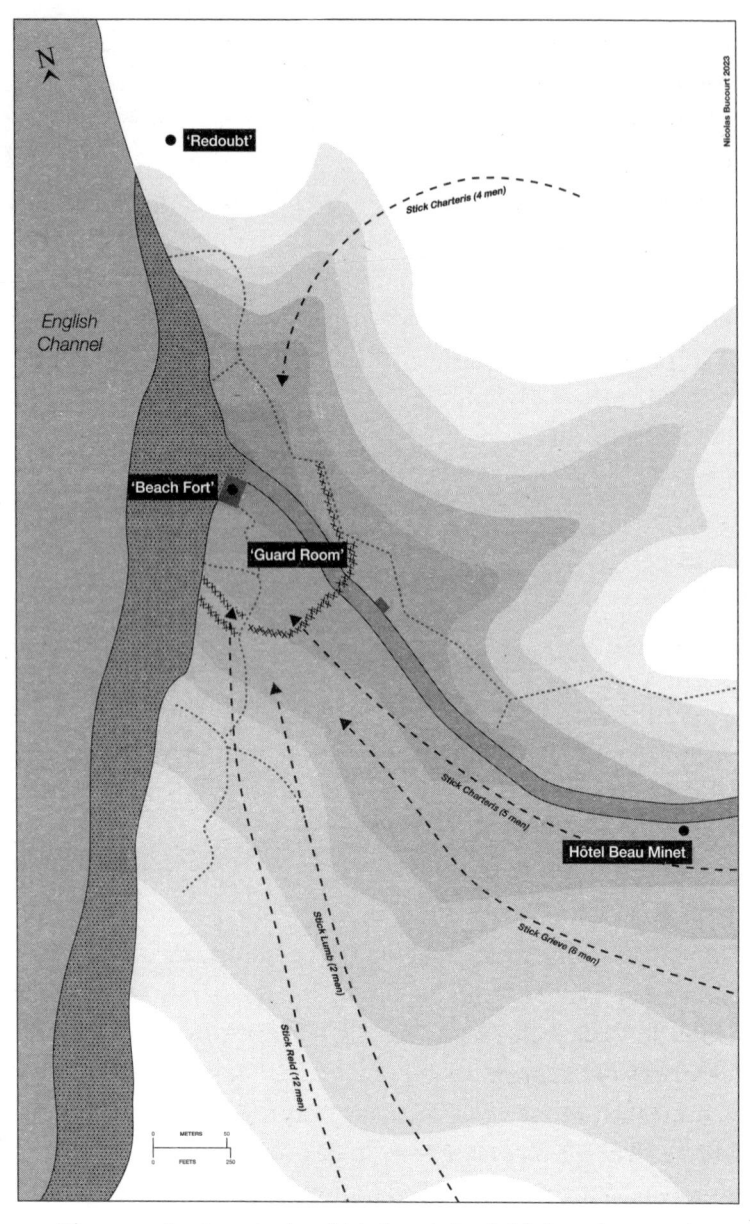

The approximate routes by which the missing 'sticks' sought to reach the beach defile at Bruneval

Peter Venters. The 'bloody German', an equally bemused Pte. Adolf Schmitz, had lost his own section as it advanced uphill from the Beau-Minet, and mistakenly added himself to that of Charteris. He now fired a single wild rifle shot towards the paratroopers before taking to his heels. Sgt. Alex Gibbins loosed his Sten gun with an instinctive twitch, almost fatally for Tom Hill, whom several rounds missed by inches. The rest of the magazine caught the thirty-five-year-old Schmitz, who fell dead. Gibbins apologized to Hill. Charteris and his men kept going north.

After the false start of Alex Reid's Rodneys, corrected by Rob Stirling, these men were now heading the right way. Accompanied by Grieve and Stewart, they were still a mile short of the beach defile when Frost and his men stormed the radar site. Suddenly the Reids heard a German voice giving a fire order, followed by an eruption of shooting. This was almost certainly the moment when the enemy posted at Beuzelin farm engaged Charteris's stick. Reid's section, pursuing a course further west, nearer to the sea, prudently kept silent and in stealthy motion.

Unbeknown to them, and further north, Sgt. Lumb and Corporal Campbell, who had been dropped on the cliff close to the defile, first moved some distance east from their landing place, then turned north on hearing firing. Since they were far closer to Bruneval, and to the defile, than were Charteris and Reid, yet took much longer than either to reach it, we may assume the two paratroopers made halting progress, hitting the ground when bursts of gunfire ripped through the darkness, as they repeatedly did. Lumb and Campbell almost certainly spent most of the next two hours hiding up or groping through woodland. Their only contribution to the operation was to remain alive and free, as the three men did not, whom they had unwisely left behind.

Charteris had aimed to strike the defile leading down to the beach between Bruneval hamlet and the sea, but his section's encounters with the Germans deflected his course sharply eastwards. Now, he used the enforced pause to send two men scouting ahead, who found a northerly track parallel with and east of that on which they had met the enemy. 'It was scrubby and difficult country,' said Charteris, 'into which we plunged, making a lot of noise. I was sure, however, that speed was more important than silence.' When they were fired upon from the Beuzelin farm, the hamlet and the defile were only perhaps three hundred yards ahead. Their new course, though, took them in a wide arc, which added at least another mile to their odyssey, over deeply broken country: only young men as fit as were Frost's paratroopers could have performed the exertions demanded of many that night.

Some of Charteris's section were already showing signs of weariness when, around 0130, they struck the road running between Bruneval and La Poterie, two hundred yards east of the Calvary which stood at a crossroads just above the hamlet. Charteris placed his Bren pair to cover the section through the dangerous moments of crossing an open, exposed, gently declining field between themselves and the road, then he and three of his men ran over together without incident. As they began swarming up the steep and wooded hillside that lay just beyond, they could soon see ahead the Gosset château, and hear firing on all sides, especially from the defile a half-mile below them, where Ross was engaged.

At that moment, much closer to hand a German machine-gun opened fire, tracer streaking up the road from the Polet farm just below the Calvary, on the edge of Bruneval. The remaining five men of Charteris's section hurriedly retreated into nearby trees, and for a time stayed there. Both groups of British soldiers could discern bullets whipping into the foliage overhead, cutting branches, though Charteris soon decided that at least some of these rounds were not aimed at them; were instead 'overs' from the continuing exchanges of fire to the north – machine-gun fire could easily carry a mile. When silence returned to their immediate vicinity, the lieutenant sent Tom Hill back to try and find the rest of the section, and bring them to join him. Hill failed – returned empty-handed to Charteris. He and his men caught their breath for a few moments, then set off north again, towards the unmistakable sound of a British Bren.

The German report on the clashes described above between Charteris's section and the defenders stated: 'Meanwhile, in accordance with orders, the platoon from Bruneval had sallied forth and divided into two groups and advanced on Hill 102 [south of the Calvary above the village].' Outside Bruneval they came under fire from 'the commandos who had landed N of L'Enfer' – Charteris's men. 'Although this platoon was unable to prevent the commandos from infiltrating between Bruneval and Hill 102, it was because of this platoon's action that some commandos did not reach the boats in time, and were later taken prisoner ... It was only because the British objective was not known that this Bruneval platoon did not take part in the action at the château [Lone House].'

All the while Charteris was still heading north towards the radar site, at last confident that he knew where he was, and increasing speed to 'a fast lollop of between six and seven miles an hour' as they reached more level ground, at the cost of desperate panting from his burdened men. Within a few minutes, the lieutenant was greeting a startled John Timothy. It was now around 0145, ninety minutes since his stick had landed. Rodney's commander updated Charteris: the radar mission was complete – Frost was leading the engineers and the rest of the main body towards the defile with the electronic components, while Timothy continued to cover their rear against German movements from La Poterie. The passage to the beach, however, was still blocked – and clearing it was the mission entrusted to Charteris in the company's orders for Biting.

The four Nelsons left Timothy; sped across the hillside to the pillboxes of Redoubt, where Charteris reported to Frost, whom he found with Vernon, Cox and the engineers, guarding their precious radar parts. Charteris thought the major seemed 'somewhat worried', and this was unsurprising. C Company's commander had experienced a crowded and difficult half-hour. Each time British soldiers moved in the defile below they attracted fire, though it was almost always mercifully high. Some confusion was caused by a voice – just possibly that of Naoumoff, in his initial excitement at having himself got down the hill unscathed – crying from down in the defile 'Come on down! Everything is all right and the boats are here!' This false statement was promptly contradicted by John Ross shouting emphatically: 'Do *not* come down! The beach defences have *not* been taken yet.'

Most of the British post-mortems after Biting were self-congratulatory. Nobody wanted to play a blame game in the aftermath of success. All the reports agreed, however, that C Company came close to defeat, or rather to fatal frustration of its escape, in its hour-long battle to break through to the beach. The paratroopers above the defile paid the price for having given the Germans – even the mere handful posted there – so long in which to take up dominant firing positions before the British appeared. Whenever the Nelsons attempted to move, the defenders released a flare, of which there seemed to be a large stock in Stella Maris, that lit up the opposing hillside, almost bereft of cover.

Enemy reinforcements, arriving from inland, could not be much longer delayed. An infantry company was on its way from Gonneville; more men and heavy weapons were moving from Étretat, delayed by vehicles stuck on the icy road that led up the steep hill out of the town. A detachment of cyclist infantry from the south was approaching the battlefield. Regimental commander Col. von Eisenhart-Rothe was also heading for La Poterie, and the now wide-awake Major Paschke had persuaded him to activate the entire formation. Large forces had not yet arrived partly because of the snow, but also as a result of lingering uncertainties about British intentions. While the Luftwaffe men at the Gosset farm understood that the paratroopers were now pulling out, the army's von Eisenhart-Rothe did not – he retained several of his units south of Bruneval, blocking the way to Octeville, which Frost's men had not the slightest intention of approaching. Confusion intensified when a patrol of the German 687th advanced on Bruneval from the south, by the same route used earlier by Charteris, was fired upon by their confused compatriots defending Beuzelin farm, and obliged to retire, believing they had encountered hostile forces.

Back at the Redoubt pillboxes, the belated appearance of Charteris with just three men did little to cheer Frost: he had hoped the young lieutenant was long since committed to the attack on Stella Maris with two entire sections. The major ordered him down the hill to join Naoumoff and the Drakes: Beach Fort and its surrounding trench system must, absolutely must, be taken, and quickly. Charteris's men – Gibbins, Hill and Laughland – were exhausted after their long, rough trek across country. To ease Hill's burdens – the corporal was carrying four filled Bren magazines in his pouches – the lieutenant took up the corporal's rifle, surrendering his own pistol in exchange. Then they scrambled downhill to the trenches facing Stella Maris. The British force there now numbered some twenty-two men, while Ross – higher up the defile in the direction of the hamlet – mustered another fifteen. They thus heavily outnumbered Sgt. Treinies and his small band, but this advantage seemed to be doing the British little good.

Frost meanwhile ordered Timothy and his sections progressively to pull back four hundred yards to the shoulder of the cliff, which they did. But this permitted Huhne and his men from La Poterie to probe forward behind them, dangerously close. The major was about to order the Rodneys to descend and join the struggle for the defile when Pte. Jack Millington appeared, bearing a message from Timothy: Germans from La Poterie had reoccupied the château, and were now shooting from there, threatening the British rear. Frost made an instant decision – they must push back the enemies closing in behind them, to gain time and space for the company to break through below. While Ross's and Naoumoff's men continued to exchange fire with the Germans across the defile, Frost ordered Cox and the engineers with their precious booty to stay under cover at Redoubt – the pillboxes. He then hastily assembled every nearby fighting man for a counter-attack which he himself led, running back uphill towards the château where some fifteen Germans, led by Lt. Huhne, had taken possession.

To the major's vast relief, as the handful of paratroopers charged onto the plateau firing, the enemy turned and fled without offering resistance, scuttling out of the château. 'The Germans,' wrote Frost, 'were still very confused and were up against they knew not what.' A Luftwaffe patrol sent from the Gosset farm by Lt. Ruben also withdrew, having merely stumbled on the body of Pte. McIntyre. Both the German soldiers and the Luftwaffe men carried little ammunition. Huhne demanded reinforcements; he was told that two cyclist infantry platoons and 50mm mortars were on their way.

Frost's counter-attack was almost counter-intuitive – he left Ross and Charteris to force the issue at the beach in order to wrest back the initiative from the nervous Germans approaching the radar site. He and his men gained some space and time by what amounted to an energetic little demonstration in the face of some of the least impressive elements of the enemy's forces.

In the defile, even as uphill Frost was seeing off Huhne's half-hearted advance, the drama reached a climax. When Charteris arrived there was a lull, during which both sides regrouped. 'By then,' said the lieutenant, 'the parties were getting a bit mixed up so we all advanced together to take the beach. I felt as naked as a baby, because I was only about seventy yards from the house which I knew to be held by the enemy ... For more than a month, I had been studying the best ways of attacking this house. I had looked at all the photographs, examined all the plans. But when the moment came to put all this into practice, reality seemed quite different from what I had imagined.' Most of the obvious access points were so steep or indeed sheer that they could be scaled only with ropes or ladders. The Germans' weapons appeared to command every approach. The British did not grasp how very few in number were the defenders.

Nor did Charteris and Naoumoff know that British reinforcements were at hand, coming from the hillside opposite. High on the cliff on the south side, Alex Reid and David Grieve, followed by their ten Rodneys, had reached a point directly above and behind Beach Fort, where they were checked by concertina wire. Reid is alleged to have told the two signallers Taffy Thomas and John McCallum – though a suspicion must linger that the two men acted on their own initiative, rather than under orders – to take their 18 set and hide up in nearby trees. Desperately the others set about forcing a passage through the entanglement with wire-cutters, a process that took precious minutes.

Even as they did so, Germans of Vormschlag's Beau-Minet platoon began firing on them from among woodland higher up the defile. A bullet pierced Corporal Vic Stewart's helmet and hit his head, causing blood to course freely down his face. The corporal fell, crying 'I've had it!' His neighbour Rob Stirling recoiled from the notion that the dead man's wallet, much thickened by pontoon winnings from half the company, should fall into German hands, and deftly retrieved this from his prostrate corporal's belt. At that moment, however, Stewart revived – realized the bullet had only grazed his scalp. He demanded indignantly of Stirling: 'Gie us my bluidy wallet back, then,' adding that if Stirling wanted his money, he would need to win it like an honest man, at the card table.

The wire-cutters were still at work around 0200, when below them Charteris and his three men made a successful dash across the road to the foot of the villa emplacement, covered by fire and a shower of grenades thrown both by themselves and Naoumoff's Drakes, and bounded up the steps on the sea side of the building. Almost simultaneously Sgt. Bill Sunley dragged aside the knife-rest gate blocking the road above, so that Ross's men could scramble through, and head down the hill. Two of Treinies' soldiers, deciding their predicament was dire, vanished into the night, and were not seen again by either side.

The sergeant now commanded just six defenders. He left two of them, Corporal Max Arndt and Fusilier Hormandinger, in a trench above and south of the villa, and ordered another man to carry their precious machine-gun up to the higher emplacement. Treinies sent yet another, Johannes Tewes, to bring more flares and ammunition from Stella Maris.

Inside the villa the German telephone rang again, and was answered by Georg Schmidt. He found himself connected to Major Paschke, the battalion commander now arrived at the *mairie* in La Poterie, who demanded to speak to Treinies. The major heard the firing and explosions; but still did not grasp what was happening, and sought enlightenment. The bewildered soldier conveyed his terror and excitement down the line to his superior, who responded with audible exasperation. When more bangs interrupted their confused conversation, the officer exhorted the telephonist to calm down and make less racket.

Schmidt countered emotionally, perhaps hysterically, that the noises were being made by the detonation of British grenades. He emerged briefly from the blockhouse rear door in search of his sergeant, but hastily withdrew again when he attracted fire. Fusilier Tewes burst in, seeking flares, tracer for the Châtellerault and ammunition clips for the riflemen; he then scrambled away, laden with boxes and draped in bandoliers. After turning out the light inside the casemate so that he himself crouched in darkness, Schmidt stayed thus through several minutes of exchanges of fire and grenade explosions that followed.

Now everything seemed to happen at once. High on the southern side of the defile, the Rodneys' wire-cutters completed a breach in the entanglement. Reid and Grieve – the latter 'a very stout fellow' in Charteris's words – charged down the hillside at the head of their seven remaining men, shouting the Seaforths' famous Gaelic battle cry of '*Cabar Feidh!*' – the stag's antler symbol of Ross-shire. They met ineffectual German fire, and were soon at the rear of the emplacements within yards of Charteris in front, and not much further from Ross's group, now also closing in. In the space of perhaps fifteen minutes, the fortunes of C Company were dramatically altered. Charteris, McKenzie, Gibbins and Laughland first tossed grenades up onto the balcony above them, without provoking any response. They found the sandbagged emplacements before the villa empty, then worked down the line of bathing huts fronting Stella Maris, kicking in doors and tossing more grenades, a fragment from one of which wounded the German Fusilier Tewes in the neck. He staggered away in search of a refuge; hid himself in an empty foxhole a few yards up the hill.

Charteris ran along the wooden terrace, meeting no one; around the back of the villa he and his men found an open door. The British soldiers burst inside and hurtled down a lighted passage. The lieutenant said: 'After that, things got somewhat confused.' Expecting to receive a burst of fire at any second, they shouted repeatedly '*Hände Hoche! Komm hier!*', and suchlike phrases learned back at Tilshead for exactly this moment. He then rushed through the door of a darkened room, which proved to contain Corporal Schmidt, with his hands held high.

Charteris demanded harshly: 'Where are the others?' The terrified prisoner gestured vaguely to other rooms, and up the hill. Jimmy Sharp, newly come with Ross's section, informed the prisoner brusquely that he was about to take a one-way trip '*nach England*'. Meanwhile Tewes, grazed by the grenade fragment, was discovered in the foxhole where he had taken refuge and was likewise seized by the paratroopers, breaching Frost's earlier injunction that only Luftwaffe personnel were worth transporting to England. A Catholic from Dortmund, Tewes was soon volubly asserting to Peter Young his hatred of the Nazis and eagerness to surrender.

Max Arndt, one of the two Germans who had stayed in the trench above Stella Maris, was killed by Rob Stirling with his fighting knife, a weapon issued to all British commandos and some paratroopers, which the bloodthirsty Stirling had been impatient to test, and indeed continued to jab into Arndt's corpse. The other defender, Hormandinger, fired once, despairingly, at Dave Grieve – the bullet creased the sergeant's lip – before this German also was felled by an exploding grenade. The British had broken through. Charteris, Grieve and the others, now in overwhelming strength, tossed grenades into every foxhole as they advanced in short bounds through the enemy positions to the Beach Fort emplacement, from which no further opposition was forthcoming. The German report described 'heavy fire from three or four commando machine-guns … after one German soldier had been killed [Arndt] and another wounded [Hormandinger] the sergeant was obliged to take up new positions'. To be more explicit, Treinies and his three surviving men abandoned their resistance and found a hiding place. There, they lay mute and undiscovered through the hour – for them, a terrifying hour – that followed. Charteris continued to hunt Germans, with the others checking and bombing every likely enemy refuge. When he met John Ross, he successfully begged more grenades, to finish the job.

Thus, when John Frost once again glissaded down the sheer hillside after mounting his successful counter-attack to frighten Huhne and his men back from the château, he found the situation in the defile transformed. Even as the major had feared he was losing control – that the whole operation was imperilled – the German weapons blocking the approach to the beach fell silent, especially the machine-gun that had troubled them so much. The deadlock in a little battle that had already lasted more than an hour had been broken by the combined efforts of Sunley, Grieve, Reid and above all Charteris. The sappers were soon skidding and sliding past them, down the frozen approach. Two men were dragging the wounded Strachan, in agony. The sergeant-major had grown chilled: John Timothy stripped off his jump smock, removed the cricket sweater he was wearing underneath and pulled this over the stricken man. Down the rough route to the beach, paratroopers supported the other casualties, to which were added Naoumoff's Sgt. Johnny Boyd, with a bullet in the foot.

Charteris took control of a confused situation, with men milling in all directions. When Corporal Campbell, of Lumb's missing section, suddenly appeared alone, having made his way down the south side of the valley, an understandably intemperate lieutenant ordered him 'with many oaths' to go back and retrieve the rest of Lumb's section, and above all to find the 18 wireless set with which they had been entrusted, and was now urgently needed to summon the navy. It remains a mystery where Lumb and Campbell had passed the previous two hours, having been dropped within a few minutes of the defile, albeit with wooded country in between. Now that silence prevailed in the immediate vicinity, the five missing members of Charteris's own section, who had taken cover rather than follow him across the Poterie–Bruneval road under fire, appeared, led by privates Grafton and Matkin, having moved cautiously along the higher ground above the hamlet, on the south shoulder of the defile. They had glimpsed some of the Beau-Minet Germans, but slipped past them without another clash.

The route to the beach had been cleared by initiative and prodigious luck: the Whitley pilots' dropping errors had proved the probable salvation of C Company. The subsequent German report on the defile battle painted a picture of stubborn resistance: 'It was not until after one to one and a half hour's fighting that the commandos were able to get through the strongpoint and the ravine to the beach with their two [in reality three] prisoners and their own wounded ... The platoon from La Poterie fought their way to the Luftwaffe Communications Station' – the Gosset farm – 'as the commandos withdrew. It was learned that the Luftwaffe personnel there had put up a stiff resistance, and only after some of them had exhausted their ammunition were the commandos able to break through to the Würzburg.' The British 'obviously intended to attack the Freya station. The skilful intervention of the La Poterie platoon, however, prevented this.' Most of this was fanciful, of course. Sgt. Treinies and his section were the only Germans who had distinguished themselves that night, by the stubbornness of their resistance. But the enemy narrative emphasizes the infirmity of German conduct. It had been a near thing for C Company, but its path to escape, and indeed triumph, now lay open at the foot of the cliff below Bruneval.

When the shooting stopped, the triumphant paratroopers enjoyed a few moments of exultation, with everybody chattering at once, exchanging experiences, rejoicing in their own survival, lighting up. Naively, they acted as if this was an exercise at home, on which the umpire had now blown the whistle. Amid their inexperience of battle, they forgot that the Germans, out there in the darkness in ever-increasing numbers, had sounded no ceasefire. Junior Charteris found Schmidt, his German prisoner, surrounded by a semi-circle of 'snarling paratroopers' in front of one of the Stella Maris bathing huts on the shingle 'as if one was in the middle of holidaymakers queueing for tickets for the beach ... they didn't realise the risks. Now that they had completed the mission that had been entrusted to them, they did not know quite what to do ... They awaited the boats as if this was the end of a scheme in England and transport would be along to take them back to camp ... The fact of the matter was, they were not very well trained.'

Bill Wood confirmed his comrades' insouciance, 'thinking they could just relax and enjoy a fag while they waited for the lorries'. Charteris brusquely insisted they must deploy defensively. He and Wood were correct that the paratroopers' inexperience of war was exposed by their spasm of delusion that they, and not the enemy, could determine when the night's work was done. Rather than lack of training, their behaviour reflected the extreme immaturity of very young men, who had just done something extraordinary.

Most of the lost paratroopers from the south appeared, some of them looking sheepish about missing the battle – Lumb and Campbell, still without their vital 18 wireless set and its operators, and likewise six of Sgt. Grieve's seven lost men. Since the latter were almost unarmed, they had the most plausible reason of any of the errant paratroopers for having stayed out of the action, confining their energies to reaching the beach at the moment of victory. The missing member of Grieve's section, John Willoughby, faced with a sudden burst of enemy fire near Bruneval, had bolted into trees up the hill west of the hamlet in search of cover, where he frightened the lights out of Thomas and McCallum by erupting into their own hiding place. The three lingered together, listening to sporadic gunfire and German voices.

Grieve's newly-arrived engineers still carried their mine-detector, and so appeared in time for Charteris to order them to check the beach – and then to report it clear. The German threat of mines had been a bluff, as reported by Pol. Frost wrote: 'The object had been achieved. We had very few casualties. We knew roughly where everyone was. We had given the enemy a good hammering ... All we wanted now was the Navy.'

11

Cook

It was after 0215, and C Company had already been in France for two hours: it had taken over half that period, since the first shot was fired, to capture and dismantle Henry, overwhelm the defile defences and convoy Cox and the engineers to within reach of the beach. They were an hour behind the timetable fixed back in England. It was extraordinary that no significant German reinforcement had already arrived on the battlefield, and well Frost understood this. Vernon's men abandoned the struggle with the clumsy trolley and instead hefted the Würzburg parts onto the engineers' shoulders, manhandling and dragging them the last yards to the beach, while the company's half-dozen wounded were also assisted down – another man became a casualty when he fell heavily on the steep, icy descent. Yet even now that they had achieved success at the radar site, Frost and his men faced the night's worst ordeal: the sea below sparkled – in Charteris's words – 'very, very empty' in the moonlight. There was no sign of Cook and his landing-craft.

Desperate appeals into their wirelesses yielded only silence across the ether. Poor communications, heavily influenced by indifferent technology – at Bruneval, the throat microphone for one 38 set fell to pieces – continued to be a weakness of the British Army, and especially of airborne forces, throughout the war. For C Company, it would be the bitterest pill of all if, having succeeded wonderfully in their purpose, they were now obliged to face the humiliation of surrender – the only plausible course – because they could not rendezvous with their rescuers. They lacked both the 18 sets intended to contact the navy: Scott, the signaller who had landed with Lumb's half-section, was adrift somewhere southwards; McCallum and Thomas, the two men with the second 18 set who had straggled from Reid's group, also remained missing. Frost's paratroopers still failed to prompt a response to incessant pleas through the feebler 38s.

They switched on an experimental 'Rebecca' beacon with which they had also been equipped, supposedly linked to a matching 'Eureka' receiver aboard the landing-craft. They had no means, however, of knowing whether its bleeping summons was being heard. Which it was not. Gathering mist out at sea reduced visibility to half a mile, and torch flashes likewise gained no response. Most of the paratroopers and engineers clustered disconsolate at the cliff base. On the hill above, sporadic shooting persisted as the Germans sustained fire, while declining to close in upon the British rearguard, whose Bren-gunners maintained deterrent bursts up the defile.

Thus C Company was forced to stay, almost supine and very bitter, for a further apparently interminable half-hour, at the mercy of enemy intervention by land or sea. At Frost's behest, John Ross fired a green Very cartridge low over the water first from the north end of the beach, then another round from the south. Still there came no reply. Timothy, who was directing the rearguard in the defile and on the north shoulder of the cliff, sent down a runner to report that headlights were visible, as German vehicles approached Bruneval from the east. Dennis Vernon left Cox and the engineers to carry the precious radar components the last yards to the beach, and himself climbed again, to assist the Rodneys.

The sappers stowed their prizes in a hollow behind the beach, now populated by clusters of men, a hundred in all, most of them peering increasingly desperately out to sea, amid guillemots and other bewildered seabirds, wheeling in confusion overhead after their slumbers in the cliff face had been broken by the firing and detonations. The soldiers began to eye a lone fishing boat, property of a local man named Joseph Lebaillif, as a possible means of escape; were dissuaded by the fact that it could carry a maximum of eight. Bill Wood heard some of his mates make bleak cracks about who might be good enough in the water to swim to England. Even Charteris, a passionate 'can-do' officer, 'began to think that we should not get back … the position was fairly serious'.

The last-resort signals agreed with the navy were red Very flares, which paratroopers fired almost horizontally from both sides of the beach. Yet these, too, evoked no response. Frost said: 'It looked as though we were going to be left high and dry once more' – as they had been before, on so many of the abortive exercises – 'and the thought was hard to bear.' He redeployed his rearguard on the shoulders of the defile, where they continued to exchange desultory bursts with the Germans. At the same time the prisoners were insistently questioned, through Peter Walker, about the whereabouts of possible enemy reinforcements, though the three proved too frightened or disoriented to give coherent explanations. Maybe also, the Germans now nursed some hopes of being delivered from captivity at this eleventh hour, before they were borne away across the sea.

If there was one period of the night when Frost almost succumbed to despair it was then, when the failure of the naval rendezvous threatened to set at naught all the courage, imagination, hard labour and now blood that had been expended upon Biting. More than a few of those on the beach vented anger and despair. The sapper Sid Jones, who had done so well breaking up Henry, exclaimed repeatedly: 'We're going to be captured! We're going to be captured!' Charlie Cox enjoyed only limited success, urging hope on his comrade. Where, where in God's name, was the navy?

Where indeed? Aboard the landing-craft a mile offshore, some of the soldiers tasked to man guns were too seasick to stand to their weapons, and instead lay prostrate and groaning as the vessels wallowed and pitched. Commander Cook, through his powerful glasses, believed that he saw German vehicles moving ashore. He glimpsed Very lights going up, but 'horizontally they were difficult to interpret with the backdrop of flashes, explosions and tracer'. The Germans' increasingly frequent release of parachute flares, lingering in the sky over the battlefield, added to the sense of confusion and peril that inspired caution in the naval onlookers. Cook and his crews saw grenades detonate; heard rifle fire and watched some of the flares being illuminated in the vicinity of 'the valley' – the road descending to the beach.

Yet the wirelesses remained stubbornly dead, as did Cook's sense of initiative. Lookouts scanned the coastline for torch flashes, and saw nothing. And thus they continued to linger, awaiting the agreed signals before closing in on the beach. It is a nice question, which many participants argued afterwards, whether the naval commander should have ordered in the ALCs, heedless of the paratroopers' silent radios. Cook's explanation was that he had no means of knowing whether the Germans still held the beach, in which case his craft could have been shot to pieces. His caution was understandable, but he certainly lacked the Nelson touch. At the very least, Cook might have ordered one craft to close in and reconnoitre the shore. If the enemy had displayed anything like their usual energy in defending Bruneval, this long final delay before the victorious paratroopers were evacuated would have spelled the failure of Biting.

It was after 0230, perhaps as late as 0245, when at last men aboard Cook's flotilla spotted blue torch flashes from the shore, and he gave the belated order to close the beach. Five of the ALCs and two support craft – LSCs, on one of which the commander himself took passage – 'rushed in at 9 knots ... The seven-minute run-in seemed like seven hours.' A sixth ALC was left behind, suffering persistent engine trouble. Ashore a signaller manning a short-range 38 set shouted that he was finally in contact: 'Sir! The boats are coming in! The boats are here! God bless the ruddy navy, sir!' The original plan, for the vessels to ground in successive pairs, was abandoned as the men ashore demanded all the boats immediately. The paratroopers, in their gratitude for glimpsing deliverance, now forgave the agonizing delay. Euan Charteris thought jubilantly, almost disbelievingly: 'By God, it's coming off!'

The infantrymen and sailors aboard the landing-craft seized the opportunity they had been awaiting for hours, to unleash their Oerlikons and Brens: they began hosing the clifftop and defile with automatic fire, creating a deafening racket, while the enraged, desperately stressed Frost shouted to them to cease fire: his rearguard was still up there – stragglers might be trying to get down. Nobody ashore, either German or British, was hit, but not for want of trying by the ALC and LSC crews, who laid aside their weapons only when Commander Cook bellowed at them through a megaphone. 'We thought you was a Jerry with a suicide wish,' cried a Welsh voice to a paratrooper, with a humour that Frost was in no mood to appreciate, 'but we gave you the benefit of the doubt.' Corporal Campbell and some of the other stragglers came close to being hit by the wild gunfire.

As the boats closed the shore, seamen in their bows probed the shallows with boathooks, testing bottom: 'We had real problems with the boulders on the rocky beach.' Their orders had stipulated that the boats should lower ramps by successive pairs. The men of C Company were supposed to board in an agreed succession. All that was now forgotten, as five of the clumsy boxlike craft grounded almost together. 'Never had such ungainly vessels looked so beautiful,' said Peter Young fervently. Cook and his officers were tormented at every moment by fears that the German destroyers and E-boats which they had earlier seen offshore might return and engage them; that defenders on the cliff could open fire with mortars or artillery, for which they were sitting targets; that Germans pressing Frost's retreat could harrow them with machine-guns, for which the moonlight made the boats painfully conspicuous targets. Cook marvelled: 'Why the Huns did not clean up our comparatively small force I shall never understand.'

Yet they did not. While the Germans continued to deliver bursts from the clifftop, their aim proved too erratic to inflict further casualties. Charteris said: 'The enemy's fire was all over the place.' It nonetheless prompted a chaotic rush for the boats, in place of the planned disciplined boarding. Beach control, such as it was, broke down. Paratroopers waded knee-deep into the icy shallows to hold the first ALC steady, bow on, as the precious Würzburg components and the wounded men were passed up its lowered ramp. The vessel which bore them put off at once. Some of the casualties proved to have been overdosed with morphia by solicitous comrades, though all survived. C Company then crowded pell-mell aboard the remaining boats.

One man fell into the sea as he struggled to get aboard a craft already backing off the beach – he was dragged out frozen and shaken; thrust into another hull. ALC3, a vessel designed for thirty, pulled away with sixty-eight men aboard – more than half of the raiding force, most of them bedraggled and waterlogged amid the surf.

Hastened by increasingly heavy machine-gun fire from Germans on the clifftop, in one boat the unseemly rush of paratroopers overthrew a seaman who was bruised and battered. At the same time the two support landing-craft renewed heavy fire from their Oerlikons and Lewises – 'a tremendous barrage', in Charteris's words – to deter the Germans from closing in. As the rearguard scrambled down from Stella Maris and the German trenches, the enemy began tossing grenades from the higher ground. Frost believed that there may also have been some incoming mortar bombs, though this seems doubtful.

The sight of two lonely figures approaching the boats raised momentary hopes that these might be some of the missing paratroopers, but instead they proved to be Timothy's men. One of them, L/Cpl. Ralph Johnston, who had all night been performing tail-gunner duties, quickened the boats' exit by reporting that he could now see lights approaching down the defile. At 0315 all the men who were coming were thought to be aboard. Charteris's half-section boarded last, followed by John Frost, final member of C Company to leave France that morning. Few such relatively junior officers had borne such a responsibility as he had done, through the three previous crowded hours. The rear ALC accelerated astern, then headed out to sea, in a rapidly increasing swell that caused waves to break into all the landing-craft, which soon had to be baled out. The wounded men, now on stretchers, suffered severely as repeated drenchings with seawater were added to their tribulations.

This last phase of the withdrawal was completed just in time, a full hour after the beach approach had been cleared and Stella Maris stormed. Lt. Huhne's order to the platoon quartered at the Beau-Minet, to head for the high ground above Bruneval, had emerged as one of the worst German blunders of the night. His decision was logical, in that Huhne dispatched men to where they might – indeed, did – meet some British invaders. If, instead, however, he had sent the platoon to reinforce Sgt. Treinies' section in the trenches covering the defile, they might well have prevented C Company from reaching the beach in time to escape. Minutes mattered. Remember that, even as the landing-craft pulled away from the beach, the best part of an infantry battalion, with heavy weapons support, was arriving at Bruneval. Huhne at the outset, though, had understood no better than did his superiors that the British were engaged upon a butcher-and-bolt mission; that they intended to quit France through the defile long before daybreak.

Some British paratroopers were still missing. Sutherland was lying wounded and stricken, up the hill at the Échos farm. Of Reid's section, Taffy Thomas and Jock McCallum, together with John Willoughby from Grieve's stick, remained in the woods between the beach and Bruneval hamlet, where on hearing both German voices and gunfire close at hand, they clung to their hiding place even when firing almost ceased below. The hapless Cornell, Embury and Scott, apparently ordered by Sgt. Lumb to stay put until he returned from his recce, were still high on the cliff south of Bruneval.

It may be suggested that none of the six – Sutherland obviously could not have moved far, if at all – displayed much initiative. But it seems unreasonable to have expected this from humble British soldiers caught leaderless in an extraordinary predicament, wherein fear of gunfire was probably a lesser component than finding themselves in a foreign land for the first time in their young lives, in darkness surrounded by a slowly closing ring of enemies. Scott, a twenty-four-year-old Londoner, met the sorriest fate: overwhelmed by misery and panic at the sight of the landing-craft departing below, he made a mad effort to descend the sheer cliff in time to join the evacuation. Instead he fell two hundred feet, and was found dying, hours later, by German soldiers. He would become only the second C Company fatality of the night.

His two shaken companions threw their section's weapons over the cliff, before starting to move, and allegedly descending to the sea. McCallum, Thomas and Willoughby indeed reached the beach while the landing-craft were still within sight. They waved, screamed, gestured in vain, receiving in return only a burst of Bren fire from the boat crews, who assumed them to be Germans. The signallers then belatedly resorted to their 18 set, contacting Cook's flotilla. The navy told them, inevitably, that there was no possibility of a vessel returning to rescue them. Disconsolate, Willoughby and the two men of Reid's section determined to surrender. Embury and Cornell, however, were bent upon attempting escape. They set off across country, their retreat unnoticed by the Germans. It seems at least possible, though contrary to their post-war testimony, that they never approached the beach, but instead struck directly across country from the clifftop where they had lingered for so long: it is hard to believe they could have descended and then climbed the defile again at this late stage, while enemy troops remained oblivious.

At the Beau-Minet hotel, as the terrified but fascinated proprietor M. Vennier peered from his window, he saw the headlights of a column of vehicles entering the hamlet. The German report stated: 'The commandos embarked just as strong reinforcements reached Bruneval.' Col. Ernst von Eisenhart-Rothe, the regimental commander, had belatedly reached La Poterie. He established a temporary headquarters in the *mairie*, where he received minute-by-minute reports from his infantry companies advancing – oh so slowly and cautiously – towards the beach defile. They reported sporadic enemy fire, probably from the landing-craft, which was serviceable in causing the Germans to be unaware that the invaders were going or gone. Only at 0345 did von Eisenhart-Rothe report to his newly-arrived divisional commander, Maj. Gen. Stever, that the British operation was over; that the attackers were now at sea.

For hours and indeed days thereafter, the Germans remained apprehensive that British saboteurs had been left behind. Many of von Eisenhart-Rothe's soldiers were set to work, tracking the paratroopers' trails through the snow and collecting abandoned *matériel* – parachutes, containers, weapons, empty magazines. Every local farm and home was visited by patrols demanding: '*Tommy là?*'

Offshore the ALCs and LSCs rendezvoused with the escorting gunboats. The engineer party's landing-craft grappled the pitching MGB 312, and with elaborate care the Würzburg parts were transferred aboard, along with twenty of Frost's men, though he himself stayed with the main body of his company. Donald Preist hastened to examine the radar components, and found that the airborne raiders had extracted almost everything that TRE could wish to work upon. He signalled: 'Samples perfect.' Then at 0326 the gunboat sped off alone for Portsmouth at its best pace, far ahead of the rest of the flotilla.

Among its passengers was F/Sgt. Charlie Cox, for whom this would be the first sea voyage of his life, and one not to be forgotten. Cox was assuredly one of the stars of the operation.

Unlike Frost's men, the little cinema projectionist from Wisbech had not entered his personal war hungry for battle or for glory. As he chattered to Preist on the passage home, he told the TRE expert how impressed he was by the manner in which the finely-engineered Würzburg components were boxed in their frame by the manufacturers, for easy extraction and exchange: 'The Jerries must have had RDF as long as us,' he said, adding tellingly, 'or longer.' Preist agreed, but said, 'Keep it under your hat, my friend.' The British were proprietorially proud of their perceived dominance in radar – which, in the earlier war years, some had even deluded themselves to be their own monopoly. In truth, some of their technology was ahead of the Germans', and would become much more so as the war advanced. But the British equipment's engineering standards lagged those of Telefunken.

Cox succumbed to seasickness, but eventually overcame this sufficiently to fall asleep in the MGB skipper's bunk. He awakened to find their engines stopped and the boat alongside *Prins Albert* in 'good old Pompey' – Portsmouth. They berthed at 1010 on a day which, for the returning raiders, had already been crowded with incident. Charles Carrington, arrived at the great naval base after an uncomfortable few hours' sleep in an armchair in the officers' mess at RAF Andover with Sam Elworthy, was among those who now quizzed the flight-sergeant, whom he described as 'a disingenuous young man ... delighted with his night's work, as well he might be'. The colonel asked the airman: was he a volunteer? 'Well, sort of.'

As the coast of France receded from the wakes of the raiding craft, Frost suffered a stab of depression, and even guilt, after hearing across the ether the forlorn voices of the signallers left on the shore: he had failed to bring everybody home from an

(Above) The men who stripped the Würzburg: RE Captain Dennis Vernon, here seen later in the war, and F/Sgt. Charles Cox. (Below) A Würzburg in action, lacking the operator's cabin fitted to the set at La Poterie.

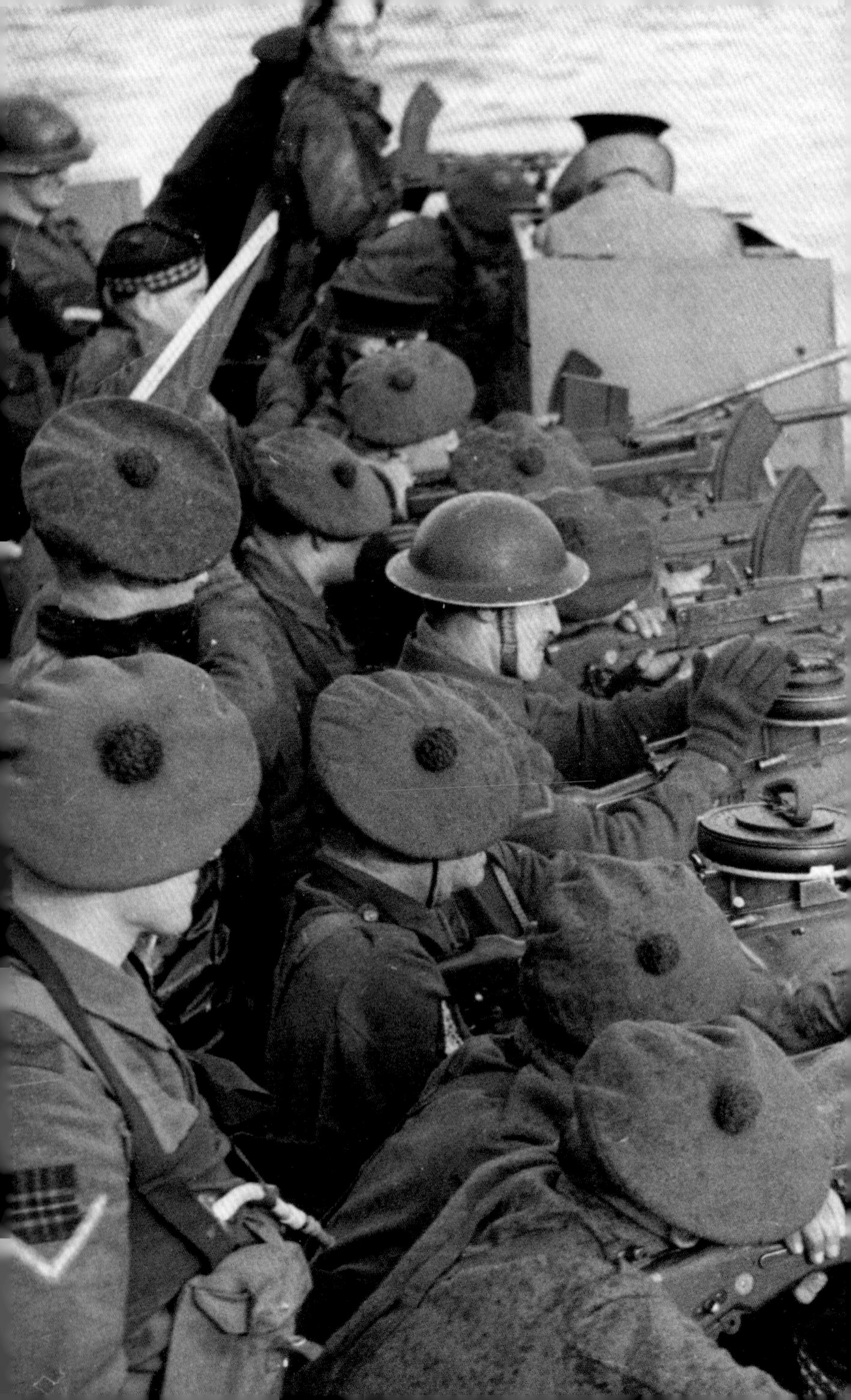

Some of the Biting attackers test-fire Boyes anti-tank rifles and Bren guns from their landing-craft.

The hapless *Gefreiter* Schmidt, appearing less grateful than he may afterwards have felt, having ended his eventful night in Stella Maris in the hands of one of the infantrymen who sailed to Bruneval in the landing-craft.

(Above) Luftwaffe personnel from the La Poterie site, conspicuously better armed than they were on the night of Biting. The little figure second right in white breeches is Heinz Meiser, who accompanied Lt. Ruben and received an Iron Cross for his contribution. (Below) The route by which the men of Charteris's missing section skirted the village and eventually reached the beach, close to where the Bruneval memorial stands today.

(Above left) HMS *Prins Albert*, the former cross-Channel ferry that became 'mother ship' for the *Tormentor* landing-craft, and (below) the ALCs as they would have looked on their retreat from the beach, though then laden with men, not equipment. (Opposite) One of the returning, triumphant MGBs comes alongside at Portsmouth, Frost on its bridge.

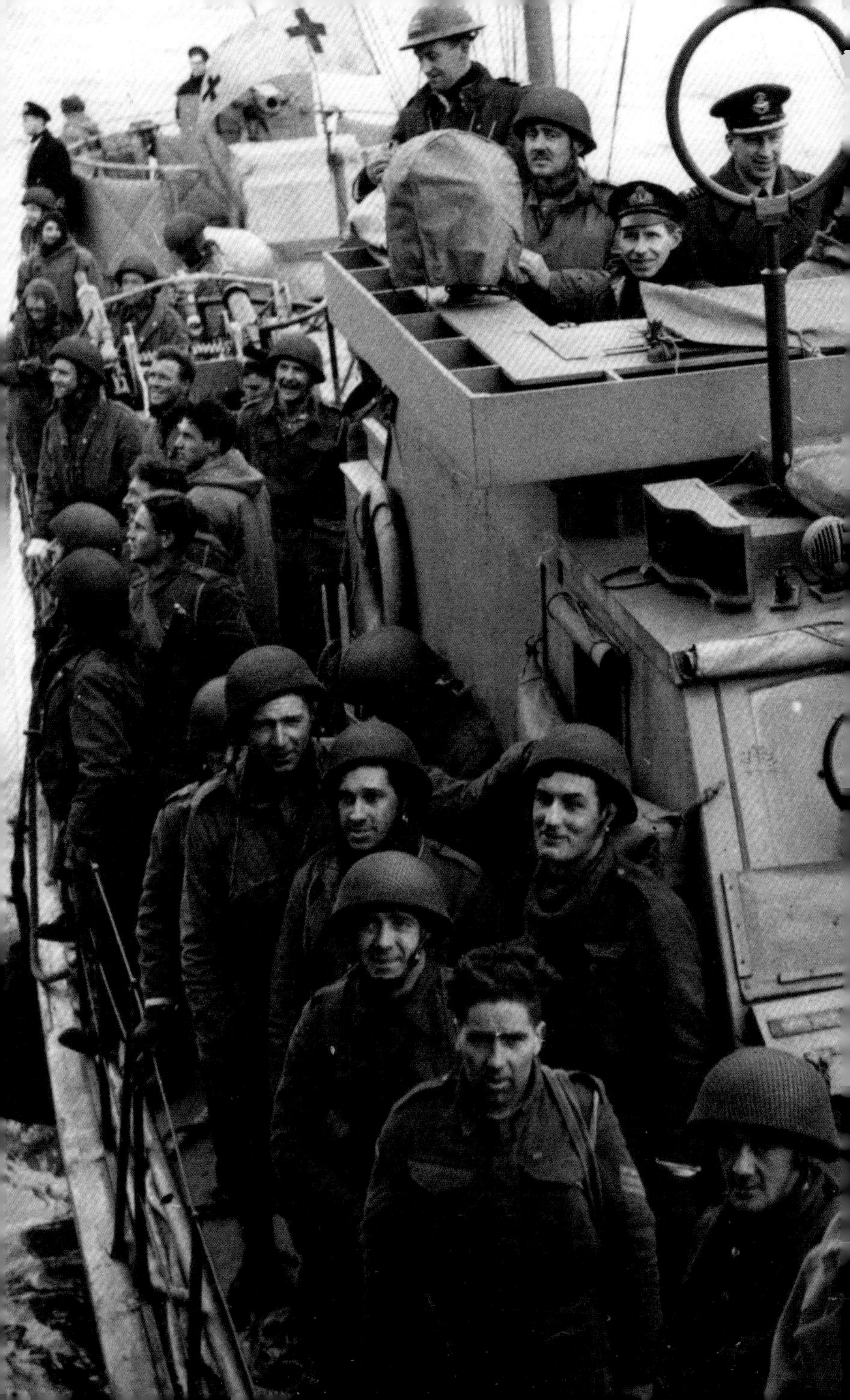

(Above left) Lt. Euan Charteris, among the undoubted heroes of Biting, photographed before he was commissioned and (right) one of the operation's victims, Pte. Hugh McIntyre, who rashly confided his participation in a letter to his brother, then fell to a German bullet. (Below) A heavily posed shot of exultant paratroopers, showing off a German helmet to Charles Pickard.

(Above left) Pte. Peter 'Walker', in reality German Jew Peter Nagel, who served as interpreter at Bruneval; (centre) Lt. Cdr. Fred Cook, RAN; (right) the doughty Sgt. Dave Grieve – note his Seaforth stag's head cap badge: he gave their war cry as he charged Beach Fort. (Below) Air Commodore Norman quizzes Corporal Jones, on the left, with Charlie Cox beside him, aboard *Prins Albert*.

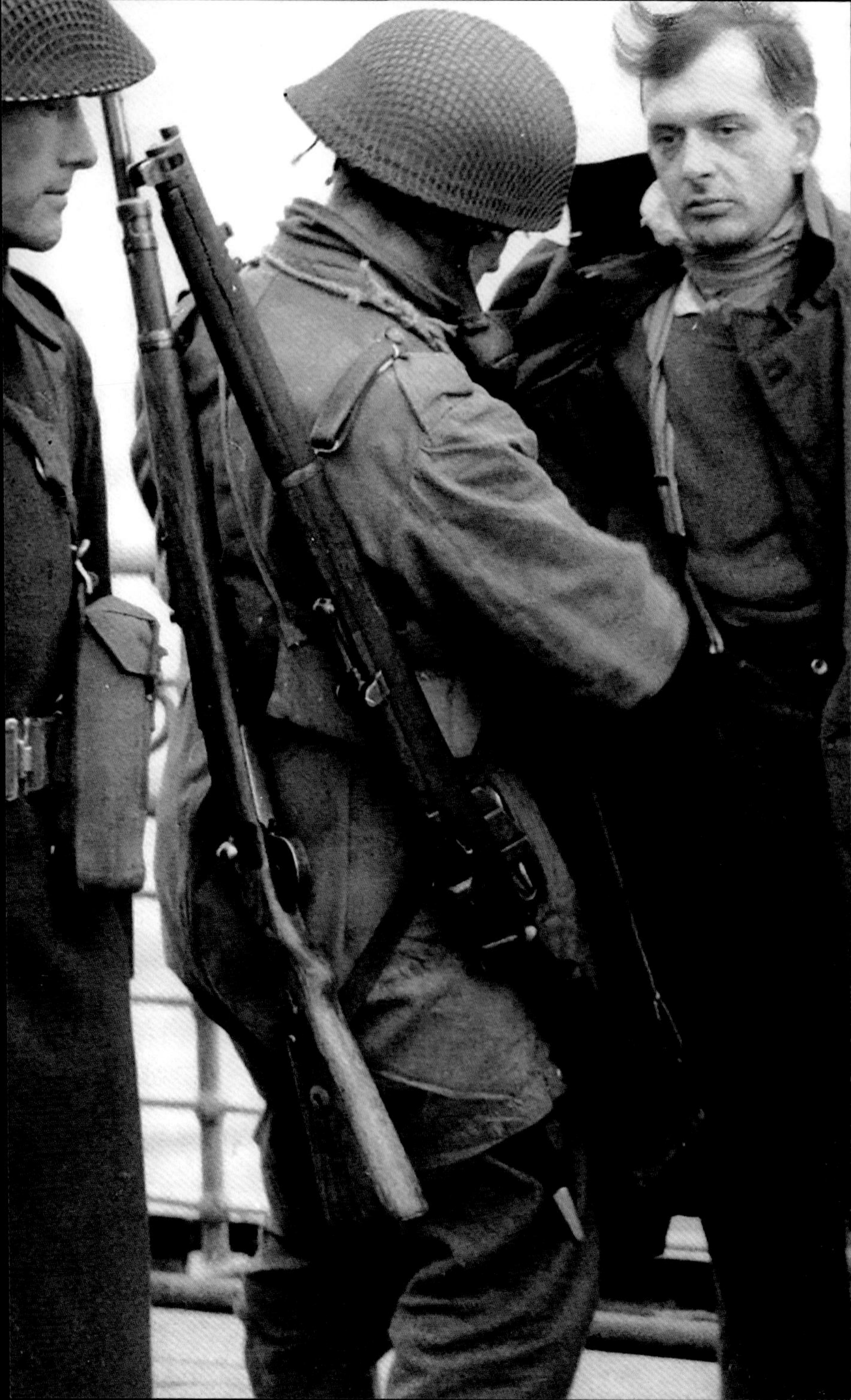

Fusilier Tewes, slightly wounded in the neck, and Heller, stripped by Peter Walker of the Luftwaffe eagle on his breast, bear the look of men who have had a trying night as they are searched by their captors at Portsmouth.

An admiring friend watches Pte. Mark Ginsberg, one of the Airborne medics who went to Bruneval aboard an ALC, enjoying the orgy of publicity that followed the raid.

(Above) The King and Queen visit 51 Squadron at Dishforth after the raid. Frost stands with George VI. (Below) Later in the war, a US paratrooper stands with John Timothy, by then a liaison officer, before a drop. Note that the American carries a reserve 'chute on his front harness, which the British always lacked.

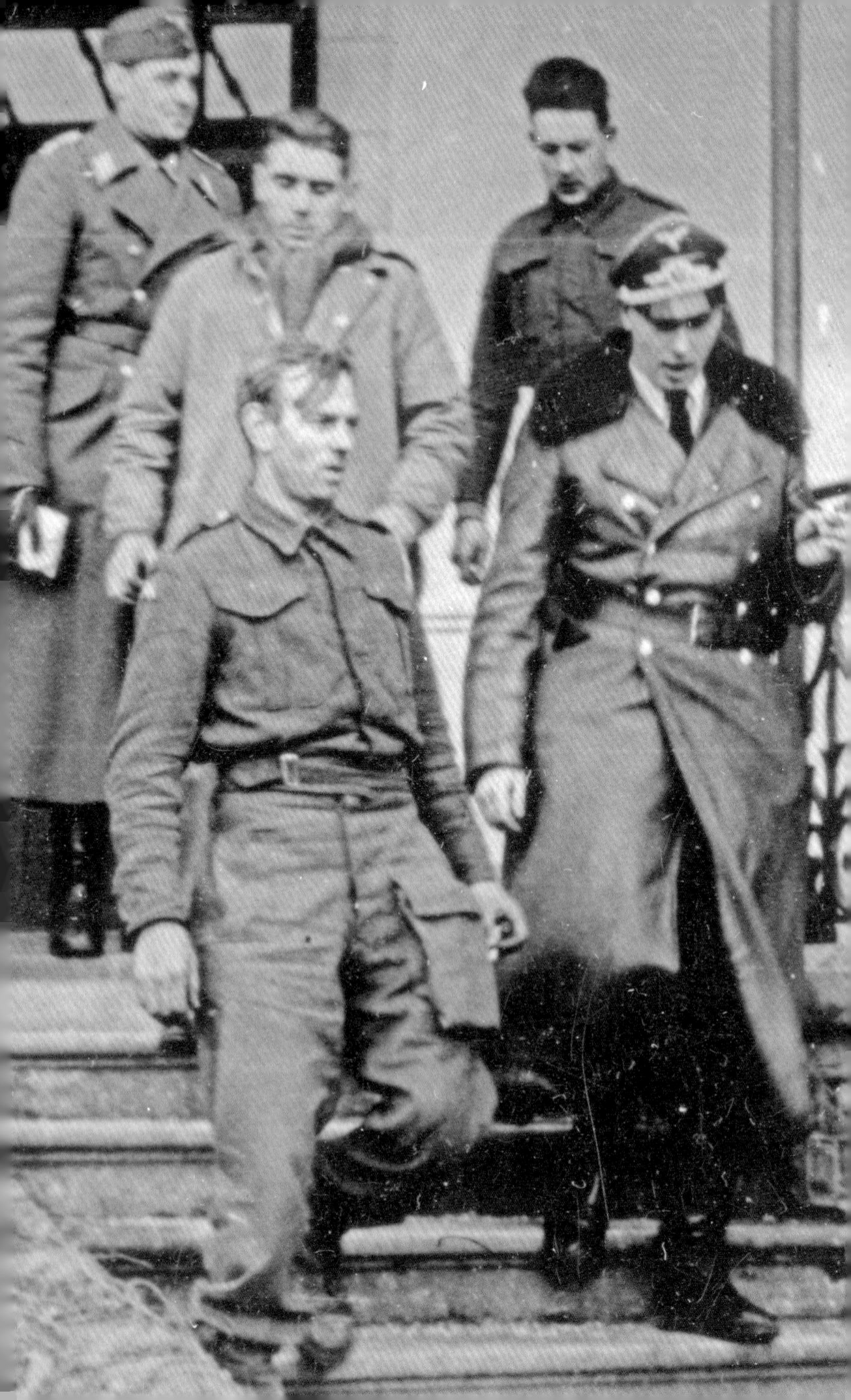

(Opposite) Three of the British prisoners captured at Bruneval – Thomas, McCallum and Willoughby – photographed with Captain von Preussen, sacked for his negligence a few days later. (Right) The impeccable 'Boy' Browning as the world remembers him: Biting's success brought closer the fulfilment of his vision of an airborne army, which he led into battle at Arnhem, with tragic consequences. (Below) The British prisoners in Normandy, here seen with Sutherland, his arm in a sling, who was wounded with Charteris. Their superiors did not approve of the matiness of such German propaganda images, but the laughter surely reflected the men's relief that they were not to be shot.

Happy Endings: (above) RSM Gerry Strachan at his 1943 wedding to army cook Ivy, and (left) John Frost at Buckingham Palace after receiving his Military Cross. He attained immortality in September 1944, defending 2 Para's foothold at the northern end of the bridge at Arnhem.

operation otherwise crowned with success. But nothing could be done to recover the stragglers. In all, six of C Company – four Rodneys and two Nelsons including the wounded Sutherland – remained behind alive as Frost's paratroopers started on the voyage – the highly perilous voyage – homeward. The bad luck which had attended Sgt. Cook's Whitley at the outset, when he was obliged to make a second run to drop his last five men, persisted to the end: two of his ten jumpers were among the missing and a third, Alan Scott, was dying beneath the cliff.

Meanwhile Frost's men, and their booty, would not be safe until beyond the reach of German aircraft and warships, of which within a few miles many and various elements were deployed. Shortly after 0400, E-boats belatedly set forth from Le Havre. Worsening visibility and sea conditions soon caused them to report that, lacking radar, they had no hope of catching up with the British until the retiring enemy vessels were within reach of their own shores, and of daylight. Offshore the swell became so heavy that Fred Cook gave orders that the four remaining MGBs should take in tow the six ALCs and two support landing-craft, to speed their sluggish passage. The naval officer later reported: 'The wind freshened from the South-Westward increasing to Force 5 during the day which made the eighty-mile passage back with two LCs in tow of each of four MGBs very tedious and hazardous.' Every wave caused the bows of the ungainly landing-craft to plunge downwards, and a foot of water was soon swilling in each hull. Thus, at never better than seven knots and often less, they ploughed their course towards home, for hours vulnerable to enemy intervention, and laden with more than a hundred seasick paratroopers, infantrymen – and three unhappy Germans.

Aboard the gunboats, all those who could find space sought warmth below decks. Fred Cook wrote in his report, 'Our main objective was to be well clear of the French coast by daylight to avoid possible Luftwaffe retaliation.' Dawn, however, found the little flotilla still only fifteen miles from Bruneval. An hour after first light Spitfires appeared overhead, and the RAF thereafter sustained a fighter umbrella, rotating aircraft through the day. Nonetheless, they were never challenged, which created yet another mystery: over the Channel, Luftwaffe pilots often displayed exemplary daring and achieved notable success. They would do so again, outfighting the British during the August 1942 Dieppe raid. By mid-morning on 28 February, hours after the raiders' departure, the German high command must have known full well what the paratroopers had done – that the Würzburg's secrets had been pillaged. But not a single enemy aircraft sought to impede the boats' progress back to Portsmouth, representing still another extraordinary failure of inter-service communication and direction on the German side.

Through the daylight hours of 28 February, most of the boats' sodden occupants vomited their hearts out, almost delirious with exhaustion and the motion. The passage, buffeted by a wind from the south-west, proved in Cook's words, 'pretty ghastly for the crews ... [ALCs] are not considered the best of craft when the operation necessitates a return tow of 80 miles in winter weather'. Two cables parted; had to be laboriously renewed. Sailors and paratroopers alike were soaked through by spray and surging waves. The naval commander, making way aft on his own MGB, chanced upon a German, horribly sick. The man's little Scots minder nonetheless refused to untie the rope binding the two together. Cook demanded: 'Scottie, what the hell are you doing?' The para responded stubbornly: 'Sirr, I've come all this way to get a Hun prisoner and I'm damned if I'm going to let this bastard get awa' the noo!'

Charteris said that during their passage he had a long conversation with Georg Schmidt, his own prisoner. The German was from Hamburg, nearing forty, and asserted volubly that far from being a Nazi, he had lots of friends who were communists.

The returning flotilla was met in mid-Channel and escorted through its last lap homeward by the destroyers *Fernie* and *Blencathra*, together with four Free French *chasseurs* – corvettes. Thus, everybody with a stake in the war effort was conceded a symbolic role. At 1600 as they approached the harbour, a roar of cheering and triumphant whistle-blowing erupted from nearby craft. The pilots of the Spitfire escort dived low overhead in salute, before banking towards home.

John Frost was one of the few passengers who did not suffer from seasickness, and so enjoyed his lunch on the bridge of the MGB which bore him home. For a time he tried vainly to sleep, as the boat pitched and rolled. Then, as they approached Portsmouth, he heard the strains of 'Rule, Britannia!' drifting across the water from the broadcast systems of their escorts, and gained the first hint that he and his men were to be received as conquering heroes. Once alongside, as the major clambered unsteadily up the ladder onto the deck of *Prins Albert*, he became the focus of a blaze of attention as journalists and photographers, together with a newsreel cameraman, crowded around: 'The limelight was strange after weeks of secrecy and stealth.' Frost and several of his men were authorized to grant interviews, though his own recording for the BBC was afterwards suppressed by the Ministry of Information's censors. All that he and the others wanted were warm beds and dry clothes, but first there was some serious drinking in *Prins Albert*'s wardroom.

The raiders had endured a night of extreme stress, but their exultation in success was untarnished by the sort of stockpiled exhaustion and trauma which overtakes men who endure days or weeks of battle, together with heavy casualties, as would become the lot of 2 Para later in the war. Fred Cook belatedly replied to Mountbatten's signal before the operation: 'Your inspiring message received pm Friday 27 Feb 1942 was much appreciated by all. Boche bitten.' Amid an orgy of mutual congratulations, Browning signalled Cook: 'I am anxious that you will all at *HMS Tormentor* consider yourselves honorary members of the Airborne Division.' Portal messaged Pickard and his fliers: 'Heartiest congratulations to all of 51 Squadron who organised and took part in Operation "Biting", a model of efficient cooperation between the services.'

Commander Cook reported to Admiral James: 'From SNO Biting to C-in-C Portsmouth: in accordance with your orders 0221/68 of 15/2/42 Operation BITING was carried out. Weather conditions on night 27th/28th February were most satisfactory until 0300 on the 28th ... Cooperation between the three services was extremely good ... I should like to remark that the Intelligence, Combined Planning and Staff work which were received were extremely accurate and helpful.' Charles Pickard wrote in his report on 51 Squadron's contribution: 'The crews of the two Whitleys which had undershot had a good party when the paratroops came back and they knew that they were all right.' This wording was a trifle disingenuous, when his own aircraft had been one of four that landed men short.

As paratroopers clambered aboard *Prins Albert* after their Channel ordeal, drinks were pressed upon them by grinning sailors and soldiers. Peter Young said: 'The German prisoners must have thought we were mad when they, too, had glasses of beer thrust into their hands as they came up the gangway.' Yet it may have been some time before the captives recognized their good fortune, in having been delivered by C Company from further participation in the war, more than likely saving their lives – 1945 would find them safely encamped behind the wire in Manitoba, while many of their former comrades from Bruneval lay dead in Russian wastes.

Arthur Humphreys, a Reuters correspondent who had sailed on *Prins Albert* to provide pool copy for the entire press, filed a triumphant story which began: 'In a daring exploit which reads like a piece of adventure fiction the parachutists destroyed – seized and brought back to this country – a radio location device being used by the Germans ... This morning I watched the arrival of the naval flotilla which carried on board a treasured prize – the climax of weeks of organization, training and waiting.' Alas for the hapless Humphreys, the censor would have none of this. Though the Germans well knew that their Würzburg had been stripped, no public crowing was permitted, about the technical objectives of the raid.

The British press nonetheless had a field day. The *Sunday Times* of 1 March was headlined 'FULL STORY OF PARATROOP RAID: HEAVY CASUALTIES INFLICTED'. *Reynolds News* proclaimed: 'We Make Our First Bridgehead'. The *Sunday Dispatch* exulted 'Our Paratroops Kill and Capture Germans and Wreck Plant'. The *Sunday Graphic* headlined: 'HOW WE LANDED 12 MILES FROM HAVRE: FULL STORY. Heavy German casualties in thrilling Paratroop Raid'. The story under it began: 'With faces blackened even to their teeth, the British paratroops who landed in France were dropped in moonlight through concentrated anti-aircraft fire. They not only smashed up the enemy radio-location station, which was their objective, but brought back prisoners. They took heavy toll of the garrison ... Not one of our aircraft or ships were lost, and casualties were light. This was the first time since Dunkirk that British infantry had landed in France.' That version was, of course, a mingling of fact and fiction typical of most wartime media reports, and emphatically so about special forces operations. German casualties were not heavy. Only three of the Whitleys encountered anti-aircraft fire. The airborne element of the attackers did not blacken their faces, and certainly did not destroy the Würzburg, which was not the idea at all.

What mattered, however, was that here was a thrilling, indisputable success for British arms, of which the tale reverberated around the world. The front page of the *Herald* of Auckland was typical of hundreds of titles around the British Empire, headlining its story 'DRAMATIC COUP – COMPLETE SUCCESS – GARRISON SURPRISED'. A week later a *Daily Sketch* sports reporter even celebrated two of the infantrymen who had manned Brens in the ALCs, and visited London ... to play football: 'In town today are two Welsh lads who last weekend were among the intrepid band who smashed the Nazi radiolocation post at Bruneval. Stanley Morgan and Cyril Toute are this time playing inside left and left back in the Brighton team playing Millwall at New Cross. The youngsters, among the supporting troops covering the embarkation of the paratroops, are on Arsenal's books.'

Across the Channel, daylight on 28 February brought hundreds of Germans into Bruneval. In the Beau-Minet hotel where part of the local garrison was billeted, four British prisoners were being interrogated, after a dispute between the Luftwaffe and the army about which service properly owned them, won by the soldiers. Meanwhile two of the dead Germans, Arndt and Schmitz, lay under the ping-pong table in the hotel dining room, covered by blankets. The previous night, when the shooting started and it became evident that British forces had landed, for a happy hour its proprietors the Venniers, who

Sunday Times

FULL STORY OF PARATROOP RAID

German Radiolocation Post Wrecked Near Havre

HEAVY CASUALTIES INFLICTED

Men Escape With Prisoners After Overcoming Coast Defence

BURMA ARMY'S BIG FIGHT
JAPANESE AIR DEFEATS
MILITARY RULE IN RANGOON

ATTEMPT TO LAND IN JAVA SMASHED
Four Japanese Warships Put Out Of Action

THE JAPANESE HEAVY CRUISER MOGAMI AND THREE DESTROYERS WERE PUT OUT OF ACTION IN AN ATTEMPT TO LAND TROOPS ON JAVA, THE LAST ALLIED STRONGHOLD IN THE EAST INDIES, ON FRIDAY.

MORE CHANGES TO COME
OFFICES LIKELY TO BE AFFECTED

CASE AGAINST THE DIVE-BOMBER
Same Work Done Better By Cannon-Fighter
By PETER MASEFIELD
"Sunday Times" Air Correspondent

REYNOLDS NEWS
GOVERNMENT OF THE PEOPLE, BY THE PEOPLE, FOR THE PEOPLE

LONDON: SUNDAY, MARCH 1, 1942

We Make Our First Bridgehead

FOR the first time since the French collapse British troops and naval forces have formed and held a bridgehead into France.
They thus made possible the successful withdrawal of a force of our paratroop troops that had carried out an important, though small, attack in France.

Australia Urges 'Help Us Now'

RED ARTILLERY HAMMERS NAZIS HARD IN CRIMEA
'Heaviest Barrage of the War'

BERLIN RADIO LAST NIGHT ADMITTED THAT THE RED ARMY IN THE CRIMEA HAD LAUNCHED AN ATTACK, ACCOMPANIED BY THE HEAVIEST ARTILLERY BARRAGE SO FAR EXPERIENCED ON THE EASTERN FRONT.

Evening Standard

FINAL NIGHT EXTRA
No. 36,654   LONDON, SATURDAY, FEBRUARY 28, 1942   ONE PENNY

British Paratroops, Followed Up by Infantry, Wreck the Nazis Radio "Eyes" Across Channel

ARMY, NAVY & RAF RAID N. FRANCE IN THE DARK

"It Was to Schedule and Very Successful"

COAL TO BE RATIONED ON MONDAY

JAP INVASION FLEET FLEES FROM JAVA

Sunday Dispatch

MARCH 1, 1942

OFFICIAL STORY OF THE RAID ON FRANCE

Our Paratroops Kill And Capture Germans And Wreck Plant

had assisted Pol to gather the intelligence for Biting, thought that this might be the start of an invasion – *the* invasion, liberation of France. They even briefly harboured delusions that the war might soon be over. Instead, in February 1944 when the Germans were creating their Atlantic Wall in readiness to repel an Allied invasion, some of Bruneval's landmark buildings would be razed to the ground. Never again under occupation was the atmosphere of the community, relations between the locals and their occupiers, as relaxed as it had been when C Company landed. Local people were ruthlessly evicted from every habitation close to German positions, and thereafter access was rigorously denied.

The British claimed to have killed over forty Germans. In reality the army reported losing just two of its soldiers killed; one seriously wounded – Hormandinger, who was hit while defending the beach with Treinies, and died some days later from his wounds; two missing – both taken prisoner by the raiders. The Luftwaffe acknowledged three men killed – Senge, Wenzel and Kaffurbitz – together with one wounded and Heller missing.

A German news broadcast on 28 February announced contemptuously: 'The relief offensive for which Britain's gravely battered [Russian] allies have been pleading for so long has confined itself to the landing of a few parachutists on the coast of northern France. They were soon forced to make a glorious retreat across the ocean, without having achieved any useful purpose.' The British thought differently.

12

The Prizegiving

1 CELEBRATIONS

John Frost reached his quarters at Tilshead more than twenty-four hours after his MGB came alongside *Prins Albert* in Portsmouth. He and his men spent the next day resting and sorting kit. Browning told Frost: 'You have put Airborne Forces on the map. From now on we should be able to get all sorts of things that have been withheld up to now.' Fine words. Yet Frost, who never thought much of Browning as an airborne forces commander, carried to the grave a belief that the divisional commander had undervalued Bruneval and C Company's achievement. That evening he was about to sink into a welcoming bath when there was a hammering on the door and an officer's voice bellowed through it: 'You have to get up to London right away because the Prime Minister wants to know the details!' The exhausted major dragged himself into service dress and climbed into a staff car for the two-hour journey to the capital, reaching the guarded and sandbagged entrance to the underground Cabinet War Rooms at 9 p.m. He was led by a Royal Marine messenger down into the depths beneath official London, past steel doors, along shadowy corridors punctuated by harshly lit offices and scurrying personnel of both sexes, all ranks and services, to find the prime minister in the Cabinet meeting room surrounded by ministers and service 'brass', including Brooke, Pound, Portal, Browning and Mountbatten, this last claiming proud fatherhood of success. In front of Churchill, who was clad in a siren suit and puffing at his invariable cigar, stood C Company's planning model of Bruneval, a duplicate which had been carried across Whitehall from Combined Ops in Richmond Terrace. 'Bravo, Frost, bravo,' said the prime minister, the British parachute force's foremost sponsor. 'And now we must hear all about it.' The major stepped forward to tell his story. Mountbatten, however, was having none of that. He himself seized possession of the narrative, and addressed the group.

To explain the assemblage of so many great men that night, to hear reports of a tiny operation, it is necessary to recall that for weeks past, they had been receiving almost unbroken ill tidings from across the world. Since Frost and his company dropped into Bruneval, the Japanese had landed in three places on Java, which they swiftly overran, and the heavy cruiser *Exeter* was sunk off Batavia. It is no wonder the prime minister was eager that his closest colleagues should share in this flush of success, achieved agreeably close to home. Churchill suddenly gestured imperiously, to halt Mountbatten's oration in mid-flow. He had noticed foreign secretary Anthony Eden and secretary for air Archibald Sinclair murmuring to each other in a corner, and addressed them as if they were errant schoolboys: 'Come over here, you two, and listen to this, for then you might learn something for once in your lives.' Eden and Sinclair shuffled sheepishly forward. When Mountbatten resumed the tale, Churchill again interrupted, to ask who was responsible for the raid's excellent intelligence brief. 'Wing-Commander Casa Maury,' said CO's chief complacently, glancing at his Cuban friend's angular features, 'who is standing beside me.' The prime minister gave the marquis what Frost described as a 'beatific smile', then demanded a cut to the chase: 'What did we get out of this?'

The chief of air staff launched a technical exposition which the prime minister once more cut short: 'Now stop all that nonsense, Portal, and put it into language that ordinary normal mortals can understand.' The hapless air marshal did his best to comply, perhaps wishing that he had caused to be present Reg Jones, the man with an inalienable claim to be garlanded as begetter of Biting. At the conclusion of Portal's account, the prime minister stood reflectively contemplating the model. He moved a finger up the cliff, then said – now obviously thinking of German intruders upon Britain's policies – 'This is the way they will come, if they come. Up and over the cliffs. Just where we least expect them. Now, about the raids. There must be more of them. Let there be no doubt about that.' Then the great man bustled out.

Mountbatten and Browning advanced together on Portal, saying in unison, apparently jesting but of course in earnest: 'More aircraft, more aircraft, more aircraft.' The chief of air staff presented his unraised hands in mock surrender, smiled and backed away. The warlords filed out, followed by the lesser mortals. A staff car bore C Company's commander away to his club, where at last he was able to take his deferred bath. He decided that he had enjoyed his hour of rubbing shoulders with the great, and would not mind more of it.

Frost and Euan Charteris received Military Crosses for their night's work – the latter's medal obviously acknowledging the significance of his intervention in the defile – while Cox got a Military Medal and CSM Strachan, who miraculously survived his wounds, a Croix de Guerre with Palm. Peter Young and

Corporal Sid Jones were mentioned in despatches, while Dennis Vernon was merely commended by Browning in his report. Sgt. David Grieve, who led the downhill charge on Stella Maris, and Sgt. Greg McKenzie, temporary owner of a Luftwaffe wristwatch, both also received the Military Medal.

To paraphrase *Alice in Wonderland*, amid success it was thought appropriate to assert that everybody had won, and thus that everybody must have prizes. Lt. Cdr. Fred Cook and two of his officers were given the Distinguished Service Cross for 'daring, skill and seamanship': nobody saw merit in asking harsh questions about the navy's almost fatally tardy arrival at the beach, and Frost never declared resentment towards Cook and his subordinates. Wing-Cdr. Charles Pickard was awarded a bar to his DSO, in recognition for his leadership of 51 Squadron on an innovative and highly sensitive mission. A cynic might suggest that it would have been more fitting to give a medal to one of the pilots who landed his paratroopers in the right place. Pickard, however, was an avowed and indeed authentic RAF hero, who featured prominently in the post-Biting newspaper publicity. The air marshals were anxious to see their service receive its share of laurels for the success of the operation, without discrimination about the contributions of individual pilots.

John Ross's absence from the list of those named for decorations may hint that senior officers were unimpressed that his Nelsons failed for so long to clear the way to the beach, until Charteris appeared. If so, such a judgement was ungenerous: for reasons that were no soldier's fault, Ross was short of firepower to cross an expanse of open hillside swept by an enemy machine-gun, and to suppress an entrenched and wired German position. Later in the war, he would be decorated for a superb battlefield performance as a company commander. The allocation of 'gongs' for the troops who executed Biting was meagre, especially in comparison with the deluge of awards made later in the year for St Nazaire and Dieppe, much larger operations but also far more costly. Frost should rightfully have received a DSO, if any man deserved it for that night's work. He wrote ruefully: 'Our ration of gallantry awards ... compared unfavourably with those given to the other Services involved, and later to all those taking part in other raids.'

Treatment of the service personnel was less mean-spirited, however, than that which was meted out to Reg Jones. 'Pug' Ismay wrote to the Cabinet Office: 'The Prime Minister wishes Dr Jones to be put forward for a high honour in the next Lists. He mentioned a CB [Companionship of the Bath].' Churchill restated this proposal in a letter to Sir Archibald Sinclair, Secretary for Air, on 3 April: 'Dr Jones's claims in my mind are not based upon the Bruneval raid but upon the magnificent prescience and comprehension by which in 1940 he did far more to save us from disaster' – by identifying the Luftwaffe's navigational beams – 'than many who are glittering with trinkets. The Bruneval raid merely emphasized and confirmed his earlier services. I propose to recommend him for a CB.'

Yet this 'high honour' failed to materialize, being downgraded by the bureaucracy to a CBE. Lord Cherwell later told Jones that when the proposal came before the Whitehall Honours Committee, the egregious Sir Horace Wilson, head of the civil service and a notorious pre-war appeaser, threatened to resign if such a lofty distinction was conferred upon a recipient graded as a mere scientific officer. The young scientist belatedly received the Companionship of the Bath in 1946, after making many further important contributions to Britain's 'boffin war'.

On the morning of 1 March, Charles Cox fulfilled orders to report to the Air Ministry, where he was met with suitable congratulations and granted two weeks' leave. A WAAF secretary sent a telegram in his name to his home at Wisbech: 'HOME TONIGHT KILL FATTED CALF'. It was almost midnight when he reached the little house to find four generations of his relations, as well as his wife Violet, gathered around the fire in the lounge. '"Hello, family", I said. "I've been in France, that's where I've been, and it's in the London newspapers tonight. How about that?"' Although later in the war Cox served in North Africa and Italy, for the rest of his life nothing happened to him as exciting or important as Biting, and we might speculate that this decent, charmingly innocent man did not regret his humdrum fate.

On the afternoon of 2 March, Reg Jones and a colleague drove in the former's old Wolseley to the Royal Patriotic Schools in Wandsworth, the PoW holding centre in south-west London where Heller, the Luftwaffe radar-operator from Bruneval, was being detained. They spent some hours sitting on the floor of a secluded room with him, reassembling the captured components in accordance with his directions. Heller said that, in his last letter to his wife, he had told her his post was so isolated the English might well make a raid and capture it. Now, he said gloomily, he was wondering if she was a fifth columnist.

Jones wrote in his report: 'Unfortunately, [Heller] is not very competent' – the man proved to have spent a significant portion of his service career in detention for assorted offences. After the war, Luftwaffe signals chief General Wolfgang Martini explained to Jones that his branch was granted only a low priority in the allocation of personnel, and thus had been obliged to accept such unsatisfactory recruits as the Bruneval prisoner. Nonetheless, the scientist reported in March 1942, 'from his description we have been able to gather the salient principles of the method of operation'.

This was, the Luftwaffe man explained to his interrogators, that a Würzburg operator was warned by telephone or broadcast from his paired Freya crew to monitor a given bearing for aircraft which had been detected at long range: 'A tram-driver's handle rotates the cabin and bowl ... The prisoner related with joy the fact that the Flak batteries in Le Havre fired blindly at an object reported by him to be high in the sky, but which he subsequently saw from his window to be a ship ... Nevertheless the station claimed to have participated in the destruction of sixty-four aircraft and two ships, and appropriate silhouettes had been painted in white inside the bowl ... The apparatus conforms closely to expectations, being simple in principle, and thoroughly, indeed beautifully, made ... Without exception the valves are extremely robustly made and reach a very high standard in every respect.' In design, as distinct from engineering, however, 'in some respects, the set lagged British RDF'.

Examination of the captured Würzburg equipment by army radar officers and scientists of the Telecommunications Research Establishment at Worth Matravers confirmed that Cox, Vernon and his sappers had pillaged almost all the set's key elements. Col. Schonland reported after a conference on 2 March that 'the equipment brought home is of great value, and the sappers could hardly have done more with a much longer time'. The aerial, cut from the 'giant mussel' as the Germans called the set's bowl, was in the words of Reg Jones's report to the Air Ministry 'the simplest possible type'. The transmitter and intermediate frequency amplifier, including a small cathode ray tube, had been captured complete. Only the indicating instruments were lacking, because these had been located in the operator's cabin, which Cox's party did not have time to explore. Nonetheless the capture of the set's operator who, in Jones's words, 'has volunteered all possible information ... largely compensated for the absence of the indicating instruments'.

Jones concluded his own report by addressing the vital question for the directors of the war effort, and explicitly the RAF's bomber offensive: what would be the most effective response to the German technology and its tactical employment? 'It appears at first sight that almost any technical counter-measure would be successful; it is certain that the device of dropping suitable reflectors, such as sheets of tinfoil, would be highly successful against operators of the calibre of the prisoner.' Here was the origin of the notion of using so-called 'Window', dropped from a diversionary force of British aircraft to simulate a major bomber attack, or merely to swamp enemy screens. It was not employed, however, until the August 1943 Battle of Hamburg because of fears that the Luftwaffe, once enlightened, might adopt the same primitive methodology to blind British radar, though in truth the Germans had long understood the potential of 'Window'.

Reg Jones and the airmen progressively grasped the 'big picture' of German electronic defences against the RAF bomber offensive. The Luftwaffe's General Josef Kammhuber had created around the perimeter of *Festung Europa* a forward defence of the Reich, based upon a chain of invisible electronic 'boxes' – the Germans codenamed them *himmelbetten*, 'four-poster beds' – each some eighteen miles wide, stretching from northern Denmark down the coasts of Holland, Belgium, France. Each box was linked to one Freya and two Würzburg radars, together with a control room fitted with a so-called Seeberg plotting table. As a bomber approached a box, one Würzburg locked onto a British aircraft and plotted its progress, while a second – such as was not installed at Bruneval – tracked an airborne German night-fighter. The controller then directed the hunter by radio-telephone towards convergence with his quarry in the darkness or, at some locations, instead provided ranging data for anti-aircraft batteries or a master searchlight. Each *himmelbett* could theoretically handle six fighter interceptions an hour.

The system worked. In the winter of 1941–42 it was refined through the progressive introduction of more powerful and accurate 'Giant Würzburgs' with twenty-five-foot-diameter perforated dishes around their aerials. At that time, when RAF Bomber Command's powers and numbers were still limited, this German defensive network represented a strong shield, and was responsible for the loss of many aircraft. Perhaps the most important technological outcome of the Bruneval raid, and of its consequent British identification of the main principles of the Kammhuber Line, was that it revealed to the RAF that a Freya-Würzburg combination could track and pursue only one aircraft at a time. Thus, Bomber Command responded by adopting so-called 'streaming' tactics – directing all aircraft of a night's attacking force through the narrowest possible corridor in the sky in the shortest possible time, to swamp the Germans' monitoring resources.

Streaming, first employed in May 1942, enjoyed significant success, though it could not save the bomber force from enduring terrible losses. Every aircraft on every sortie was obliged to pass hours forging through the darkness above the continent, offering the defenders repeated opportunities to shoot it down, despite the increasingly formidable array of radar jamming technology deployed by the RAF. Moreover, in the last eighteen months of the war German night-fighters achieved many of their successes by roaming the skies unguided by ground controllers. At a phase of the struggle when the night sky over Europe would often be crowded with hundreds of potential targets, these 'Wild Boars' located a bomber through visual sighting or their own short-range aircraft-mounted radar. The pinpointing of a British aircraft frequently signalled its doom. Wild Boar tactics were relatively crude, but inherently impervious to electronic counter-measures. A bomber crew's eyesight became its best weapon in preserving their lives. Nonetheless, in 1942 all that lay a distance in the future: given that the entire strategic air war represented a deadly tennis match between measure and counter-measure, with the balance shifting every few months or even weeks, capture of the Würzburg endowed the British with an important short-term advantage.

There were further consequences of Bruneval. First, the Germans felt compelled to expend resources on strengthening the defences of every radar installation within reach of raiders. These were encircled with dense barbed-wire entanglements, readily visible to PRU pilots and on the images which their cameras brought home. Therefore, Jones and his colleagues could soon be confident of all Freya-Würzburg locations. At Bruneval, a replacement Würzburg set was re-sited within a single wired compound shared with the two Freya arrays. In April the Gosset château – the Manoir de la Falaise or 'Lone House' – was blown up by the Todt Organization, to remove a conspicuous landmark from the Normandy coast. On the debit side, the British were alarmed to recognize that their own Telecommunications Research Establishment, home to the nation's most closely-guarded electronic secrets, was as vulnerable to enemy raiders in its coastal location outside Swanage as had been Bruneval to C Company. Thus, the TRE was transferred to a new inland base, at Malvern in Worcestershire, where its successor organization remains to this day.

Although John Frost and his men were saluted for their success, the army bureaucracy was remorseless in complaints about the perceived shortcomings of C Company's fulfilment of its responsibilities. The major wrote wearily: 'We got into trouble over equipment lost during the operation. We were on a peacetime system of accounting, and it was difficult for some to understand that almost inevitably things go missing in the confusion and flurry of action against a live enemy which includes a hasty evacuation by sea in the dark.' C Company had abandoned or lost in Normandy most of its useless wirelesses, together with the engineers' trolleys and other equipment, three Brens, two Stens and eleven rifles, for all of which they were persecuted through weeks of increasingly satirical paper exchanges with uniformed functionaries who had never heard a shot fired in anger. Frost was accused of losing eighteen pairs of binoculars that his men had not even taken to France. The glider pilots' quartermaster at Tilshead was unwilling to accept that C Company had been in action, even when reading a newspaper that blazoned an account of the raid.

Moreover, Heller, the captured Luftwaffe technician, became in the security of captivity sufficiently truculent to complain about Sgt. McKenzie's confiscation of his wristwatch. Amazingly the War Office decided to demonstrate that Britain faithfully obeyed the rules of PoW custodianship. Staff contacted C Company and insisted the watch should be returned. Now it was McKenzie's turn to be the aggrieved party, because he asserted that he had spent five shillings on having the German 'ticker' repaired, which nobody offered to refund him.

Six of the seven paratroopers left behind at Bruneval survived the war as prisoners. Following the death of Scott and surrender of McCallum, Willoughby and Thomas on the beach, the

Germans, who had found the signaller nearby, breathing his last, drafted the prisoners to carry his body up to the hamlet. Sutherland was discovered in the morning by Paul Delamare, owner of the farm where he had taken refuge, to whom he now introduced himself simply as 'Tommy! Anglo!' Soon in agony from his wounds, Sutherland asked Delamare to fetch Germans to whom he could surrender. The farmer duly called soldiers, saying '*Tommy! Blessé! Ici!*' Both the Luftwaffe and Wehrmacht treated the four paratroopers with surprising goodwill and even joviality. The divisional commander, Gen. Stever, quizzed them in English. The men relaxed on finding that they were not to be shot, and Madame Vennier the Beau-Minet's owner reported: 'They laughed – seemed excited by their adventure.'

Meanwhile Cornell and Embury walked for several days, receiving a mixed reception from local people and shivering through nights in the woods, before finding Resisters courageous enough to hide them, then to help them attempt to escape. A family named Lechevallier gave them notable assistance before Maurice Lajoye and his partner Madame Regnier, later his wife, guided them first by train to Paris – where, in a notable display of bravado, they were taken to see some of the great tourist sites – and then towards the Vichy Unoccupied Zone. At the last leap, on 9 March 1942 crossing the bridge at Bléré, Indre-et-Loire, a hundred yards short of relative safety, they were arrested and made PoWs. Their heroic guides were dispatched for the remainder of the war respectively to Buchenwald and Ravensbrück concentration camps, from which they returned broken in health.

The only French people to profit from the Bruneval raid were young farm boys who found and secreted a parachute discarded by C Company, from which they fashioned silk shirts, re-dyed in blue, that became the envy of the neighbourhood.

2 THE WHEEL OF FORTUNE

On 1 August 1942 a decree was promulgated from the War Office that Britain's airborne infantry should thenceforward assume membership of a new Parachute Regiment, of which Bruneval was later declared to have been the first battle honour. Soon afterwards these soldiers were ordered to forsake their former unit headgear and adopt maroon berets. The 'paras' became, as they remain to this day, one of the most celebrated elite elements of the British Army.

More than a few of those who participated in Biting died on later Airborne battlefields, notably including Tunisia, Sicily and Arnhem. Frost's 2 Para, of which he assumed battalion command in November 1942, fought through the North-West Africa campaign in which Sgt. David Grieve MM perished, aged twenty-eight, among sixteen officers and 250 other ranks who became casualties.

Another of the dead was Euan Charteris, killed on 3 December, aged twenty-one, after being dispatched on a mission to British lines from the encircled battalion, of which he was then intelligence officer. He was one of three brothers, all of whom served in the wartime army. It is unlikely that they were then aware of the controversial reputation of their father, because only after the Second World War was Brigadier John Charteris's key role as Field-Marshal Earl Haig's 1914–18 intelligence chief subjected to critical scrutiny by historians, himself exposed as a prime mover in some of Haig's bloodiest blunders. In all probability, the Charteris boys knew their father only as a much-decorated soldier, whom they should aspire to live up to. Assured it is that Euan was a remarkably courageous young man and imaginative leader, whose role in Biting was critical. John Frost felt his loss keenly, especially because he believed the Tunisian deployment to have been a waste of expensively-trained airborne soldiers, there squandered as cannon fodder. Meanwhile Sgt. Johnny Boyd, hit in the foot at Bruneval, was killed especially cruelly, not by Germans but instead by Greek communists in Athens in January 1945, when the war's ending was within sight.

Other prominent contributors to Biting also fell: Tony Hill, the photo-reconnaissance pilot who captured the first identifiable images of the Bruneval Würzburg, was fatally injured during a sortie over the Le Creusot works, dying in a French hospital on 12 November 1942. Reg Jones wrote: 'I felt his loss more than any other in the whole war.' Air Commodore Sir Nigel Norman, who directed the RAF element of Biting, was killed as a passenger in an aircraft take-off crash in May 1943, aged forty-two. Sgt. John Pohe, the 51 Squadron Maori who dropped Dave Grieve south of Bruneval, was later shot down and became a PoW. He participated in the March 1944 Great Escape from Stalag Luft III, and would be one of fifty recaptured prisoners executed in cold blood by the Germans, as deterrent examples to others.

Gen. Charles de Gaulle said to an intimate, André Gillois, after France's liberation: 'Between ourselves, the Resistance is a bluff which has succeeded.' On 8 April 1942 a memo from the War Office's director of military intelligence to Sir Stewart Menzies, chief of MI6, observed: 'The report from "Rémy" on the enemy deployments [at Bruneval] was a remarkable document and contained information of the highest value, such as we seldom obtain.' Rémy himself, exultant on learning of the success of the raid while he was in London, dispatched a personal signal of congratulations to Pol – Roger Dumont – the agent who had travelled to Bruneval and probed its defences. Rémy's message, drafted in his room at the Waldorf

Hotel after a sybaritic lunch at the famous Écu de France restaurant, read: 'TO PACO FOR POL CONGRATULATIONS SUCCESS BRUNEVAL WHICH HAS RESULTED DESTRUCTION IMPORTANT GERMAN INSTALLATION WHILE TAKING AND KILLING NUMEROUS BOCHE.'

This signal was decrypted by the Germans a few weeks later – Gaullist BCRA codes were notoriously vulnerable – and proved to be Pol's death warrant. Its sentiments were richly justified, but the message should never have been sent. It precipitated Roger Dumont's arrest, and eventual execution by firing squad at Mont-Valérien on 13 May 1943. He wrote to his family an hour before his death: 'All that I have done I have done as a Frenchman. I regret nothing.' Elsewhere, Rémy's mother and three of his sisters suffered a long imprisonment in Fresnes, while three other sisters were deported to the female concentration camp of Ravensbrück. They were liberated at the end of the war, but Rémy's brother Philippe, also deported, was killed in Lübeck Harbour days before the British Army arrived there in April 1945.

Charles Pickard once recalled the lines famous among his kind, from Kipling's 1919 poem entitled 'R.A.F. (Aged Eighteen)': *Laughing through clouds, his milk-teeth still unshed/ Cities and men he smote from overhead./His deaths delivered, he returned to play/Childlike, with childish things now put away.* Following Bruneval, Pick and the other aircrew of 51 Squadron returned to bomber operations from their base at Dishforth in Yorkshire, where they played a favourite after-dinner game in the officers' mess. The CO was hoisted upside down to plant soot-smeared footprints on the walls and ceiling as his pilots roared with alcoholic laughter. Pickard was obliged to explain the joke and the footprints when George VI visited the squadron a few weeks later. The king also witnessed a demonstration parachute drop by men of 3 Para, and Johnny Frost was presented to him.

Pick met his own almost inevitable death on 18 February 1944, when leading a sortie which garnered both fame and controversy, dubbed after the event as Operation Jericho. Nineteen twin-engined RAF Mosquito light bombers, escorted by Typhoon fighters, sought to liberate French Resistance prisoners held in Amiens prison. The attack required extraordinary aiming precision, to demolish the wall without killing the captives. In the event, of 832 prisoners in the jail 102 would be fatal victims of the bombs, a further seventy-four were wounded, while 258 escaped, of whom seventy-four were political prisoners or members of the Resistance. Pickard, who was designated as airborne controller, was 'bounced' by a German FW 190 fighter, from which cannon fire tore off the tail of his Mosquito. F-Freddie plunged into the ground ten miles north of Amiens, immolating Pickard, together with his devoted comrade and navigator Alan Broadley. Pick's widow Dorothy returned to Africa after the war and eventually died in Rhodesia in 1999. Their son Nick became a successful musician with his own sound studio, dying in 2009.

Jericho almost certainly cost more lives than it saved. Nobody, including the French Resistance and SOE, ever admitted to requesting such a rescue mission, a hare-brained conception comparable with Gen. George Patton's March 1945 dispatch of a US armoured column to liberate his own son-in-law from Hammelburg PoW camp, which likewise precipitated a bloodbath. Moreover, of those who escaped from Amiens two-thirds were soon recaptured by the Germans. The RAF did not initiate Jericho, so presumably the proposal came from an unidentified element of the secret world, which afterwards found it prudent to keep silent. It was tragic that Pickard, after surviving so much, should have been permitted as a group-captain to assume airborne command of such an operation. Like so many wartime stars, however, he had come to know no other life. He invited such a death, almost exactly two years after Bruneval.

Others lived, to share in victory. CSM Strachan remained on a hospital danger list for weeks, but eventually regained sufficient of his health to return to 2 Para in August 1943 as its regimental sergeant-major, the triumph of an iron Scottish will over a grievously damaged body. He later dropped into Arnhem, was again hit, and spent the last months of the war as a PoW before rejoining his old regiment, the Black Watch. Strachan's Bruneval wounds continued to trouble him, though, and were responsible for his sudden death following surgery in 1948, aged forty-two, leaving a widow, Ivy, an army cook whom he had married five years earlier, and two small children.

Lt. John Timothy finished the war as a major with three Military Crosses, thus becoming one of the most decorated officers in airborne forces. His wartime adventures after Bruneval would fill a considerable volume. On leaving the army he returned to Marks & Spencer, for whom he had worked until 1940: for seven years he managed its Wakefield branch. He retired in 1973, never married, and died in 2011.

Charles Cox richly deserved not only the Military Medal which he was awarded for Biting, but his good fortune in living happily ever after. When the war ended he started a little electrical shop and survived until 1997. He was salt of the earth.

Peter 'Walker', or rather Nagel, the interpreter who served Frost so well at Bruneval, performed the same role on the St Nazaire raid, but was less lucky. He was captured by the Germans and spent the rest of the war as a PoW, though he preserved an identity as an infantryman named Walker. Nagel died in 1983, aged sixty-seven.

Bren-gunner Charlie Branwhite was reunited with his three children only in 1946, four years after the death of their mother, his wife Helen. Pte. Eric Freeman became one of Nottingham's senior magistrates. Pte. Frank Embury, one of those left behind, who endured more than three years as a PoW, returned to his home town of Stoke-on-Trent, married and became a father of twins; found work first in a local abattoir, then in a pottery factory, before dying in 1987. His son says that he seldom spoke about his wartime odyssey, or perhaps nightmare.

The adventures of Tom Hill's mate Tom Laughland, a Glaswegian corporal who served in Charteris's Nelson section, had scarcely begun at Bruneval. He fought until captured in North Africa; escaped in Italy to rejoin 2 Para, dropped into Arnhem, where he was again captured at the bridge. After the war he completed a bricklaying apprenticeship, travelled widely before retiring to Scotland. In 2012 he celebrated forty years of marriage, finally dying aged ninety-three.

John Ross received a DSO following a December 1942 North African battle in which the company of 2 Para that he commanded was reduced to five men. He also later received an MBE, for his fine conduct in the German PoW camp where he spent almost two years, after being captured in Sicily. He became a post-war solicitor in Dundee and a deputy lord-lieutenant of Tayside, living until 1993.

Dennis Vernon finished the war as a major with a Military Cross, after surviving much action with airborne forces in North Africa and Italy. On being demobbed, he resumed his career as a civil engineer, 'prospering without any fuss or bother, in peace as in war', according to George Millar when they met.

Peter Naoumoff was captured in North Africa, and remained a PoW in Germany until he was liberated almost three years later. Returned to civilian life, he worked extensively abroad and died in 1986, aged sixty-five.

Lt. Cdr. Fred Cook returned to his native land in 1943, to direct the Australian Navy's embryo amphibious training centre. Mountbatten became a godfather to his son, born after the war, and Cook continued to serve until he retired as a captain in 1960. The naval commander of Biting died in 1985.

Charles Chauveau, the motor dealer who had accompanied Roger Dumont to reconnoitre Bruneval, escaped German vengeance and sustained his role in Resistance until the liberation. By a sad irony, however, his garage business in Le Havre was destroyed in a 1 April 1942 RAF bombing raid. He died in 1963.

Rémy – Gilbert Renault – somehow survived two further missions in France as a secret agent. His wife Édith and baby son Michel escaped with him to England by sea after the earlier of these, in June 1942. He finally quit his field role in January 1943, thereafter staying in exile until France's liberation. Renault proved able to overcome the strictures, indeed fierce criticisms, of some former Resistance comrades, notably Pierre Brossolette, to become a nationally recognized hero. Later, however, he went spectacularly politically astray. He revived his old monarchist enthusiasm, and broke with de Gaulle over the latter's unwillingness to pardon Marshal Pétain, in the cause of national reconciliation. Renault died in 1984, aged eighty, having made himself a highly controversial, contrarian figure. Historian Sébastien Albertelli has written that Rémy was 'the principal creator of his own legend through his prolific [post-war] literary output'. Yet there was substance in that legend, to which the triumph of Operation Biting made a substantial contribution.

Reg Jones was appointed in 1946 to the chair of natural philosophy at Aberdeen University, a role in which he specialized in improving the precision of scientific instruments. He briefly returned to intelligence under the 1951–55 Churchill government, but was unable to work comfortably with the peacetime secret services, most of whose senior personnel were conspicuously less gifted than himself. Jones's daughter Susan earned fame in her own right when she was three times crowned Miss Scotland in national beauty pageants, while also gaining a degree in mathematics at Aberdeen.

Publication of R.V. Jones's 1978 memoir *Most Secret War* made him belatedly a national figure. In 1994 he became a Companion of Honour, though he was never honoured by Oxford or Cambridge universities. The CIA created a special intelligence award in his name, of which in 1993 he was the first recipient. James Woolsey, the agency director responsible, said in expressing his own admiration for Jones: 'He did not have any trouble speaking truth to power. He didn't know any other way. This may be one of the reasons he was formally unrecognized [in his own country] for so long.' Jones died in 1997, aged eighty-six.

As for Johnny Frost, C Company's commander survived not only the bitter fighting in North Africa but also the bloody Sicilian campaign, in which the Parachute Regiment suffered terribly. Thereafter, at Arnhem Frost secured immortality, holding positions at the north end of the bridge through three days and nights before he and his men were obliged to surrender by losses, his own wounds and the exhaustion of their ammunition. After seven months in captivity, he returned home, having been one of a tiny handful of men who participated in all four of 1st Airborne Division's major operational drops. In 1947 he married Jean Lyle, whom he had first met during the war, and encountered again in Palestine where she was shot and wounded by a terrorist of the Stern Gang while working for the Women's Voluntary Service, and Frost was serving with his unit. The couple had two children, Hugo and Caroline, and after leaving the army as a major-general in 1967 he took to farming. He was urged to stand as a Conservative candidate for Parliament, but his wife sternly and surely wisely vetoed the idea. Instead, well into middle age he rode a 400cc Suzuki motorbike, and avidly consumed books of military history.

Frost died in 1993, aged eighty-one. Although one of Britain's most famous wartime soldiers, he once confided how grateful he was never to have been considered for a VC, because he witnessed the lifelong unhappiness, and even guilt, that such a distinction could confer upon the Cross's recipients. Few men better deserved their happy and fulfilled later lives than did Frost. He was no Wellington nor even Montgomery, but instead the best sort of British professional soldier – brave, effective, inspirational, absolutely committed to the fulfilment of any mission to which he pledged himself.

One of the last surviving Bruneval airborne veterans, Corporal Tom Hill who had dropped with Euan Charteris, died in March 2014.

Operation Biting, second jump into action – after the Tragino aqueduct – by Britain's embryo airborne forces, as well as being only the second significant raid mounted under the auspices of the Combined Operations Command, might be described as a series of small miracles, such as are seldom granted to those committed to any act of war. The first was that Rémy's agents were able to visit Upper Normandy; secure accurate intelligence about the defences around the Würzburg site; then return to Paris and report this to London, without being captured or their purpose divined by the Germans.

Gliders would have been far better suited to landing a concentrated force to execute Biting, but given their operational unreadiness in February 1942, it is remarkable that eight and a half of the twelve 'sticks' that comprised Frost's company were dropped by parachute in darkness in the right place. The Whitley pilots were assisted by their objective's proximity to the coast, so that in moonlight it was relatively easy to identify landmarks. Consider the consequences had Frost, Cox and Vernon been dropped where Charteris, Reid, Grieve and their men found themselves, as chance might easily have decreed: the assault would have been doomed. There was also no wind to blow the jumpers off course, once their canopies deployed. Largely thanks to the snow cushion, no paratroopers suffered jump injuries. Donald Peveler, one of Pickard's flight commanders, wrote later that such an operation properly demanded visual beacons to mark the landing zone.

Most important of all, though many Germans witnessed C Company descending from the sky over Normandy, their superiors were amazingly slow to do anything effective about it. The winter weather contributed significantly to the difficulties of moving reinforcements to Bruneval, but so did infirmity of command. Whereas Mountbatten received bouquets, across the Channel his cousin Captain Prince Alexander-Ferdinand von Preussen, commanding the Luftwaffe's 23 *Flugmelde* responsible for the radar sites, was formally reprimanded by his superiors for unauthorized absence from his post of duty on the night of 27/28 February. In a photograph of him taken next day in Étretat with three British prisoners the prince, back from Paris, appears relaxed and cheerful, but on 7 March he was dismissed from his command. He survived the war, dying in 1985, though youthful hopes went unfulfilled that his own early support for Hitler might induce the latter to make him a new kaiser.

Among humbler defenders of Bruneval, the Luftwaffe's Ruben, Meiser, Deckert and Ermoneit received Iron Crosses, second class. The army's investigator, a general, produced an extraordinary whitewash report on the British raid, asserting that everybody on the German side had fulfilled their duties as expected: 'The troops did everything in their powers to prevent the enemy from executing their mission ... I expressed my complete satisfaction that the division totally fulfilled its responsibilities.' Col. von Eisenhart-Rothe, the 685th's regimental commander, was soon afterwards promoted to brigadier-general, but Gen. Joachim Stever, the 336th's divisional commander, was sacked. Less than three months later the formation was redeployed to the Eastern Front, where it fought until finally destroyed at Sevastopol in May 1944. Many of those in its ranks who had been stationed around Bruneval in February 1942 never came home from Russia – no more was ever heard of Sgt. Treinies, who had stubbornly defended Stella Maris, nor of the ineffectual Lt. Huhne. There is no record of any Wehrmacht decorations being awarded for the defence of Bruneval.

The worst consequence of Biting was that it gave Britain's warlords, notably Browning, Mountbatten and their staffs, an inflated notion of their ability to breach the walls of *Festung Europa*, and an insouciance about the powers of the enemy to frustrate them. Amid the exhilaration of success, there is scant evidence in the written reports of hard questions being posed about the muddle of the drop, C Company's near-fatal sluggishness in breaking through to the beach, the indifferent showing of the navy – and thus, how near the operation came to failure.

The Bruneval plan devised in Richmond Terrace by Casa Maury and Hughes-Hallett assumed that Fred Cook's landing-craft could cross the Channel in both directions, very slowly, while between passages the raiders conducted a three-hour land battle, without the enemy intervening, even after the evacuation. This indeed proved the case on 28 February, but would never happen again. Even Reg Jones and his staff displayed naivety, by inviting Dennis Vernon to take flashlight photographs while under enemy fire. Meanwhile, the hour-long resistance mounted by the handful of Germans at Beach Fort – the villa Stella Maris – showed what havoc the enemy might have wrought had the soldiers billeted in Bruneval responded to the 0025 alarm by manning the pillboxes which the paratroopers found empty, instead of hastening in the opposite direction towards Hill 102, the higher ground east of the hamlet. The absence of any senior army officer from the locality probably went far to explain the confused reactions. It was as unlikely that in a single night all these elements of good fortune should have favoured the British, as that John Frost should have drawn four aces in a mess poker game.

The success of Bruneval caused airborne forces, and explicitly Browning, to assume the principle held good that it was acceptable to land parachute attackers at a significant distance from their objectives, to achieve a tidy drop. Here again, on 28 February 1942 C Company enjoyed a success never repeated, by securing surprise in overrunning the Würzburg site, despite having been seen landing forty-five minutes earlier, more than half a mile away. At Arnhem in September 1944, Browning embraced the plan for 1st Airborne Division to land early in the afternoon between five and eight miles from the vital bridge for which the British came, to please the RAF who were apprehensive about enemy flak closer to the objective. A despairing Polish Maj. Gen. Stanisław Sosabowski appealed against the madness of such a course, exclaiming in the midst of its exposition: 'But the Germans, general … The Germans!', only to be mocked.

On the day of the Arnhem drop the men of 2 Para, commanded by Frost, did not approach their objective until 2000, by which time the Germans – unsurprisingly to anyone save Browning and his staff – had secured the Rhine bridge, and defied all subsequent efforts to dislodge them. Frost and his gallant but doomed battalion were thereafter confined to the north bank, a stepping-stone to nowhere. In fairness to Browning, foremost blame for the Arnhem disaster lies with his superiors – Montgomery, the American Lewis Brereton and the RAF chiefs who imposed an impossibly flawed air plan – but Browning was the man in charge on the day.

With the exception of Bruneval, all the most brilliant airborne successes of the war were *coups de main* achieved by landing men on top of their objectives – the Luftwaffe operation at Eben Emael in 1940; German commandos' rescue of Mussolini from captivity on the Gran Sasso mountaintop in September 1943; and the 5 June 1944 British descent on Normandy's Caen canal bridge. It is notable that all these successes were achieved by troops delivered in gliders – precursors of modern helicopter-borne assaults – rather than by parachutists. The only slender chance of success for the 1944 Market Garden objective of securing a Rhine crossing would have lain in accepting the losses inescapable if some American and British gliderborne troops or even parachutists had been landed immediately alongside the Dutch bridges – in the midst of Arnhem, Nijmegen and other crossings – instead of miles away. Such a tactic would, in the end, almost certainly have proved far cheaper in lives.

Arnhem, which made Frost a legend portrayed by Anthony Hopkins in the film *A Bridge Too Far*, destroyed the reputation of 'Boy' Browning in the eyes of almost all those who knew the inside story of what took place. There was the poor planning; Browning's strained relations with his American counterparts, especially the great Maj. Gen. Jim Gavin, who thought him a posturing caricature of an English gentleman and wrote in his diary: '[Browning] unquestionably lacks the standing, influence and judgement that comes with a proper troop experience … His staff was superficial … [British senior officers] never get down into the dirt and learn the hard way.'

Then there was the misjudged appointment of Roy Urquhart, who lacked experience of parachute warfare, to command 1st Airborne; Browning's own subsequent failure to 'grip' the battle – to respond swiftly to the unfolding calamity which destroyed half his command. John Frost also deplored the decision to launch Operation Market Garden in daylight: experience at Bruneval and elsewhere had convinced him the Germans disliked fighting in darkness, a vulnerability that should have been exploited.

Moreover, many of 1st Airborne's units had suffered grievously in the Mediterranean fighting, and others were of less impressive quality than those of 6th Airborne, which distinguished itself in Normandy. Above all, in the eyes of insiders, there was Browning's obsessive determination to lead into battle a sky army such as he had striven since 1941 to bring into being; to earn for himself the laurels for which he yearned, after five years of war in which he had never led troops in action. This hunger caused him recklessly to dismiss the overwhelming intelligence evidence of a strong German armoured presence at Arnhem such as must spell doom to Airborne troops almost bereft of mobility and heavy weapons, and to commit his divisions to a project which, from the outset, most of his subordinates thought misconceived.*

---

* The author has addressed the Arnhem story at length in *Armageddon: The Battle for Germany 1944–45* (Macmillan 2004).

Today Browning's reputation has arguably fallen too low. He devoted himself single-mindedly to transforming the embryo battalions of the early war years into the large parachute forces which Britain possessed by 1944. The success achieved by 6th Airborne Division on D-Day and in the weeks that followed should be cast in the balance of Browning's record against the disaster at Arnhem. He was an efficient, forceful manager, whose misfortune it was to fail the decisive test of a wartime general: that of high command in battle. He yearned to prove himself at the head of fighting men and when he did so, was found wanting. Ismay – the scepticism of the prime minister's chief of staff being perhaps surprising – described Browning as 'a first-class leader, but as wild and disorganized as Mountbatten'.

After the war Browning left the army and became private secretary to Princess Elizabeth, remaining in her service at Buckingham Palace when she ascended the throne in 1952. She and her husband Prince Philip esteemed him as some of his fellow soldiers did not. The general experienced persistent difficulties with alcohol abuse, and was obliged to retire from royal service after suffering a nervous breakdown. He was never a man at ease with himself, yet his marriage to Daphne du Maurier survived and even, in its peculiar fashion, prospered. She grieved deeply when he died in 1965.

Mountbatten was more fortunate. On 2 March 1942 he sent a note to the prime minister, emphasizing the role in Biting of his polo chum 'Bobby' the marquis: 'The plan for this operation was devised by Wing-Commander Casa Maury, and submitted on January 1.' Two days after this missive Churchill, still basking in the afterglow from Biting, summoned Mountbatten and told him he was to assume the enhanced title of Chief of Combined Operations and join the Chiefs of Staff Committee, with the acting ranks of vice-admiral, lieutenant-general and air marshal.

Admiral Sir Dudley Pound, First Sea Lord and chairman of the Chiefs, was so appalled by this elevation that he wrote at length to Churchill, saying he feared it might not enjoy the support of the navy: 'I am afraid I feel so strongly that it is wrong that I cannot shoulder this responsibility.' Pound disliked even more the alternative, that people might reach the correct conclusion – that the appointment was made against his advice, which must weaken his authority. Worse, Mountbatten could be thought to have secured his advancement because of his royal blood. 'Apart from the above, the Service will not understand a junior Captain *in a shore appointment* [emphasis in original] being given three steps in rank.'

The prime minister dismissed not only Pound's strictures, but also the objections of Alan Brooke and others. The appointment was duly made. There was rejoicing only among Mountbatten's courtiers in Combined Ops, notably including 'Jock' Hughes-Hallett, the naval officer later held responsible for much of what went wrong with the August 1942 Dieppe raid, who said: 'My own reaction was one of exhilaration, almost exultation. At one stride our organisation had penetrated the very centre and citadel of power.' Cabinet minister Leo Amery believed the appointment presaged Mountbatten's eventual promotion to run the Chiefs of Staff Committee.

Amery proved mistaken – Alan Brooke assumed the chairmanship in succession to Pound – but the politician's view reflected the prevailing mood in Whitehall. Mountbatten was a rising star in the only firmament that mattered, that of the PM, and a lot of important and sensible people did not like it. Brooke wrote that he and his colleagues were always filled with trepidation when it was known that Mountbatten was to visit Chequers and bend the prime minister's ear: 'There was no knowing what discussions he might be led into ... and let us in for.' When Lord Louis as CCO consequently attended the Chiefs of Staff Committee and reported on his weekend discussions with the prime minister, there were sometimes unpleasant surprises.

Combined Operations never again secured such an undisputed success as that achieved at Bruneval. A month later, on 28 March 1942, Mountbatten's command presided over a much more ambitious attack on the port of St Nazaire. This succeeded in its objective, blocking the dry-dock's lock gates to prevent their use by German capital ships. But the defenders from the outset harrowed British attacking vessels with fire. Losses were heavy – of 622 soldiers and sailors committed, 168 were killed and 210 taken prisoner. Doubts persist about how much the lock mattered to the German naval war effort, though they expended substantial effort on its repair. The award of five Victoria Crosses to participants, dead and alive, was believed by cynics* to have been intended to assuage the grief caused in a bloody shambles, by identifying candidates for glory.

Much worse was the calamity at Dieppe in August, for which to this day nobody has identified a credible purpose, save that the seaside resort was quite wrongly judged vulnerable to attack. Of six thousand men committed, most of them Canadian, 980 died and over two thousand became prisoners. Mountbatten's sponsorship of Dieppe, which killed many good men, should have damaged his reputation much more gravely

---

* Air Chief Marshal Sir Arthur Harris in 1977 forcefully expressed to the author his contempt for the St Nazaire decorations list, as an example of the Royal Navy's ill-judged self-promotion.

than it did, had it not seemed at the time to be in the national interest to shield from blame a certified hero. If Mountbatten had been disgraced, his principal sponsor, the prime minister, must also have been tarnished.

Thereafter, as the Allied war effort turned towards major amphibious landings in North Africa, Sicily, Italy, France, raiding went out of fashion. Its principal purpose – to sustain an impression or illusion of momentum in Britain's struggling war effort – became redundant, as huge operations supplanted gestures. Combined Operations, and Mountbatten himself, could claim to have played a part in identifying the difficulties and addressing the challenges posed by amphibious landings, but the principal players in the raiding game were gamblers, entrusted by the prime minister with the lives of men as stake money.

Bruneval remained unique, as an operation which received indispensable assistance from German lassitude and incompetence. Never again would the enemy prove so obliging. At both St Nazaire and Dieppe, local forces showed what havoc energetic defenders could inflict upon seaborne invaders. Both bloodbaths had a profound psychological impact on planning for D-Day in Normandy. These 1942 demonstrations of how amphibious assaults should not be done caused 1944 commanders and their staffs to make the most meticulous preparations, and to concentrate overwhelming force, to ensure success.

Mountbatten and his colleagues in Richmond Terrace could assert with justice that for Operation Overlord resources were made available to the Allies which simply did not exist two years earlier. Moreover, much that went wrong in early combined operations reflected not merely commanders' and planners' misjudgements, but also wider institutional failures in the British armed forces that were much mitigated by the time of D-Day. Nonetheless Mountbatten did foolish things for which he was fortunate to secure forgiveness – Churchill shipped his favourite east to become Supreme Commander in South-East Asia before his shortcomings as CCO had become widely known. Such Richmond Terrace acolytes as the Marquis de Casa Maury vanished from the counsels of the great.

Mountbatten in his new role achieved considerable success not as an operational warlord, which he never was, but instead as maître d' for Britain's floundering Asian war effort, a figurehead function to which his talents were well suited. He provided an infusion of glamour in a theatre that badly needed it. In the wake of Arnhem, 'Boy' Browning was dispatched to become his chief of staff at the supreme commander's enormous headquarters in Ceylon, modern Sri Lanka, a droll final wartime pairing for the two principal conductors of Biting.

Mountbatten subsequently held naval commands before becoming in 1947 the last viceroy of India, and later First Sea Lord and chief of defence staff. As Admiral of the Fleet Earl Mountbatten of Burma, in 1979 he was murdered by the IRA off the coast from his home in the west of Ireland. His career had always tottered only narrowly on the credit side of absurdity, but his end possessed a tragic sort of dignity that must have gratified him. He performed best in roles which required showmanship. As Chief of Combined Operations in 1942, he endowed the post with an energy which was serviceable, though he was unsuited to bear responsibility for the execution of naval and military operations. He parlayed plausibility, royal connections and public popularity to rise ever higher, despite the failures with which he had been associated. Noel Coward had much to answer for, in making Mountbatten a celebrity, through *In Which We Serve*. After it was showered with

American awards, including a special Oscar for Coward, and beat *Casablanca* to become the New York Critic Circle's Best Film, its real-life star became almost unsackable.

Charles Carrington, who was not given to extravagant praise of any portion of Britain's war effort in either of the great conflicts in which he participated, afterwards described Biting as 'the most successful combined operation, both in its planning and execution, that I have seen in ten years of active service'. The Germans agreed, acknowledging in their after-action report: 'The operation of the commandos was well-planned and executed with great daring ... The British displayed exemplary discipline when under fire. Although attacked by German soldiers they concentrated entirely on their primary task. For a full thirty minutes one group did not fire a shot, then suddenly at the sound of a whistle they went into action.' Long after the war, Mountbatten was enchanted to receive a letter from *fallschirmjäger* commander Gen. Kurt Student, who said that he had been watching the great man's television autobiography, in which he claimed personal credit for conceiving the Bruneval assault. The German officer applauded, and said he could confirm that 'the successful execution by Major Frost sent a great shock through Hitler's headquarters'.

C Company's mission had a clear, limited objective, as less successful later raids did not. John Frost lamented that never again did Britain's warlords organize a company-strength 'party' on the modest scale of Bruneval – preferring larger and grander schemes, wherein whole brigades or even divisions were engaged, with far less impressive results. A historic lesson about special forces, now as then, is that they should remain special, and thus small. In the course of the war, and not least because of the apparently interminable four-year intermission between Dunkirk in May 1940 and D-Day in June 1944, many of the 'private armies' which Churchill encouraged at the conflict's outset were permitted to balloon beyond their rightful functions or usefulness, and to continue in being after their original roles had become redundant. This applied to Commandos, the Special Air Service, the Long Range Desert Group. Brooke wrote after the war: 'I remained convinced ... that the commandos should never have been divorced from the army in the way they were. Each division should have been responsible for maintaining a battle patrol capable of any commando work that might be asked of it.'

Though Brooke was more enthusiastic about airborne forces, arguments also persisted about the scale and rightful employment of these. For all the glamour associated with winged warfare, lack of mobility and heavy weapons imposed chronic limitations, if airborne formations were obliged to engage in sustained combat. Massed parachute drops enjoyed barely a quarter-century of prominence in the mainstream of armies, before silk canopies were supplanted by helicopters as the principal instruments for transporting soldiers by air into battle. It was a distinguished wearer of the maroon beret and survivor of Arnhem, Col. Geoffrey Powell, who later expressed a personal conviction that the British Army in North-West Europe should have used the bold and eager volunteers who formed the parachute formations to stiffen its line units. 'Eisenhower would have been better served in the autumn of 1944 by another half-dozen infantry or armoured divisions ... than by First Allied Airborne Army ... It is not easy to justify the scarce resources which the Americans and the British devoted to their fine airborne forces, and to the aircraft which flew them into battle.'

Back in February 1942, however, the Bruneval raid offered Britain's novice paratroopers an outstanding, almost unique opportunity to demonstrate the potency of surprise assault from the sky. When the prospect facing Britain was still so grim, it was a great thing for the nation's war effort that such eager warriors as Johnny Frost and his men, together with Reg Jones, Rémy, Roger Dumont, Charles Pickard, Charles Cox and the other remarkable personalities who played their parts, were at hand to conceive and execute a brilliant little coup which lifted the spirits of Churchill's people, and impressed their enemies as had few actions of the British Army since the onset of war.

Appendix I

Maj. John Frost's Orders for Operation Biting February 1942*

SECRET
NOT TO BE TAKEN IN AIRCRAFT

OPERATIONAL ORDER 'BITING'
by
Major J D Frost, Commanding 'C' Coy 2nd Parachute Bn.

TOPOGRAPHY — Scene of operation to be explained on model.

INFORMATION — Enemy.
From aerial photographs no sign of weapons heavier than MGs [Machine-Guns] can be seen. Until recently these appeared to be sited for defence against seaborne invasion only, but in the last three months three blockhouses have been constructed on the North shoulder of the exit from the beach. These are all thought to cover the valley and are connected to each other by communication trenches, work on these still

---

* No attempt is made here to comment upon or correct misstatements in Frost's briefing, especially about details of the defences at Bruneval.

continues. This group will be called REDOUBT.

There appears to be a strongpoint at the mouth of the beach exit, consisting of two blockhouses, four LMG posts and a roadblock. This group is likely to be sited for all-round defence, it is connected by communication trenches to a further LMG post one hundred yards up the valley. This group will be called BEACH FORT, it is surrounded by wire two metres thick.

Further inland there is a house on the edge of a depression running North from the Valley. This being the main perimeter of wire, is surrounded by wire ten metres thick. This house is believed to contain two MGs and is permanently manned. This will be known as GUARDROOM.

There are more possible LMG posts as shown on the model. The garrison consists of 30 men under an NCO. Five sleep in the GUARDROOM and the remainder in the village in a house some 500 yards from the beach.

To the North of the valley is a lone building which will be known as LONE HOUSE, 50 yards west of LONE HOUSE is the main objective which will be known as HENRY, LONE HOUSE is believed to contain 20 signallers.

North of LONE HOUSE is an enclosure of trees and buildings, believed to contain a number of signallers, this will be known as RECTANGLE.

OWN TROOPS
120 all ranks (see loading schedule)

OBJECT:
1. To capture various parts of HENRY and bring them down to the boats.

APPENDIX I

2. To capture prisoners who have been in charge of HENRY.
3. To obtain all possible information about HENRY and any documents referring to him which may be in LONE HOUSE.

METHOD — The force will be divided into three main parties, each party to be allotted a definite task.

No 1 NELSON

1. Task — to capture and hold REDOUBT, BEACH FORTRESS and GUARD ROOM and to cover the withdrawal of the remainder of the force to the beach for embarkation in ALC's.
2. DZ — NELSON will be dropped in the area due East of the track running North & South (Model).
3. Direction — The aircraft will be flying from South to North.
4. FUP [Forming Up Point] — The line of the track and the hedge running North & South in the re-entrant due East of the DZ.
5. Action — OC NELSON will detail 3 light sections to approach as near as possible to the 3 objectives enumerated in the task paragraph. The heavy sections will move to and take up a position on the spur due East of the REDOUBT so as to cover the road leading from the village and give support for the assault on the GUARDROOM and BEACH FORTRESS.
6. Timing — 1st NELSON stick will be dropped at 0015 hrs. The whole party will move to their objectives as soon as possible after forming-up.

7. <u>Co-ordination</u> — It is of vital importance that the enemy at LONE HOUSE and HENRY should be taken by surprise. Therefore NELSON will take every precaution to make no noise of any kind until either:
i. The attack on HENRY begins, or
ii. Successive blasts on a whistle are heard, or it becomes absolutely necessary to fire on the enemy. However should any section commander find it possible to occupy any one of the objectives silently, he will at once do so.
8. RE [Royal Engineers] Immediately it is possible, Lieut Ross will move to the beach with RE personnel and stores [mine-detectors] to:
i. Clear and make a route through minefield (if any)
ii. Establish HQ and checkpoint.

No 2 <u>JELLICOE, HARDY, DRAKE</u>

1. <u>Task</u> — Move to LONE HOUSE and deal with HENRY. Immediately all possible material has been taken, information and prisoners captured. To withdraw to the beach and prepare to embark.
2. <u>DZ</u> — as for NELSON
3. <u>Direction</u> — As for NELSON
4. <u>FUP</u> — As for NELSON
5. <u>Action</u> — DRAKE will move towards and take up a position West of the RECTANGLE in order to prevent enemy movement towards LONE HOUSE. HARDY will move to, and surround HENRY (Less RE party) RE party will follow JELLICOE.
6. <u>Timing</u> — JELLICOE, HARDY and DRAKE will be dropped at 0020 hrs.

7. Co-ordination — On the Sound of 4 blasts on the whistle, HARDY will force their way into LONE HOUSE, collect all enemy into a room on the ground floor and await further orders. RE party will commence their task with HENRY, JELLICOE will be responsible for their protection while doing so and will give any assistance they require.

No 3 RODNEY

1. Task — To prevent with 2 sections any attempt by the enemy to attack HARDY from RECTANGLE and to support with 2 sections, NELSON, in the event of an attack from the village.
2. DZ — As for NELSON
3. Direction — As for NELSON
4. FUP — As for NELSON
5. Action — RODNEY will take up position on the ground to the West of the FUP so as to be able to carry out both tasks. He must be able to reinforce either detachment in case of emergency.
6. Timing — RODNEY will begin dropping at 0025 hrs.
7. Co-ordination — No noise or firing until HENRY has been taken or the signal — 4 blasts on the whistle — is heard.
8. RE and Signals — OC RODNEY is responsible for ensuring that RE and Signal personnel are guided to area of BEACH FORT, where they will be met by Lieut Ross and will then carry out their duties (See Signal Instructions).

WITHDRAWAL FOR EMBARKATION

1. Immediately HARDY have completed their task they will move to the beach by the most direct route.
2. JELLICOE and DRAKE will follow at 50 yards intervals.
3. However should OC RE have any doubts concerning HENRY, and should the situation warrant it, JELLICOE, HARDY and DRAKE will remain in position until a small party named NOW arrive from the beach, inspect HENRY and complete their task. The withdrawal will then continue according to plan.
4. RODNEY will receive orders to withdraw by M/T or runner when HARDY etc have reached the beach. OC RODNEY will however prepare to withdraw as soon as he sees LONE HOUSE area evacuated.
5. RODNEY will move by the more direct route.
6. NELSON will withdraw immediately RODNEY are clear of the beach.

BEACH CONTROL

1. OC parties are responsible for the disposition of their parties on the beach.
2. RE personnel will lay tapes to guide parties through the minefield (if any). Lieut Ross to ensure that guides are in position when required.
3. Section Commanders will report their sections present or otherwise to Lieut Ross, at the checkpoint (BEACH FORT).
4. Parties will embark under orders from the Beach Control Officer — appointed by Lieut Ross.

5. The Beach Control Officer will ensure that parties get to their boats as quickly and vigorously as possible. He will ensure that each boat takes its correct load, and will inform the Naval Officer in Command as soon as the boat is correctly loaded, and ready to leave. He will give the Naval Officer all possible assistance.

GENERAL
1. No prisoner will be taken off, other than signallers.
2. Ammunition will be conserved as far as possible.
3. Sentries will be dealt with silently, whenever possible.
4. The password will be 'BITING'.
5. It is emphasised that the whole operation fails unless HENRY is effectively dealt with and the parts required are captured. All ranks must be fully aware of this.
6. On the ALCs the senior officer or NCO is in command of all troops. He is responsible to the Naval Officer in Command of the ALC and will ensure that all orders given by the NO are implicitly obeyed.

INTERCOMMUNICATION
1. Os i/c NELSON, HARDY, DRAKE and RODNEY will communicate with each other by:
i. No 38 W/T Set
ii. Whistle
2. Signallers with RODNEY will communicate with the Naval Force by:
i. D/F transmitter

ii. No 18 W/T Set
iii. Visual (torch)
iv. Very pistol
3. The senior signaller will decide which equipment is to be used where two similar equipments are available.
4. Signals containers can be identified by a green light and will be painted with 4 black and white bands.
5. Signallers will RV with RODNEY in accordance with para
6. On orders being given by O i/c RODNEY to take up battle posn signallers will accompany RODNEY.
7. Comm will at once be established with the Naval Force by No 18 W/T Set.
8. As soon as notification has been received that the beach is clear, signallers will leave RODNEY and proceed to the beach. No 18 W/T sets will be carried without being dismantled.
9. On arrival at the beach a REPORT CENTRE will be opened as near as possible to checkpoint at BEACH FORT.
10. D/F transmissions will begin immediately on taking up posn at check point. The drill for establishing D/F transmissions will be in accordance with Appx.
11. As soon as Naval craft are heard to be approaching. D/F transmissions will cease and the signaller i/c D/F apparatus will signal in the direction of the craft with a signalling torch using the white light. The signals to be sent on the torch will be the same as those sent on the D/F transmitter.

12. In the event of Comm with the Naval Force failing, signals will be fired by Very pistol but only under orders of O i/c NELSON
13. Very light signals
i. To indicate the direction of the beach to the Naval Force:
ii. Two green lights will be fired, one to the right and the other to the left along the base of and below the cliffs.

ADMINISTRATION
1. Normal morning routine.
2. 1000 hrs. Pack containers — check weapons and arms.
3. 1400 hrs. Containers to Thruxton.
4. 1700 hrs. Tea.
5. 1930 hrs. Move to THRUXTON by MT.
6. 2030 hrs. Arrive THRUXTON.
7. 2100 hrs. Tea & refreshments.
8. 2115 hrs. Fit statichutes.
9. 2140 hrs. March to aircraft.
10. 2200 hrs. All troops emplaned by.
11. 2215 hrs. First aircraft takes off.

Feb '42
JOHN FROST
Commanding 'C' Coy 2nd Parachute Bn

Appendix II

Order of Battle for C Company 2nd Parachute Battalion 28 February 1942

Wave I — W/Cdr Pickard
Group NELSON — 2/Lt Charteris

Whitley 'G'
Captain — W/Cdr Charles Pickard
Nelson I (dropped 0015)
#01 — **2/Lt Euan Charteris**
#02 — Cpl Thomas Hill
#03 — Pte Charles Branwhite
#04 — Pte Peter Venters
#05 — Sgt Alex Gibbins
#06 — Pte Donald Sutherland
#07 — Pte Peter McCormack
#08 — Pte Jack Grafton
#09 — Pte Tom Laughland
#10 — Pte Henry Matkin
Special equipment: 1 38 wireless

Whitley 'B'

Captain — Fl/Lt C Towsey
Nelson II (dropped 0014)
#01 — Sgt David Tasker
#02 — L/Cpl Hughie Dickie
#03 — Pte William Wood
#04 — Pte Bill Sturges
#05 — **Sgt James Sharp**
#06 — Pte Robert Coates
#07 — Pte James Henderson
#08 — Pte Albert Synyer
#09 — Pte William Goold
#10 — Pte Fred Barnett

Whitley 'U'

Captain — Fl/Lt G R Coates
Nelson III (dropped 0014)
#01 — Sgt William Sunley
#02 — Cpl William McLennan
#03 — L/Cpl Archie Kerr
#04 — Pte William Shaw
#05 — **Capt John Ross**
#06 — Pte James Calderwood
#07 — Pte Alan Ewing
#08 — Pte Albert Heron
#09 — Pte William Grant
#10 — Pte Thacker
Special Equipment: 1 38 wireless set

Whitley 'T'
Captain — Sgt John Pohe
Nelson IV (dropped 0015)
#01 — Pte John Willoughby
#02 — Sgt Leslie Ellis
#03 — Sap Vic Mitchell
#04 — Pte Eric Freeman
#05 — Pte William Fleming
#06 — Pte Frank Creighton
#07 — Pte David Horne
#08 — Pte Sidney Hughes
#09 — **Sgt David Grieve**
#10 — Cpl Victor Stewart
Special equipment: 1 mine-detector, 5 anti-tank mines

Wave II — S/Ldr Peveler
Group DRAKE — Major Frost

Whitley 'F'
Captain — S/Ldr Donald Peveler
Jellicoe (dropped 0020)
#01 — Sgt Gregor McKenzie
#02 — L/Cpl William Burns
#03 — Pte Henry Flitcroft
#04 — Pte Richard Drape
#05 — **2/Lt Peter Young**
#06 — Pte Frank McCausland
#07 — Pte James Wilson
#08 — Pte William Addie
#09 — Sap Norman Manning
#10 — L/Cpl R Heard
Special equipment: 1 Trolley

Whitley 'Y'
Captain — Sgt E Clow
Hardy I (dropped 0020)
#01 — **Major John Frost**
#02 — Sgt George Fleming
#03 — Cpl Sam Taylor
#04 — Pte Andrew Young
#05 — CSM Gerald Strachan
#06 — Pte James McLeod
#07 — L/Cpl Robert Dobson
#08 — Pte John Hayhurst
#09 — F/Sgt Charles Cox
#10 — Sap Stanley Halliwell
Special equipment: <u>1 Trolley</u>, <u>1 38 wireless set</u>

Whitley 'E'
Captain — Sgt Gray
Drake (dropped 0039)
#01 — Sgt Neville Lutener
#02 — L/Cpl Alex Webster
#03 — Pte Robert Beattie
#04 — Pte Michael Herwood
#05 — Sgt John Boyd
#06 — **2/Lt Peter Naoumoff**
#07 — Pte Frank Murphy
#08 — Pte John Bond
#09 — Pte Frank Welsh
#10 — Pte Frank Williamson
Special equipment: <u>1 Trolley</u>

Whitley 'Q'
Captain — Sgt Hughes
Hardy II (dropped 0020)
#01 — Cpl Sid Jones
#02 — Sgt William MacFarlane
#03 — Cpl Geoff Heslop
#04 — Pte Thomas Galey
#05 — **Lt Dennis Vernon**
#06 — Pte Robert Keyes
#07 — Pte William Gordon
#08 — Pte Hugh Mcintyre
#09 — Pte Martin Conroy
#10 — Peter Nagel (interpreter)
Special equipment: 1 38 wireless set

Wave III — S/Ldr Meade
Group JELLICOE — 2/Lt Timothy

Whitley 'O'
Captain — S/Ldr Meade
Rodney I (dropped 0024)
#01 — Sgt MacLeod Forsyth
#02 — Cpl Bernard Walker
#03 — L/Cpl Ralph T Johnston
#04 — Pte James Stephenson
#05 — **2/Lt John Timothy**
#06 — Pte William Hutchison
#07 — Pte Richard Scott
#08 — Pte Henry Crutchley
#09 — Pte Fred Greenlough
#10 — Pte Jack Millington
Special Equipment: 1 38 wireless set, 1 Eureka beacon

Whitley 'P'
Captain — P/O Mair
Rodney II (dropped 0026)
#01 — Pte Sydney Ramsey*
#02 — L/Cpl William Fleming
#03 — Pte Patrick McCann
#04 — Pte Tom Higgins
#05 — **Sgt Robert Muir**
#06 — Pte John Judge
#07 — Pte Gavin Cadden
#08 — Sap Francis Hornsby
#09 — Pte George Collier
#10 — Pte Ernest Richardson
Special equipment: 1 mine-detector, 1 Eureka beacon

Whitley 'M'
Captain — P/O Jeff Haydon
Rodney III (dropped 0024)
#01 — Cpl. David Finnie
#02 — Pte Rob Stirling
#03 — Pte Peter Buchanan
#04 — Pte Ernest Lough
#05 — **Sgt Alex Reid**
#06 — Pte W Craw
#07 — Pte James O'Neill
#08 — Sap Fred Harris
#09 — Pte David Thomas
#10 — L/Cpl John McCallum
Special equipment: 1 18 wireless set

---

* This is the most complete company roll and dropping order that can be compiled, but doubts surround the correctness of a few names such as Ramsey and spelling of – for instance – McKenzie.

Whitley 'X'
Captain — Sgt Andy Cook
Rodney IV (dropped 0025 & 0030)
#01 — Cpl Henry Campbell
#02 — Pte George Cornell
#03 — Pte Alan Scott
#04 — Pte Frank Embury
#05 — **Sgt Tom Lumb**
#06 — L/Cpl Robert Findlay
#07 — Pte Joseph Eden
#08 — Pte George Stacey
#09 — Sgt Alex Bennett
#10 — Pte Allan Ward
Special equipment: <u>1 18 wireless set</u>

Appendix III

Maj. Gen. Frederick Browning's After-action Report on Operation Biting, March 1942

[UKNA WO106/4133]

OPERATION 'BITING'

REPORT BY
MAJOR-GENERAL F A M BROWNING, DSO
COMMANDER, THE AIRBORNE DIVISION

INTRODUCTION
1. The Air Ministry had information that the Germans had a new type of 53cm RDF equipment, which was playing an important part in the control of German 'flak' and probably in the control of searchlights. It was a serious menace to our aircraft. Counter-measures to give adequate protection to our aircraft were being investigated but these were hampered by the lack of information about the enemy apparatus.
2. An object, presumed to be one of these 53cm sets was reported to be situated at THEUVILLE (49° 40' 28" N, 09' 41" E) a little north of LE HAVRE. It was believed to consist of a paraboloid (9ft diameter) and a small cabin

(about 6ft x 5ft x 4ft) mounted rotatably on a trolley.

3. The above information was given to Commodore, Combined Operations (Commodore The Lord Louis Mountbatten, GCVO, DSO) who, after consulting GOC The Airborne Division, obtained the approval of the Chiefs of Staffs Committee to an operation by parachute troops to capture this RDF set. The Chiefs of Staffs agreed on 21 Jan '42 that one operational Whitley Squadron from Bomber Command RAF, one company of parachute troops and sufficient light naval craft to evacuate the force by sea, should be made available. It was later decided to include some personnel of 5 Corps to act as escort to the ALC's; they were not to take part in the operations on land.

TRAINING

4. 'C' Coy. 2 Parachute Bn., under command of Major J D Frost, Cameronians, were selected for the operation, though both 1 Parachute Bde and the company were then under the impression that they were required only for training in combined operations with Royal Navy and RAF. Major Bromley-Martin was detailed as Liaison Officer at HQ The Airborne Division, with the tasks of detailed preliminary planning and obtaining of equipment.

5. Having been delayed for a few days by snow, 'C' Coy moved South from HARDWICK CAMP to TILSHEAD CAMP (SALISBURY PLAIN) on 24th Jan '42 and commenced training immediately. The first part of their programme, as originally drawn up, was interrupted by the weather, with

heavy falls of snow and intense cold. The
result was, that when the Coy. moved to
INVERARAY for preliminary training with Royal
Navy on 9th Feb '42, they had not been able to
do any parachute drops and very little
satisfactory ground training. At INVERARAY,
elementary combined training was done with
Royal Navy and inter-services signal codes
were arranged.

6. The Coy. arrived back at TILSHEAD on 14 Feb
'42, and were then kept very busy doing their
own ground training, one drop as a company
from the aircraft which would carry them on
the operation, and combined training with
Royal Navy and RAF. Much time had to be wasted
in travelling by road between TILSHEAD and the
South Coast, as the weather was very
treacherous and no less than four unsuccessful
attempts were made to carry out the required
training with the MGBs and ALCs of Royal Navy.
This wasted time would have been of great
value to the Coy. for ground training [in
battle tactics].

7. Apart from the normal training carried out by
each of the Services, it was considered
advisable that they should all be able to
train on ground similar to that on which the
operation would take place. A suitable place
was found at Golden Ball Hill 5784 (on the
South MARLBOROUGH DOWNS) which, with some
alterations, resembled the actual place
sufficiently both from the air and from the
ground, though distances were not correct and
slopes too gradual [in reality exercises were
carried out slightly south of Golden Ball

Hill, closer to the canal]. In future, it should be noted that, for ground training, it is often more important that distances should be correct than anything else.

Three beaches on the South coast between SWANAGE and WEYMOUTH were selected by Royal Navy as being suitable for practices. After further reconnaissance from the air and ground aspects, it was agreed that they should be used, weather permitting, in the following order of priority:

i. ARISH MELL COVE 2801
ii. ½ mile East of REDCLIFF POINT 1502
iii. BOWLEASE COVE 1302

113 Inf Bde (Brigadier D C Butterworth, DSO) through H, 38 Div, 5 Corps and Southern Command, were detailed to clear the beaches sufficiently of mines, scaffolding and wire. They were most helpful in doing this, which meant a very great deal of apparently wasteful work for them. Gunnery Wing, A F V School, LULWORTH, were also most helpful in allowing the use of their training ground and in providing excellent accommodation and meals at short notice.

OTHER TROOPS TAKING PART
8. Other troops taking part in the operation were:
i. 5 ORs per ALC to act solely as escort to the ALCs. Each of the parties were armed with four Bren LMGs (with 500 rounds per gun) and four anti-tank Rifles (with 40 rpg). To provide the required numbers and reserves, one officer and

25 ORs from each of 8th Monmouth Regt. and 11th Bn. Royal Fusiliers joined HMS Prince Albert at INVERARAY on 10 Feb and remained on board her or in the ALCs until 1 Mar '42. 20 ORs from each R'ment actually accompanied the ALCs but did not land or attack the beach defences.

ii. 1 Officer and 20 ORs. Medical personnel from 181 Fd Amb, the Airborne Division. They also joined HMS Prince Albert at INVERARAY on 12 Feb and left her on 1 Mar '42. They accompanied the ALCs during the operation (see Appendix 'K').

PROVISION OF EQUIPMENT AND WEAPONS

9. The provision of special equipment and weapons required was rendered very difficult for two reasons:

i. The fact that much of this equipment was very new and only in the experimental stage and that it had to come from many different sources. As the Division becomes better equipped, this difficulty will not be so acute.

ii. For security reasons, the need for both new and standard equipment not actually held by the Division could not always be quoted as an operational requirement and questions by inquisitive staff officers had to be parried. It is essential that in future HQ Combined Operations should be empowered to demand.

A list of special equipment obtained (other than Engineer or Signal) is given at Appendix 'B'. A list and description of Engineer and Signal Equipment is given in Appendix 'J' and 'K'.

10. Containers were obtained and provided by AFEE Ringway under special arrangements made by them. These arrangements were not then produced in any numbers. All containers were specially marked and fitted with coloured lights turned on by impact, to assist in easy identification. The packing of every container was worked out by AFEE who also calculated CG positions, for every aircraft lending and supplied packing diagrams and loading schedules. These are attached at Appx 'C' and 'F'.
11. Statichutes were provided by 38 Wing RAF, both for practices and for the operations.

INFORMATION
12. All information about the RDF Station, the enemy's dispositions, and defences, and all photos and models of the ground and buildings, were provided through HQ Combined Operations. Apart from anything else, this is essential for reasons of security and no enquiries can be made direct to other sources by personnel of the Airborne Division.

A summary of all the intelligence is contained in Airborne Div. Operation Order No 1 and in an additional intelligence summary attached to that order.

Additional photos, of which there is only one copy, are attached. The model of BRUNEVAL and district (scale 1/2000) is held at HQ The Airborne Division. Another model of the house and the RDF Station was returned to HQ Combined Operations. All photographs and models, which were really excellent, were provided by CIU Medmenham, through HQ Combined Operations.

SPECIALIST PERSONNEL

13. Certain specialist personnel were required to deal with the RDF Station. Flight Lieutenant Priest was given a temporary commission in the RAF so that he could accompany the force and provide expert scientific knowledge if required; he was taken over in an ALC and was not allowed to drop by parachute, as his capture by the enemy could not be risked. In fact, he did not land but his knowledge was of great assistance.

F/Sgt Cox, RAF, a RDF specialist, was trained in parachute jumping at PTS RINGWAY and actually dropped with 'C' Coy. to assist in dismantling the RDF apparatus. His work was excellent throughout.

No. 13801753 Pte. Nagle, 93 Pioneer Coy., a German fighting against Hitler, also joined 'C' Coy. and dropped with them. His knowledge of the German language and the psychology of Germans proved of great assistance.

All the above specialists were obtained through HQ Combined Operations.

SECURITY

14. The success of the operation proved that there had been no leakage of information to the Germans. Nevertheless security was by no means perfect.

When the operation was first planned, only a very few essential people knew that it was contemplated at all, what was the object of the operation and the fact that the Airborne Division was taking part. Secrecy was to be preserved by using a 'cover story' to the effect that training was being carried out in a new phase of combined operations. Further, it was understood that no army personnel outside the Airborne Division was to take part; the resources of the Airborne Division were entirely adequate and no waste of specialists would have been involved in any way.

Three main reasons contributed to breaches of security as training progressed:

i. Difficulties in obtaining essential weapons, amn. and equipment without quoting operational requirements. This was reduced to the minimum by HQ Combined Operations, who, as far as possible, obtained all that was required for the Division.
ii. The necessity for beaches in Southern Command to be cleared of mines, scaffolding etc, for training. This work was very extensive and had to be done by, or with the knowledge of, the local troops.
iii. The fact that the 'cover story', that the whole object of everything was 'combined training', was not adhered to by GHQ Home Forces. Their letter No. HFS/CC/122/Ops (P) dated 28th Jan. 1942, which was not seen by the Airborne Division until after it had been sent, was the first indication to anyone outside HQ Combined Operations and HQ The Airborne Division, that British parachutists

were ready for or about to take part in an operation.

There were a few cases of officers and ORs mentioning unnecessarily that an operation was to take place, or hinting to that effect. They did not realise that the fact that an operation is even being considered is as much of a secret as the details of that operation. They did not appear to realise that their carelessness or desire to 'show off' might result in a disaster and loss of life. Action has been, and is being, taken to prevent such mistakes in future.

Security would be far more easily preserved if:

i. Troops from units outside the Airborne Division need not be used.
ii. The Heads of departments at the War Office and GHQ Home Forces which must be concerned with an operation, ie Operations, Intelligence, Staff Duties, could be told that an operation by the Airborne Division was planned and that when requirements backed by the HQ Combined Operations were submitted, they must be met on the highest priority. No officers except heads of departments should be told under any circumstances that an operation is to take pace, and they should be forbidden to pass on any information to either senior or junior officers without permission from CCC.
iii. A 'scrambled' telephone could be provided at HQ The Airborne Division.

CO-ORDINATION OF PLANNING

15. The co-ordination of all planning, including preliminary training and provision of equipment, was done by HQ Combined Operations until Commander-in-Chief, PORTSMOUTH, took over, as Supreme Commander. Copies of minutes of all meetings held at HQ Combined Operations are attached at Appx. 'D'.

ORGANISATION OF COMMAND FOR THE OPERATION

16. 16. Commanders of the forces of Royal Navy, Army and Royal Air Force taking part were nominated as under:

Naval Force Commander — Commander F N Cook, RAN
OC Parachute Troops — Major J D Frost, OC 'C' Coy., 2 Parachute Bn.
RAF Force Commander — Group Capt. Sir Nigel Norman, Bt. OC 38 Wing, RAF

Commander-in-Chief, PORTSMOUTH (Admiral Sir W M James, KCB) was nominated as Supreme Commander and Operation HQ was in his Operations Room at FORT WALLINGTON.

All troops on board HMS Prince Albert and the MGBs and ALCs were under the orders of Commander F N Cook.

Wing Commander P C Pickard, DSO, DFC, commanded 51 Sqn RAF, Lieut. Commander W G Everitt, RN commanded 14th Motor Gunboat Flotilla, and Lieut. Commander H B Peate commanded HMS Prince Albert.

Group Captain Sir Nigel Norman and Lt. Col. A G Walsh, GSO1 The Airborne Division, were at the HQ of Commander-in-Chief, PORTSMOUTH, throughout the operation.

38 Wing RAF had arranged direct telephone communications with 51 Sqn's aerodrome at Thruxton and with RAF TANGMERE.

RE, SIGS, MED

17. Separate reports are attached

Their orders for the operation are included in Airborne Division Operation Order No. 1

PRESS REPRESENTATIVES

18. HQ Combined Operations arranged for three representatives of the Press to sail in HMS Prince Albert, under the orders of SNO. Two were allowed in the ALCs. None were allowed to land. Their reports were subject to control by HQ Combined Operations direct.

ORDER TO CARRY OUT THE OPERATION

19. On 27th Feb. '42, the following message was received at HQ The airborne Division, following a 'disguised' telephone message received at 1500 hrs.

MESSAGE CYPHER

(IMMEDIATE)

To: HQ 11 Gp, HQFC, HQBC, GOC Airborne Div., SOUTHERN COMD. Rptd. Admiralty. 257 Commodore Combined Ops.

From: C-in-C PORTSMOUTH

MOST SECRET (.) following is repetition my 1507 A
27th Feb. (.) Begins added HMS PRINS ALBERT
TORMENTOR senior offr 14th Motor Gunboat flotilla
GOC Airborne Div. Southern Comd. HQ Bomber Comd.
rptd HQ 11 Group. HQ Fighter Comd. HQ Bomber Comd.
rptd Admiralty 257 Commodore Combined Operations
from C in C PORTSMOUTH (.) Carry out operation
BITING tonight
27 Feb.

TOO. 1507
A/27 ends.

TAKE-OFF AND FLIGHT IN AIRCRAFT

20. The take-off and flight in aircraft went
exactly according to plan. Some flak was met
in the area of ST. JOUIN and some damage was
done to aircraft but not to personnel. This
has been reported in detail by the Air Force
Commander.

DROPPING OFF PARACHUTISTS

21. Two aircraft dropped their parachutists South
of the dropping zone. Estimates of how far
South they were dropped vary between 1500
yards and 3 miles. One aircraft dropped 15
minutes late. The remaining aircraft dropped
their parachutists according to plan. All
containers were dropped successfully and were
found quickly. There was no enemy AA fire on
the dropping zone and none of the parachutists
were fired at as they dropped.

ACTION AFTER LANDING

22. NELSON (less that part which had been dropped short) moved off unopposed to attack the beach defences. They were partly successful but could not complete their task owing to shortage of personnel.

HARDY and JELLICOE formed up and moved off according to plan. During this time a few shots were heard and it appeared that some of the enemy were aware of the attack. HARDY surrounded and took the House and found it empty except for one German in the attic — he was killed.

JELLICOE surrounded the Radio location set; the crew of 5 men offered little resistance but all were killed [incorrect] with the exception of one Luftwaffe man who was taken prisoner. From him it was learnt that there were 100 Germans in the Rectangle and approximately one company in the BRUNEVAL area. The lighthouse at Cap d'Antifer had warned them that a parachutist raid was taking place.

In the meantime RODNEY and DRAKE had dropped. DRAKE moved to their positions near the Rectangle and when they received orders to withdraw, threw grenades and opened fire on the enemy in the Rectangle.

Some of RODNEY were in the aircraft which dropped short and RODNEY were therefore slightly under strength. However, they took up their positions in reserve without difficulty.

After the RE and RAF RDF experts had taken what was required from the RDF set, HARDY, JELLICOE and DRAKE withdrew Southwards about half way to the beach, when it was learnt that the beach defences had not yet been taken completely by NELSON.

The Company Commander detailed a party under Lieut. Young from HARDY, JELLICOE and DRAKE to assist NELSON to take the remaining beach defences.

This was done successfully and soon afterwards 2/Lieut. Charteris, who was in charge of that party of NELSON which had dropped short, arrived with 4 of his men and took over the beach according to plan.

RODNEY, who had been engaged with some enemy fire from the Rectangle, then moved to the beach under the orders of the Company Commander.

HARDY and all technical experts, with the equipment which they had collected, also moved down to the beach. The remainder of the company was arranged in defensive positions near the beach while contact was made with the Navy.

This was done by No. 38 Wireless Set and a Very Pistol, as the signallers with No. 18 sets were amongst those who had been dropped short.

As soon as the ALCs arrived, orders were given for the whole company to withdraw and embark. This was done successfully with the exception of a small party, including the signallers mentioned before who had not yet reported to the beach.

At about 0300 hours it appeared from various vehicle lights that were seen that reinforcements were arriving just North of the Rectangle and possibly a counter-attack might have been put in at about 0330 hours. The troops actually left the beach at 0315 hours.

At 0815 hours a wireless message was received from Commander Cook that the operation had been successful.

RETURN SEA VOYAGE

23. One MGB, with the RDF equipment and technical experts, returned independently at high speed and reached HMS Prince Albert off SPITHEAD at 1000 hours 28 Feb.

The remainder of the force arrived at 1630 hours on 28 Feb, the sea being moderately rough most of that day.

No. 11 Group Fighter Command had fighters protecting the returning boats from about 0815 hours 28 Feb until they were all back. In consequence, no German aircraft interfered in any way.

PRISONERS

24. 3 German prisoners were brought back in the boats, including one man of the Luftwaffe.

CASUALTIES

25. German casualties are estimated at a minimum of 40 killed.

Our own casualties were as follows. There were no casualties amongst 5 Corps troops in the boats, the Royal Navy or RAF.

<u>Killed</u>

3252284 Pte. McIntyre, H — 'C' Coy, 2 Parachute Bn.
Pte. Scott — /Wounded.

Wounded

2751640 CSM Strachan, G — 'C' Coy, 2 Parachute Bn.
3195970 Sgt. Boyd, J — 'C' Coy, 2 Parachute Bn.
2929915 Cpl. Heslop, G — 'C' Coy, 2 Parachute Bn.
2879337 Cpl. Stewart, V — 'C' Coy, 2 Parachute Bn.
2037582 L/C Heard, R — Air Troops, RE, 1 Parachute Bde.
2928756 Pte. Grant, W — 'C'Coy, 2 Parachute Bn.
3058375 Pte. Shaw, H — 'C'Coy, 2 Parachute Bn.

Missing (ie left in France, no details available)

2930416 L/C MacCallum, J — 'C' Coy, 2 Parachute Bn.
2879968 Pte. Sutherland, J — 'C' Coy, 2 Parachute Bn.
4745152 Pte Willoughby, J — 'C' Coy, 2 Parachute Bn.
5951642 Pte. Thomas, D — 'C' Coy, 2 Parachute Bn.
4622613 Pte. Cornell, G — 'C' Coy, 2 Parachute Bn.
5047949 Pte. Embury, E — 'C' Coy, 2 Parachute Bn.
5347681 Pte. Scott, A — 'C' Coy, 2 Parachute Bn.

26. <u>GERMAN TROOPS AND DEFENCES</u>

See Appx. 'O'.

27. SUCCESS OF THE OPERATION

The operation was completely successful.

A preliminary report on the value of the RDF equipment captured is attached to Appx. '1'. Since that report was written, it has been ascertained definitely that all the equipment required was captured and brought in very good condition.

The prisoner of the Luftwaffe who was captured had spent some time previously in a German Concentration Camp and was willing to talk. As he is a RDF expert, the information he has given has been sufficient to complete the whole picture.

28. PUBLICITY

In addition to the reports of the three Press representatives who accompanied the boats, one officer, one NCO and one Pte. of the parachutists reported to HQ Combined Operations to give interviews to the Press. They were allowed to describe the operation in full, except that they were forbidden to reveal the fact that RDF equipment was brought back; that is still secret information.

The BBC were to have broadcast a talk by Major Frost, but, although recorded, the talk was later forbidden by the Ministry of Information.

29. DESCRIPTION OF OPERATION TO WAR CABINET AND CHIEFS OF STAFF

At 2100 hours on 2 Mar 42, GOC the Airborne Division, with GSO1 and Major J D Frost, attended a meeting of the War Cabinet and Chiefs of Staff at which the following were present:

The Rt Hon W L S Churchill, PC,CH, TD, LLD, MP — Prime Minister
The Rt Hon R A Eden, PC, NC, MP — Secretary of State for Foreign Affairs
The Rt Hon Sir James Grigg, PC,KCB, KCSI — Secretary of State for War
The Rt Hon A V Alexander, PC, CH, MP — First Lord of the Admiralty
The Rt Hon Sir Archibald Sinclair Bt., KT, PC, CMG, MP — Secretary of State for Air
The Rt Hon C R Attlee, PC, MP — Deputy Prime Minister
Capt. The Rt Hon O Lyttleton, PC, DSO, MC — Minister of Production
Admiral of the Fleet Sir Dudley Pound, GCH, GCVC — First Sea Lord
General Sir Alan Brooke, CB, DSC — Chief of the Imperial General Staff
Air Chief Marshal Sir Charles Portal, KCS, DSO, MC — Chief of the Air Staff
Commodore the Lord Louis Mountbatten, GCVC, DSO — Commodore, Combined Operations
Wing-Commander The Marquis of Casa Maury — SIC, HQ, Combined Operations

Appendix IV

Extracts from the Report of the Telecommunications Research Establishment on the German Technology Captured at Bruneval

1. INTRODUCTION

This report follows the Interim Report on the Technical Results of the Raid on Bruneval … (Most Secret) and is a purely technical description of the station. Information about methods of jamming this and other stations together with observations of a more operational nature will be contained in a separate report entitled 'Report on the Investigation of Enemy Short Range RDF Stations', TRE ref 6/R/13. Certain information in this present report was extracted from a Prisoner's Report.

2. GENERAL LAYOUT OF THE STATION

All the equipment was mounted on a mobile trailer. On this trailer was a single paraboloid 2.8 metres in diameter, to the back of which was fixed all the apparatus with the exception of the presentation equipment. The latter was inside the operating cabin which was mounted to the rear and slightly to one side of the paraboloid.

The paraboloid was movable both in azimuth and in elevation, the first being done either manually by a hand-wheel in the operating cabin, or electrically by an operator-controlled push-button. Elevation was done manually only. D/F was obtained by working on the maximum of the lobe.

Power for the apparatus was obtained from the French 50 cycle AC mains. All the apparatus is designed to work off AC, probably at 175 volts; the power supplies were not captured but the modulator unit contains a transformer which required this primary voltage.

On this particular site, the trailer was parked about 50 yards from the edge of a 300 ft cliff, thus enabling very low angle radiation to be obtained in a seaward direction.

The transmitter, receiver, modulator, and some power supplies were mounted in boxes on the back of the paraboloid on shockproof mountings. All the boxes were captured with the exception of the power supply, and comprise:

 i. The T/R Box
 ii. The Modulator Box
 iii. The Receiver IF Amplifier Box

The T/R box is made of cast aluminium and is 24½" x 10½" x 6¼". It contains three separate withdrawable units; the transmitter, the receiver mixer, and the receiver local oscillator, as shown in Plate I (Appendix). At the back of the box is the common T and R feeder system and the connection to the main feeder.

The modulator box measures 13" x 12¾" x 6¾" and contains the transmitter modulator only.

The receiver IF box measures 6½" x 7" x 12½" and contains about half the total IF amplifier. The other half was probably contained in the presentation equipment (which was not captured) inside the cabin.

Also on the back of the paraboloid was a small switchboard consisting of 10 push-buttons for switching the apparatus on and off.

The contents of the three boxes will now be described in detail.

3. DETAILS OF TRANSMITTER MODULATOR

a. General

Modulation of the transmitter is effected by super-imposing on a fixed negative grid bias voltage a positive pulse which brings the grid cathode potential to zero at the start of the pulse. During the pulse the oscillation is biased back to a value depending on the amount of grid current, and the energy of the pulse is formed by the tail of the modulating pulse. There is no squegging in the circuit.

The width of the pulse given out by the modulator is about 2 microseconds and can be changed to about 1½ microsec. by means of a relay in the modulator unit.

The HT voltage is applied to the oscillator continuously.

b. Circuit and Performances

Circuit is appended. To see how the actual modulation is performed, it is easiest to consider first the functions of valves 6 and 7. It will be seen that these two valves are in series and that between the anode of V6 and the cathode of V7 there is a resistance W27 across which is developed the grid cathode potential applied to V7.

Production of the pulse is effected by switching Valve 6 on and off. During the quiescent period V6 is conducting and anode current flows through it and through the chain of resistances, W22–26, from the cathode of V7 up to the earth line. There is a small potential drop across W27 sufficient to cut off V7. Thus the oscillator grid which is connected to Pin 15 is held negative by approx. 800 volts which is the voltage applied to Pin 16 from an external power supply which was not captured.

The magnitude of the bias voltage applied to pin 16 is estimated at 800 because:

i. The discharge tube between pins 15 and 16 flashes over at 800 V. Thus if the pulse produced across these pins were more than 800 V. in amplitude it would flash over.
ii. The valves flash over inside at about 1000 V. between anode and cathode.
iii. The monitoring CRT becomes defocussed beyond the limits of the focussing control (W.66) if the line voltage is increased beyond about 900 V.
iv. Assuming a normal deflection sensitivity for the monitoring CRT of 30 V./cm. (unfortunately the CRT plate assembly was broken during its journey to England) the deflection voltage in the Y plate could not be greater than 60 volts; otherwise the picture would not all be on the tube.

Actually when the bias voltage on pin 16 is -800 the deflection voltage is about 60 volts.

Now consider what happens when V6 is cut off. There will no longer be any anode current flowing nor will there be any negative potential drop across W27, therefore V7 will conduct and the grid of the oscillator will now be tied down to the earth line through V7 which will have a low impedance and will pass the negative grid current taken by the oscillator.

At the end of the pulse V6 is turned on again and V7 is turned off thus biassing the oscillator grid back to its previous value.

The purpose of the time constant C21 and W33 in the grid line is probably to prevent excess anode dissipation in the oscillator valve due to accidental CW oscillation.

The discharge tube G which flashes over at 800 volts is probably a device for preventing 'blocking' of the oscillator due to reverse grid current because it will not allow the mean grid cathode potential of the oscillator to go more than a few volts positive.

The rest of the modulator is a generator of pulses of sufficient amplitude to turn V6 on and off on its control grid, plus a circuit for providing negative going pulses which are used for blacking out the presentation CRT and for suppressing the receiver during the transmitted pulse.

Starting at the beginning a negative going square wave is applied to the grid of V1, probably of only a few volts amplitude, from an external source which is probably the presentation equipment. A positive going wave front is

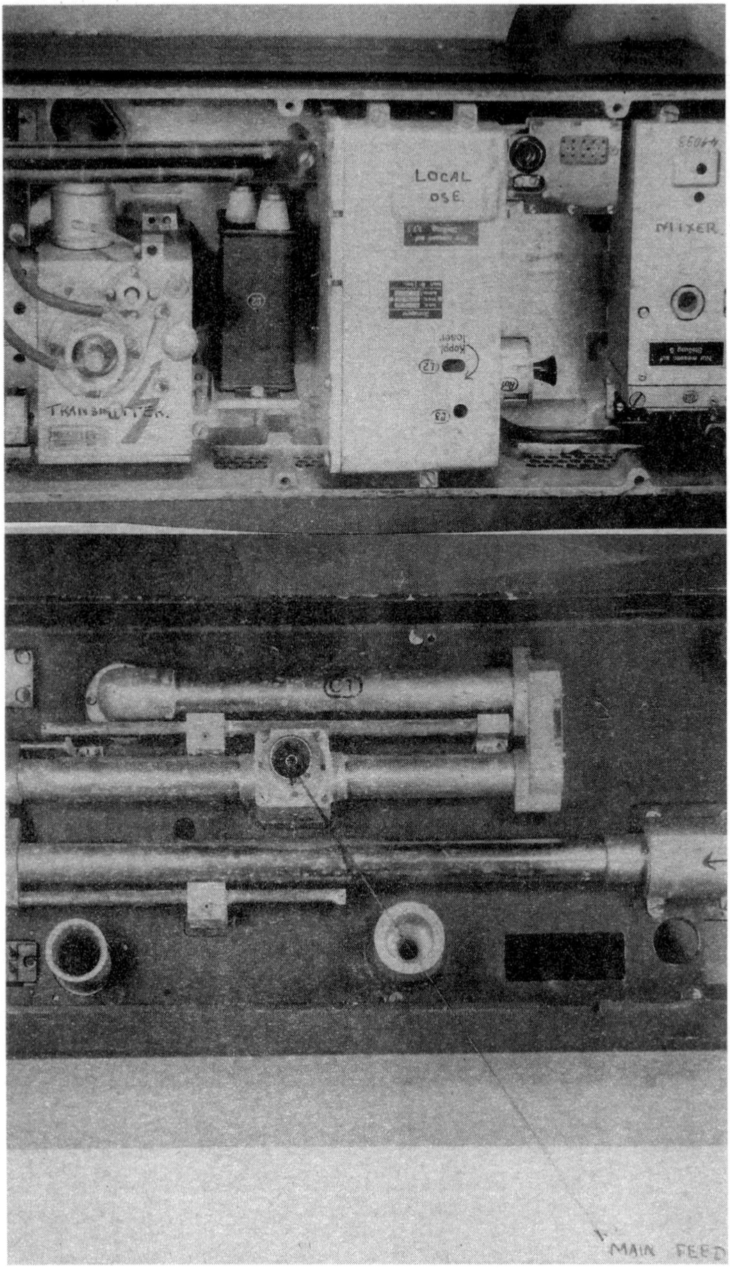
LOCAL
MIXER
TRANSMITTER.
C1
MAIN FEED

therefore applied to the grid of V2 which has a small transformer in its anode circuit, the secondary of which is connected to the grid of V3 which is normally biased beyond cut-off. This pulse transformer produces a small positive going impulse of about 1 microsec. in width on the grid of V3 and this valve amplifies it and applies a larger but negative pulse to the grid of V4 via a relay operated pulse widening circuit (W12, C7, C6) which enables one of two pulse widths to be applied to the grid of V4. This valve amplifies the pulse further. The circuit then branches, the anode of V4 being fed through condensers to:

i. The grid of V5 which is an amplifier feeding the grid of V6. This is the modulator part of the circuit.
ii. The grid of V8. This is the beginning of the blacking-out part of the circuit.

The action of valves 5, 6 and 7 has already been described. Valves 8, 9 and 10 are used for producing across the anode load of V10 a negative going pulse of amplitude very nearly equal to the bias voltage on Pin 16 (-800 volts approx.). This black-out pulse is wider than the modulating pulse owing to the presence of W51 and C29, in the grid circuit of V9, and actually is about 3 microsec. wide, but decreases with the modulating pulse when the relay is operated. The output from V10 is taken to two pins Nos. 14 and 17 in the circuit diagram; between Pin 14 and earth a negative pulse of about 40 volts is produced; this is probably used for blacking-out the presentation CRT during the transmitted pulse, and between Pin 17 and earth the amplitude is nearly 800 volts approx. This large pulse is used for suppressing the receiver during the transmitted pulse.

A cathode ray tube is used for monitoring. A simple time-base is provided by the anode voltage wave front of V1 which is applied via a slowing-up circuit to one X-plate only, and one Y-plate is switched by means of the key switch on the front of the modulator to measure either the modulator pulse (condenser network C36, C37 and C40) or the black-out pulse (network C38 and C39).

It is known from Intelligence listening and confirmed indirectly by information from a prisoner-of-war that the unit is designed to work with a pulse repetition frequency of 3750 per second.

A transformer for supplying the valve and CRT heaters and the bias for the grid of V5 is incorporated in the modulator unit and is intended for use with a primary voltage of 175 volts at 50 cps. Another feature of interest is the small testing panel on the front of the unit to which the measuring points as indicated on the circuit diagram are brought out.

Two details of the circuit are difficult to understand.

Firstly, the bias voltage on the grid of V5 and V10 was measured and found to be -300 volts. Thus in order to drive the grids of V5 positive a positive pulse of at least 250 volts is required at the anode of V4. This would mean that the H.T.line on valves 1,2,3,4, 8 & 9 would have to be 300 volts plus the drop across V4. It was found necsssary to raise this voltage to 400 before V5 started to conduct during the tip of the pulse.

Now at this H.T. voltage the anode resistances of V1, V4 and V5 are definitely over-run and the total screen and anode current of valves 1,2,3,4, 8 and 9 amounts to 250 mA approx. Further, it is difficult to see why the bias voltage on V5 needs to be 1300, as with the working screen voltage of 150, the valve cuts off at -40. As the pulse across W16 has very steep sides it does not seem necessary to bias back V5 and drive it hard on the grounds of obtaining a good pulse shape. Therefore during the tests an external resistance of 100 K. was put across the bias unit output as shown dotted in the ORT diagram (Fig. 1). This reduced the bias to -100 volts and allowed the HT on the other valves to be reduced to 150 at which everything ran at a reasonable temperature.

The second peculiarity of the circuit is that the network W43, W44, and lamp Roll is obviously intended as a means of observing whether the bias voltage on Pin 16 is actually present. The front of the containing case is cut away to show Roll which is a neon tube which flashes over at 150 volts and become non-conducting at a voltage only 2 or 3 volts less than this.

But for 150 V. across the lamp, the bias voltage would have to be -6000 which it definitely is not. This has so far not been explained.

c. Valves and Cathode Ray Tube

The valves in the modulator are all of the same type, namely Telefunken LS50's. Those are dealt with in detail in the Valve and CRT section of this report. This valve is a pentode and characteristics as measured at TRE are appended. The valve is of exceedingly robust construction like all the valves in this equipment. All the leads are brought out through the base.

The CRT is similar to our VCR91 and has a green screen.

d. Method of Construction of the Unit

The unit is of extremely robust construction and makes full use of aluminium alloy castings and pressings, bakelite mouldings and ceramic terminal blocks. Details of the construction can be seen from the appended photographs of the unit. Points of interest are the method of holding the valves in position which is virtually foolproof, the method of holding the CRT in position which incorporates a mechanical device for ejecting the CRT and the fact that ceramic valve holders are used throughout, although there are no ultra high frequencies present. Also the small size of some of the fixed condensers with respect to their voltage rating is particularly note-worthy, ie C33 is a 1 microfarad 25)450 volts condenser measuring 1" x 1" x 1". The excellent manufacture of the output connections is also of interest.

4. DETAILS OF TRANSMITTER

The transmitter proper is a single valve oscillator modulated on its grid and using a simple Colpitts circuit. The anode circuit consists of a tuned line which is very short owing to the valve inter-electric capacity. A variable ceramic condenser which can be tuned externally forms the only tuning control on the equipment. The HT is fed through a ceramic condenser bushing of interesting design, and the grid is fed in through a smaller bushing of low capacity to ground.

The power is taken off by the serial feeder which is tapped on to a lumped resonant circuit, coupled inductively on to the main tank circuit. The serial feeder is attached to the oscillator unit by means of a large concentric plug.

The valve is a Telefunken LS180. The grid and anode are brought out through the top of the valve through double seals (to reduce the lead out inductance) and the filament is brought out through the base of the valve (see photographs). The filament is a double spiral. The grid is a parallel wire cylinder (squirrel cage) and the anode is heavily finned for cooling.

The filament is thoriated tungsten and takes 12½ amperes at 6.2 volts AC.

The maximum anode voltage is not known exactly but is definitely above 11 kV.

The frequency limit is not known but probably lies in the region of 750 Mc/s.

a. Test Results

The following figures were obtained on test:

    Pulse width — 2 microsec
    Recurrence freq. (fr) — 250 per sec
    Anode voltage (Va) — 9 kV
    Bias voltage — 800 volts
    Mean Anode current Ia (mean) — 1.25 mA
    Peak anode current IA (peak — 2.5 amps
    Power input Wi (mean) — 11.25 watts
    Power input Wi (peak) — 22.5 kW
    Watts in load lamp — 2.25
    Peak Output (kW.) — 5.6
    Mean watts dissipated — 8.45
    Anode efficiency — 25%

Allowing for the higher recurrence frequency used in operation, the probably working conditions are as follows:

Width — 2 microsec
fr — 3750 per sec
VA — 10 kV
Bias voltage — 800 V
Ia (mean) — 21 mA
IA (peak) — 2.68 amps
Wi (mean) — 210 watts
Wout (mean) — 52.5 watts
Wdiss. (mean) — 157.5 watts
Wi (peak) — 26.8 kW
Wo (peak) — 7.0 kW
Efficiency — 25%

This is a conservative estimate and it is possible that the efficiency was slightly higher than 25%.

b. Methods of Construction

As can be seen from the photographs the oscillator is a separate unit which can be plugged into the T and R box. It is made entirely of aluminium castings and is completely enclosed so that there is no power lost by radiation.

The design of the circuits shows no great novelty of technique but it is considered that they are both efficient and simple in construction. It is difficult to see how the valve could have been made to give appreciably more power by any other form of construction.

5. DETAILS OF RECEIVER
The stages in the three receiver units are as shown in block form in Fig.3.

The initial frequency changer is a double diode, Telefunken LG2, with a $\lambda/4$ balanced line circuit between anodes, the signal being fed on to the circuit from a screened twin feeder.

The local oscillator employs two Telefunken LD2 valves operating in a tuned-plate tuned-grid circuit on about 146 Mc/s. This oscillator drives a Telefunken LD5 valve used as a quadrupler which feeds, through a length of cable, a high Q resonant circuit made of lumped concentric L and C elements, mounted on the rear of the frequency-changer box. The oscillator feed to the mixer is by means of a small probe, roughly a $\frac{1}{4}\lambda$ long, projecting from the concentric circuit to between the ends of the diode line.

The output of the mixer is at 25 Mc/s. and the first four stages of the IF amplifier provide amplification at this frequency. These stages are followed by a second frequency changer reducing the IF to 6.5 Mc/s. Following this mixer are three stages of amplification at 6.5 Mc/s., the output being fed at low impedance into a concentric cable. The bandwidth of the IF amplifier is 0.5 Mc. at 6 db. down.

On test the receiver gave a noise factor of 20 db. corresponding to a noise voltage of 4.1 microvolts in series with 30 ohms.

a. Frequency Changer
The frequency changer is a double diode Telefunken LG2 valve used in a $\lambda/4$ parallel line circuit housed in a cast box.

The signal from the aerial is fed through a concentric line into a transformer, the balanced output of which feeds through a short screened twin line to the leads marked A in Plate IV and so to the diode line. The parallel resonant line, B, consists of two ceramic tubes plated with some white metal, presumably silver. The line is grounded at one end and tuned with a small balanced preset variable condenser, E, at the other end, the coarse adjustment being provided by a shorting strap, S.

Connections are run from the anodes down the centres of these lines probably by a metal coating on the inside. After passing through the screen these inner leads are connected to the terminals F from which points the feeds are taken to the primary of the balanced to unbalanced IF transformer. The secondary of this transformer is connected to the output plug at D in Plate IV. The coupling in the transformer has an adjustment which appears from the sealing paint on the locking screws to be preset before going into service.

The local oscillator voltage is injected into the circuit by a probe C in Plate IV which couples loosely to the diode ends of the line. The other end of the probe is fed by the high Q concentric circuit which selects the required fourth harmonic component from the output of the local oscillator which is fed between the units through the short length of flexible cable H. (Plate V).

During the transmitter pulse the diodes are cut off by a large negative pulse of about 800 V. which is applied to the centre of the primary of the IF transformer and so through the inner of the lines to the anodes of the valve, this being possible as there is no DC connection in the mixer circuit between the inner lines and earth.

The suppression pulse is supplied from across a 5000 ohm resistance in the Impulse Generator Unit. As the cathode of the LG2 is grounded this 5000 ohm resistance is the only resistance in the mixer circuit and acts as bias resistance for diode. The current flowing in this circuit during working conditions is about 200 croamps.

b. Local Oscillator

The beat frequency oscillator consists of two parts, an oscillator and a frequency multiplier which quadruples the oscillator frequency.

The oscillator itself is a push-pull tuned-plate tuned-grid circuit using two Telefunken LD2 valves, working on about 146 mc/s. The circuit is mounted in a ceramic frame plated on the inner side with copper, the whole assembly being housed in a cast iron box.

The tuned circuits are made of U-shaped ceramic plates coated with a white metal, apparently silver. The assembly is shown in Plate VI and the circuit in Fig. 4. While the oscillator and quadrupler assembly is mounted in the T and R box there is no means of adjusting the oscillator frequency or of changing the valves. If the unit is removed from the T and R box there is a hole through which the grid tuning condenser can be reached. This condenser is indicated at K in Plate VI. The plate turning condenser, just under the coupling loop, J, cannot be reached except by removing the whole unit from its cast iron box.

The oscillator is preset in frequency by changing the capacities of C11, C12, C13 and C14 the condensers being actually formed between part of the plate and grid inductances (X and Y) and the coated ceramic plates, Z, mounted on the silver coated ceramic shaft. By rotating the shaft the capacity of these condensers can be varied. Once the proper values are found the shaft is clamped and sweated to the copper plating lining the ceramic box.

The oscillator valves require an anode voltage of the order of 300 V. and when running in this circuit they draw about 50 mA. Provision is made for possible metering of the cathode current of each valve and also the grid current and plate current of both osc. valves, and grid current of the quadrupler.

Drive on the quadrupler is obtained by a small tuned hairpin loop, J, coupling to the anode circuit of the oscillator. The grid of the quadrupler has a certain amount of fixed bias and some self-bias. Conditions are arranged so that the total bias is such as to give maximum fourth harmonic component. The output is fed to a socket into which is plugged a cable. This cable is roughly $\lambda/2$ long in actual linear dimensions and is coupled at the other end by a small loop into the concentric circuit mounted on the back of the mixer box.

This concentric selector circuit is of rectangular cross section, the inner wall consisting of two concentric tubes with a small clearance forming a lumped capacity which tunes to about 585 Mc/s. with the inductance of the axial rod. The resonant frequency may be slightly changed by a small plate trimming condenser P.

In view of the extremely specialised form of construction of this unit the frequency stability is probably very high, (this will be measured later), in fact much higher than is required in this equipment.

It is therefore considered very probably that the unit was designed originally for communications purposes, especially as it is known that the enemy have a communication system on frequencies of the order of 600 Mc.

c. IF Amplifier

The IF amplifier is made up of nine units letters A-J, all using Telefunken RV12P2000 low consumption pentodes.

The output of the mixer is fed from the plug D through a concentric cable to the plug L on the IF amplifier unit. This connects directly to the grid of the first amplifier valve. Units A, B, C, and D are 25 Mc/s amplifier stages, employing single tuned circuits, apparently stagger tuned (no response curve). Unit C is an oscillator working on 18.5 Mc/s. Unit F is a pentode converter with cathode injection reducing the IF to 6.5 Mc/s, which is amplified by Unit G, H, and J. The output of J is fed through a stop-down core transformer, tuned on the primary to the output socket M. The best results are obtained by terminating this in 200 ohms.

Each stage is made as a unit and it is only necessary to take out 4 screws and unsolder 4 or 5 connections and the unit is free. Unit E, the second oscillator, is arranged to plug in. The reason for this was not at first seen until an occasion arose to remove Unit F. In order to remove Unit F, Unit E must be removed first to be able to unsolder a connection. In all the other units connections to be unsoldered in event of removal are readily accessible.

Each unit has its own drawn metal shield can. This can is held on by one screw. It is made to fit snugly by a bevel on the base plate. The sub-assembly parts of these units are very well designed for mass production. Wiring is extremely neat and the whole layout is very clean. Tuning condensers are ceramic and after being once adjusted are fixed by sweating.

From the lightness and general method of construction of this unit it is thought very probably that it was originally designed for aircraft use in another equipment, possibly for communications. Evidence in support of this is the output socket which is not congruous with the rest of the amplifier, and appears to have been added, and the fact that the IF amplification for the RDF receiver is carried out in two separate units. It seems likely that this particular unit as originally constructed had the extra stages, probably an amplifier. There is room for these on the chassis when the output socket is removed as can be seen from Plate IX, and with this alteration the amplifier would have sufficient gain by itself to work headphones.

6. AERIAL AND FEEDER SYSTEM

The aerial is a centre-fed half-wave dipole. Its reflector and the supporting structure containing a balance to unbalance transformer in the form of Pawsey stub is shown at Plate X.

The main feeder is an air spaced concentric of 70 ohms characteristic impedance with an outer diameter of about 1 inch. This branches into the Pawsey stub which is made in the form of a U with square section outer sheathing. There is a shorting bar across the limbs of this, forming a matching device by putting a variable inductance across the dipole. In the boat position of the shorting bar (which was as found) the standing wave on the main feeder was 2:1, and in the worst position 4:1.

The common T and R system is formed by the branch from the main feeder to the T and R through two adjustable phasing loops. The line to the R passes through a small balance to unbalance transformer of interesting design and then feeds the first tuned circuit which is connected to the double diode. It is arranged that the length of feeder between the junction point and the receiver first tuned circuit is [equation], and a large suppression pulse (-750 volts) is applied to the diode anodes simultaneously with the transmitted pulse. Thus an open circuit is transferred to the junction point … during transmission.

The transmitter phasing loop is adjusted so that during reception a very large impedance is presented to the junction point.

As a system this is very efficient because no power is lost during either transmission or reception, but it is limited by the inverse voltage that the receiver diode will stand. This ability to withstand inverse voltage can only be obtained at the expense of increased transit time loss due to the anode-to-cathode clearance being necessarily larger than usual, and for power outputs of the order of 100 kW. it is doubtful whether the system would be practicable. For small power it is excellent.

The dipole itself is made adjustable in length from 17.5cm to 24.5cm by sliding 0.42 dia brass tube over .31 in. dia tube.

The reflector is of curious design being made of sheet metal 95 cm. long by 15cm.wide. It is mounted 0.75cm. (0.165 in) in front of the dipole and its function is to redirect energy back into the paraboloid.

The whole aerial system is very strong and well finished. Castings are used wherever possible with consequent reduction of machining time and waste material.

7. FREQUENCY COVERAGE OF THE APPARATUS

This is extremely important from the point of view of jamming by us.

It is clear that the operator of one of these stations cannot make any rapid adjustment of frequency at all because there is no external control of receiver local oscillator frequency.

By removing the units and adjusting them however, a considerable variation of frequency can be obtained, the limit being set by the transmitter. The extreme frequency range of this is 531 Mc/sec. to 566 Mc/sec. To change the frequency by this amount would require adjustments to at least the local oscillator and quadrupler (4 tuned circuits) the aerial phasing loops, and the aerial balance to unbalance transformer. This would require the services of a skilled technician and would take some time to carry out.

If the transmitter unit were replaced also the frequency range would be much larger; probably 500 Mc/sec. to 700 Mc/sec. approx.

Thus the variation of frequency due to thermal drift of the local oscillator becomes of major importance when considering spot-frequency jamming unless a jamming system is used which automatically or manually tunes the jamming transmitter to the RDF frequency more or less continuously. This thermal drift will be measured later.

8. NOTES OF VALVES AND CATHODE RAY TUBES

All the valves and all the equipment were made by Telefunken, and the monitor CRT by Loewe Radio. Without exception the valves are extremely robustly made and reach a very high standard in every respect. With the exception of the transmitting valve and the small pentode used in the IF amplifier they are all mechanically similar externally, using ring seals in the base for all the leads-out and a die-cast aluminium alley cap which is accurately lined up with the pins so that a strong and foolproof valve holder can be used. (See photographs, Plates XI-XVII). Details of interest are the use of tungsten for all the pins and the fact that the pins are tapered for easy insertion into the holder.

Taking the valves in turn:

(i) The Transmitting Valve
This is called LS180 and some figures have already been given in Section (4) for ease of reference but are tabulated hereunder.

Max. anode voltage — above 12 kV. DC under
  oscillating conditions
Anode dissipation — 150–200 watts
Filament volts — 6.2
Filament current — 12.5 amps
Filament omission — 10 amps
Amplification factor — 30–50
Frequency limit — probably about 750 Mc/s

Grid and anode are brought out through the top of the valve, each by a double seal to reduce inductance. The filament, which is thoriated, is brought out at the bottom. A photograph is appended (Plate XII), unfortunately the valve had sprung a leak before this was taken, possibly due to mechanical stress resulting from a flash-arc during an over-voltage test.

Points of interest are the parallel wire grid, the heavily finned anode and the fact that the frequency limit is high for this type of construction, compared with British valves. The maximum anode voltage is also higher than is used in British valves of this type.

(ii) The IF amplifier pentode

This is called RV12P2000 and is well known to us. See Plate XVIII. This valve is used very frequently in German radio equipment. It is a pentode of fairly poor performance with a slope of 1.5 mA/V, but it is very small and easily produced.

(iii) The receiver double diode (LG2)

A static characteristic of this has been taken and is appended. The conducting DC resistance is about 2000 ohms.

The valve is … is very robust. Each anode is brought out to two pins and inside the valve consists of a bent metal sheet giving very low loadout inductance. The cathode is a large unipotential rectangular bar and is also brought out through two pins. The fact that as a mixer on 600 Mc. the valve gives a very good performance in spite of the rather large electrode clearance of about 0.5 mm shows perhaps that transit time loss is not so serious, and loss due to large leadout inductions and mutual inductances is more serious, than has been imagined.

(iv) Local oscillator valve (LD2)

These, and the quadrupler valve LD5, embody what is sometimes referred to as 'Micromesh construction' as the anode is split along a line parallel to that of the cathode and the grid loops protrude through this slit and are all fastened to a single supporting bar. Thus the grid inductance is reduced to a minimum. The anode is of popular shape and is well finned for cooling, and the pins are tungsten with silver thimbles over them to reduce contact resistance. The use of tungsten and hard glass seals reduces the dielectric loss which would be obtained if ordinary soft glass were used. As can be seen from Plate XIII, which is a photograph of the data sheets published by Telefunken, the valve is 25% efficient as an oscillator at 50 cm and 4 watts of CW are available at this wavelength. (Photographs at Plate XVIII).

(v) Quadrupler valve (LD5)

This is similar in construction to the LD2 except that the electrode axis is perpendicular to the axis of the glass bulb. This enables the grid and anode each to be brought out through two pins instead of one, thus reducing leadout inductance still further.

The fact that these two valves, the LD2 and LD5, combine such an excellent performance with mechanical rigidity and a standard form of base must be regarded as a technical achievement of a very high order. See Plate XIX.

(vi) Modulator valve LS50

These pentode valves were found to vary from sample to sample, and any particular valve on test showed considerable 'creep' with rise of screen and anode temperature. All the valves tested showed marked fluorescence when working in the $V_G=0$ region.

It can be seen from the curves and the photographs that the valve has a very low impedance for its size, and makes an excellent general purpose valve for modulation, as an oscillator, and an amplifier probably up to frequencies of up to 50/100 Mc/s/sec.

(vii) Cathode Ray Tube

This is 2" dia.monitoring tube made by Loewe Radio and is designated 2LB7/15 OPTA'.

Unfortunately the tube electrode structure was damaged during capture so that deflection sensitivity could not be measured. It was possible on test to produce a spot however and the beam-forming electrode voltages were measured. The tube has a green screen and appears to be similar to our VCR91 and has a side-contact base.

9. THE PRESENTATION EQUIPMENT

Unfortunately this was not captured owing to lack of time. Considerable knowledge has been gathered (from prisoner-of-war reports) however, which show that the tube used was about 4 inches in diameter only and that the time-base was circular with radial deflection of signals.

The receiver gain was usually operated at a high level, giving about 1 cm of noise on the tube. Owing to the high recurrence frequency used (3750 pulses per second) it would be possible to see signals below the noise level.

It will be seen that the time-base is blacked out during and after the transmitted pulse. This is presumably done by the voltage across W57.

As the tube is so small, and as the time-base length is 40 Km. as shown, range measurement cannot be carried out to better than about 0.5 Km. by the average operator.

It seems certain that the equipment in the operating cabin included a 3750 c.p.s oscillator which not only provided the circular time-base but also provided the negative going firing wave for the transmitter modulator.

As far as can be gathered no devices for anti-jamming were used.

10. THE REPORTING SYSTEM

This was very simple. The 53 cm station was linked up with the 240 cm station about ¼ mile further along the cliff edge by a landline, and control was effected from there. When an aircraft approached within 40 Km it was handed over to the 53 cm set for further plotting, and apparently the 53 cm plots and the 200 cm plots were passed along the same landline to the local operations room.

The 53 cm operator's microphone was mounted above the CRT and for receiving he used a loudspeaker.

11. CALCULATIONS OF PERFORMANCE

1. Range
Known data:

i. Aerial gain
Paraboloid is 2.8metres dia. λ = 53 cm.
48.6 microvolt/m. to give signal equal to noise.
As the bandwidth of the receiver is 0.5 Mc. this gives a noise factor of 20.3 db.

ii. Target area
Assumed to be 4 sq. metres for normal aircraft head-on.

This is of the right order since normal max. range is 40 Km but 60 Km has been seen. (Corresponding to effective A of about 8 sq.m. instead of 4, or signal below noise level, which would be detectable on account of the high pulse recurrence frequency).

2. Jamming power required
Jammer on every aircraft. RDF station assumed to be pointing at aircraft … = 0.17watts per channel
Receiver bandwidth is 0.5 Mc.

Taking max. frequency range to be covered by jammer as 53.0 cm. to 56.5 cm. (567—531 Mc. = 36 Mc)

Therefore Average Power required from jammer is: 12.2 watts (radiated from aerial).

12. CONCLUSIONS

As regards operational performance and general RDF technique, the equipment does not show any original trend or novel feature; it is straightforward and in no respects is it brilliant. Compared with British RDF technique, in many ways, it lags behind; the lack of split for D/F, the poor accuracy of range measurement, and the crude height-finding system illustrate this clearly. On the other hand it must be remembered that the equipment was made in 1940 and designed in 1939 or earlier in all probability. Also, it was originally designed as an RDF aid to Observer Corps posts where great accuracy was not required. Further, in 1939 RDF on 50 cm. in England was not sufficiently developed to give a maximum range of 50 Km. on aircraft — we did not reach that stage until 1941. Nevertheless, in general and considered as a weapon of defence, this equipment has shown us nothing new.

In certain technical details, mechanical construction and general engineering design however the apparatus is outstanding and is worth careful study, especially by those engaged in development and production.

The robustness of the equipment is very notable. Not only is the whole equipment mounted in a very strong box, but each individual unit within this box is of sturdy construction. Even the removable components, such as the valves, are of more robust construction than we are accustomed to expect.

This robustness is in part achieved by the very general use of castings in aluminium and light alloys, and of mouldings. For this manufacturing technique to be economical it is necessary for a stability of design to exist, such as can only be achieved by careful and probably lengthy development. When it has been achieved however it is possible to use one unit in a number of different equipments. This construction by sub-units of generalised design has advantages for maintenance. Retrospective modifications may also be carried out by replacing units by improved designs.

In this equipment, for example, the IF amplifier unit and the local oscillator unit were probably not designed for this application … In the IF amplifier of the German equipment a large number of one type of valve is used, a large number of another type is also used in the modulator. On our standards the equipment is extravagant in the total number of valves.

The overall performance of any RDF system depends mainly of two characteristics, the peak pulse power of the transmitter and the signal-to-noise ratio in the receiver. For the German equipment the pulse power is 5 kW., which may be compared with 100 kW. available in our corresponding 50 cm. transmitter employing two NT99 valves. The noise level in the German receiver is 20 db. above thermal noise; in our latest 50 cm. receiver the noise level is less than 12 db. above thermal noise. This represents a gain of more than six times in our favour in the receiver, and twenty times in the transmitter. Judged by these standards the German equipment is of a low performance, but it must be remembered that the equipment was probably designed in 1939 and at that time the great drive on RDF had hardly got underway and we could not even have matched the performance of the German equipment.

One of the main interests in examining this equipment has been to discover any means by which it may easily be jammed. Unfortunately the prospect of this is not very hopeful. While the apparatus is constructed so that it is not possible to change the radio frequency at all quickly, it is nevertheless possible to tune over a wide range, and our listening tests have shown that these equipments are in fact set up over a considerable frequency range.

Acknowledgements

My first debts are to my splendid publishers HarperCollins in London and New York, and especially to Arabella Pike and Iain Hunt. My agent Andrew Wylie has provided staunch support as always. Most of my research for Biting has been carried out at the National Archives, the Imperial War Museum and the Airborne Assault Museum at Duxford, where Ben Hill and Jon Baker have been especially helpful. For a professional historian, it means much to be able to consult named individuals such as themselves at a given institution, as is no longer possible at the National Archives.

I am indebted to Tim Carson for giving me access to Manor Farm in Wiltshire, where his family has lived for the best part of two centuries and on the heights of which C Company trained before Operation Biting, when it was quartered at Tilshead, and to his brother David who contributed useful fragments of local information about Alton Priors in wartime. I exchanged very helpful emails with Major-General Ashley Truluck about the detail of that training programme, and also had a wonderfully fruitful email conversation with the expert battlefield guide Col. Paul Oldfield, who has made a close study of Bruneval. I am especially grateful to him for reading and commenting upon my draft MS, to which he has provided significant corrections. In October 2023 we shared a delightful outing to Alton Priors, to walk the ground scrambled over by C Company eighty-one years earlier.

Caroline Jones, archivist of Wellington College, most kindly found me material and photos of Euan Charteris. Hugo Frost was generous in giving me his time, to recall memories of his splendid father.

I must again emphasize my debt to the 2012 book *Raid de Bruneval: Mystères et vérités* by Alain Millet and Nicolas Bucourt, which offers all manner of fascinating facts and insights, based on the latter's almost lifelong study of the raid. With a few exceptions, I have accepted their version of most of the night's events, and especially of the routes taken across country by elements of C Company which landed short of the dropping zone, though of course some of this must remain speculative.

My secretary Rachel Lawrence remains the pillar of support which she has provided for most of the past thirty-seven years, and my wife Penny is the rock upon which everything in my life rests, not least the commitment to keep writing books in my seventy-ninth year.

References and a Note on Sources

A warning seems appropriate about the text above. While it exploits the best available sources, many details remain obscure, especially about the struggle in the defile before the beach approach was cleared, because personal memories were fallible or flawed. I have sought to piece together a jigsaw with many pieces missing. In Biting's immediate aftermath several of the leading participants composed personal accounts – Frost, Vernon, Cox, Charteris, Young, Pickard and Cook. Interviews were also recorded with the three German prisoners, albeit not greatly enlightening or coherent. Few of the Germans who occupied the radar site and Bruneval defences in the early morning of 28 February 1942 gave post-war testimony – many lay in Russian graves. We shall never know for sure about the experiences of some participants, especially those of five of the six members of C Company who became PoWs, because their own accounts are incomplete or less than wholly convincing – only the wounded Sutherland's fate is self-explanatory and conclusive. None of those who missed the beach evacuation is believed to have attended post-war reunions of Bruneval veterans.

Meanwhile the contemporary German narratives are fragmentary, and obviously designed to be exculpatory. Some of the story has required informed guesses, based on the circumstantial evidence – this is especially true about the timings of events on the ground, for which no complete record was ever made. Moreover, while we may be sure that, once back in England, plenty was said among the interested parties and their commanders about the blunders and misfortunes, in the wake of success nobody wished to parade dirty laundry by committing adverse comments to paper.

In the references below, UKNA denotes the UK National Archive and IWM the Imperial War Museum. I have conducted my own research in the French historical accounts cited in the bibliography, and thus quotations derive from my own free translations. I hope that these justly reflect the original texts.

Introduction

xiii 'As you reach each window' Brooke, Alan *War Diaries 1939–45* ed. Alex Danchev and Alan Todman Weidenfeld & Nicolson 2001, 26.x.41

xiii 'beyond the compass of our stride' Churchill to Auchinleck 30.x.41 *Churchill War Companion Documents* Vol. 3 p.1392

xvii 'we in Combined Operations' Millar, George *The Bruneval Raid* Cassell 2002 p.xiii

1: Reg

2 'My childhood was steeped' Jones, R.V. *Most Secret War* Penguin 2009 p.39

6 'Tell him from me' ibid. p.83

10 'The path of truthful duty' Jones, R.V. 'Temptations and Risks of the Scientific Observer' *Minerva* Vol. X, No. 3 p.446

10 'Are we not tending to lose our sense of proportion' UKNA DEFE40/2 Harris memo of 1.ii.41

11 'He told me how impressed' Jones p.183 *Most Secret War*
18 'Look, Charles' ibid. p.236

2: Dickie

21 'Enterprises must be prepared with specially-trained troops' WSC 6.vi.40 *Churchill Companion* Vol. 3
24 'What can you hope to achieve' Terraine, John *The Life and Times of Lord Mountbatten* Arrow Books 1968 pp.112–13
24 'You are to give no thought to the defensive' Fergusson, Bernard *The Watery Maze: The Story of Combined Operations* Collins 1961 p.88
25 'The Chief of Combined Operations always remained an agent' Smith, Adrian *Mountbatten: Apprentice War Lord* I.B.Tauris 2010 p.306
27 'He is a pretty wonderful man' Ziegler, Philip *Mountbatten: The Official Biography* Collins 1985 p.171
28 'I have been greatly criticised' ibid. p.172
28 'owing to a series of misfortunes' quoted Ziegler p.132
29 'Mountbatten was not a good flotilla leader' ibid. p.145
29 'He conducted at least two protracted love-affairs' ibid. p.53
30 'Mountbatten delighted in the planning' ibid. p.167
31 'the PM is ruining him' Bruce Lockhart, Robert *Diaries 1939–45* ed. Kenneth Young Macmillan 1980 p.191
32 'a wholly irrational prejudice against you' Bishop, Patrick *Operation Jubilee: Dieppe 1942 The Folly and the Sacrifice* Penguin 2021 p.98
32 'There was no justification' Brooke diary 5.iii.42 p.236
32 'A strange character' Smith p.307
33 'Mountbatten was by all odds' *Wedemeyer Reports* New York 1958 pp.108–9

33 'I want him to exercise influence' Churchill Papers 20/53 letter to Pound 5.ii.42
35 'must be judged a marked failure' Churchill Papers 20/88 Companion Volume 17 p.43
36 'Procedure: CCO [Mountbatten] has bright idea' UKNA AIR39/43
36 'Mountbatten was a likely lad' Ziegler p.207

3: Boy

40 'John Frost wrote' Frost *Nearly There* Pen & Sword p.70
41 'in the hope that he would not hit the water' Gale, Richard *Call to Arms* Hutchinson 1968 p.117
42 'Gentlemen, someone once described' Saunders, Hilary St. George *The Red Beret: The Story of the Parachute Regiment at War 1940–45* Michael Joseph 1952 p.32
43 'It simply and almost, it seems, apologetically' ibid. p.41
43 'the next recollection I have' *By Air to Battle* p.9 Air Ministry 1943
44 'The RAF at Ringway' St. George Saunders p.46
48 'He is the best-looking thing I have' Forster, Margaret *Daphne du Maurier* Kindle edition Random House 2015 p.92
48 'is trying to teach me' ibid.
48 'My dears, I am delighted' ibid. p.94
49 'couldn't see the sense in military life' ibid.
49 'I feel I mustn't leave Tommy too much' ibid. p.101
49 'She wanted what she thought she had married' ibid. p.102
49 'Can you picture me going around the married quarters' ibid. p.116
50 'a sour old army wife in an Indian hill station' ibid. p.155
50 'She didn't understand half the things he talked about' ibid. p.164

51 'ebullient … indeed a *beau sabreur*' IWM81/11/1
Carrington MS memoir *Chairborne Soldier*
52 'He possessed all the virtues' Powell, Geoffrey *The Devil's Birthday: The Bridges to Arnhem 1944* Buchan & Enright 1984 p.38

4: Rémy

1'THE MOST EXTRAORDINARY SECRET AGENT I EVER MET'

56 'The English are pigs' Lecompte-Boinet, Jacques *Mémoires d'un chef de la Résistance* Felin 2021 p.99
57 '*mauvais coucheurs*' de La Vigerie interviewed in the 1968 documentary film of Marcel Ophuls *Le chagrin et la pitié*
57 'None fitted the conventional picture' Amouroux, Henri *La vie des Français sous l'Occupation* 1961, Kindle edition p.73
57 'Resistance was still, and for a long time to come, ill-organised' Lecompte-Boinet p.104
58 'lacked all social status' Kerrand, Philippe *L'étrange colonel Rémy* Champ Vallon 2020 p.73
59 'We were betrayed, dishonoured' Rémy, Colonel *Le Refus: Mémoires d'un agent secret de la France Libre* France Empire 1998 p.39
60 '*Nous commençons à zéro*' Kerrand p.84
60 'I have worked in business' Rémy p.52
62 'the most extraordinary secret agent' quoted Kerrand p.88
63 'became a magnificent turntable' Rémy p.76
64 'His biographer Philippe Kerrand is almost contemptuous' Kerrand p.120 and *passim*
65 'He suggested that German soldiers' ibid. p.100
65 'this operation would be spearheaded by 150,000 paratroops' ibid. p.136

65 'a certain number of the reports you have sent us' ibid. p.162
65 'My informants were whispers' ibid. p.186
67 'The network inspired by [Rémy] was several times' Baumel, Jacques *Résister* Albin Michel 1999 p.103
67 'given the considerable risks he took' Kerrand p.181
67 'every network had its quota of traitors' Guerin, Alain *Chronique de la Résistance* Omnibus 2000 p.676
67 'avalanche of contagious illnesses' Lecompte-Boinet p.90
68 'We did as you asked us!' Rémy *Le Refus* p.186
69 'Why are you crying?' ibid. p.301
69 'the foundation stone of our secret operations' *Le Figaro* 31.vii.84
70 'the Germans deployed' Pollack, Guillaume *L'armée du silence* Tallandier 2022 p.198
71 'Broadway ran such men as Gilbert Renault' Jeffery, Keith *MI6: The History of the Secret Intelligence Service 1909–1949* Bloomsbury 2010 see pp.394–5
72 'He suggested the French Service of the BBC' Kerrand pp.203–4
73 'If he talks, there is likely to be a massacre' Rémy p.299
73 'Ask, and it shall be given' ibid. p.314

2 BRUNEVAL

75 'swift execution of orders was often rendered impossible by agents' Pollack p.196, letter of 21.viii.41
76 'the nature of the questions' Rémy p.339
81 'I love the work that I do' Kerrand p.191

5: Johnny

1 C COMPANY

- 83 'a man who knew just exactly' Frost, John *A Drop Too Many* Cassell 1980 p.40
- 84 'he hoped eventually to enter politics' Millar p.184
- 85 'My own first thought' Frost p.2
- 86 'I had not very much idea' ibid. p.17
- 87 'It was action that was wanted' Gale p.116
- 88 'a wild crew' Millar p.6
- 88 'What struck me so forcibly' Frost p.28
- 90 'Why, that's the surest way of becoming a prisoner' ibid. p.36
- 90 'We smiled at each other' ibid. p.30

2 TILSHEAD AND INVERARAY

- 94 'I didn't like this at all' ibid. p.38
- 95 'someone else would be found' ibid. p.39
- 96 'This was to be a combined operation' ibid. p.40
- 100 'the guardroom door yawned' ibid. p.47
- 100 'Sir, shouldn't we tell Cook' IWM Cook 95/5/1
- 101 'He wished to show that line infantrymen' IWM family publication *My War* by Bill Westcott, 1998
- 102 'Even the subalterns had enough' Frost p.41
- 102 'The possibility of being left stranded' ibid. p.41
- 103 'We were left in no doubt' ibid. p.42
- 103 'The slightly-built "Hun's" real name' Jewish Virtual Library, Martin Sugarman

6: Charlie

111 'It seems incredible, even at this distance of time' Jones *Most Secret War* p.238
112 'Don't be worried too much' ibid.

7: 'Party' Planning

1 'PICK'

114 'it mightily impressed the enthusiastic young officers' IWM Carrington 81/11/1
115 'He disliked publicity stunts' ibid.
115 'Our chief complaints against the Air Staff' Kennedy *The Business of War* p.178
116 'Carrington believed that if the principal exponent' IWM Carrington 81/11/1 *Chairborne Soldier* MS
121 'When this war is over' Forster p.163

2 THE ENEMY

129 'A small enemy force, probably not more than 10' Bromley-Martin copy of Biting operational order, sold at Spinks sale 17001 lot 433 12.iv.17
134 'As long as they can dig and shoot!' MH conversation with Hugo Frost 20.ix.23
136 'There had been a vexed debate' Foot, M.R.D. and Langley, J.M. *MI9: The British Secret Service That Fostered Escape and Evasion 1939–45* Bodley Head 1979 pp.84–5
137 'Lulworth was "a very bad show"' UKNA AIR39/43
138 'It will be a great pity' UKNA PREM3/73
138 'The last rehearsal' Frost p.43
140 'We are all thoroughly miserable' ibid. p.47

8: The Jump
144 'I suppose you know there's to be a commando raid' IWM Carrington 81/11/1
145 'Aha! You have no idea' Frost p.47
145 'fleetingly, during pauses in the conversation' ibid. p.48
146 'We paraded as a strange new bombload' ibid. p.48
146 'I feel like a bloody murderer!' ibid. p.49
147 'They marched past like Guardsmen' Pickard personal narrative Airborne Assault Museum
147 'We knew so little … The Germans were to us' Frost p.49
148 'Morale in the aircraft was terrific' IWM PA Young 17/2/1
148 'So have we sung many times' Frost p.50
151 'We could not believe our good luck' IWM Cook 95/5/1
153 'At Carlton Gardens Passy, and indeed de Gaulle' Rémy pp.163–4

9: Henry
174 'unfortunately we failed to spend quite as much time' Frost p.62
176 'Then we were seen' IWM Young 17/2/1
186 'it became extremely uncomfortable' Frost p.51

10: Junior
194 'It was scrubby and difficult country' Charteris personal narrative Airborne Assault Museum
195 'a fast lollop' ibid.
198 'The Germans were still very confused' Frost p.52
199 'By then the parties were getting' Charteris personal narrative
207 'The object had been achieved' Frost p.53

11: Cook

210 'began to think that we should not get back' Charteris personal narrative
210 'It looked as though we were going to be left' Frost p.54
212 'By God, it's coming off!' Charteris personal narrative
213 'Never had such ungainly vessels' IWM PA Young 17/2/1
213 'The enemy's fire' Charteris personal narrative
222 'Your inspiring message received pm Friday 27 Feb 1942 was much appreciated by all' IWM Cook 95/5/1
222 'The German prisoners must have thought' IWM PA Young 17/2/1

12: The Prizegiving

1 CELEBRATIONS

227 'You have put' Frost *Nearly There* p.73
231 'Our ration' Frost *Nearly There* p.74
231 'The Prime Minister wishes Dr Jones' UKNA PREM3/73
231 'Dr Jones's claims in my mind' Churchill Papers 20/67, *Documents* Vol.17 p.481
232 'Now, he said gloomily, he was wondering if she was a fifth columnist' Jones *Most Secret War* p.244
233 'in some respects, the set' UKNA AVIA26/1872
237 'We got into trouble' Frost p.59
237 'The glider pilots' quartermaster' ibid. p.40
238 'Their heroic guides were dispatched' letter published in 3.ii.46 edition of regional newspaper *Havre Libre*

2 THE WHEEL OF FORTUNE

240 'I felt his loss more than any other' Jones *Most Secret War* p.232

240 'Between ourselves, the Resistance is a bluff' Gillois, André *Histoire secrète des Français à Londres* Hachette 1973 p.164
241 'All that I have done' Millar p.201
245 'the principal creator of his own legend' Albertelli, Sébastien *Les services secret du général de Gaulle, le BCRA 1940–44* Perrin 2009 p.46
246 'He did not have any trouble' *New York Times* obituary of R.V. Jones 19.xii.97
247 'Although one of Britain's most famous' MH conversation with Hugo Frost 20.ix.23
247 'One of the last surviving Bruneval' Paradata, Airborne Assault Museum, Duxford
248 'such an operation properly demanded' Peveler in *RAF Journal* May 1944
250 'But the Germans, general!' Beevor, Antony *Arnhem: The Battle for the Bridges* Penguin 2018 p.27
252 '[Browning] unquestionably lacks the standing' quoted *Armageddon* p.40
253 'a first-class leader' Bruce Lockhart p.527
254 'My own reaction was one of exhilaration' Hughes-Hallett interviewed on *Mountbatten Life & Times* prog. 5, Reel 3, p.4
254 'the appointment presaged Mountbatten's' Amery, Leo *The Empire at Bay: The Diaries of Leo Amery 1929–45* ed. John Barnes and David Nicholson Hutchinson 1988 13.iv.42
255 'There was no knowing what discussions' Brooke diary p.242 28.iii.42
258 'the most successful combined operation' IWM Carrington *Chairborne Soldier* MS
258 'the successful execution by Major Frost' Millar p.xiii

259 'I remained convinced ... that the commandos' Brooke diary p.185 note on entry for 25.ix.41
259 'Eisenhower would have been better served' Powell p.252

Bibliography

Albertelli, Sébastien *Les services secrets du général de Gaulle, le BCRA 1940–44* Perrin 2009

Amery, Leo *The Empire at Bay: The Diaries of Leo Amery 1929–45* ed. John Barnes and David Nicholson Hutchinson 1988

Amouroux, Henri *La grand histoire des Français sous l'Occupation* 1987 Kindle edition

— *La vie des Français sous l'Occupation* 1961 Kindle edition

Baumel, Jacques *Résister* Albin Michel 1999

Beevor, Antony *Arnhem: The Battle for the Bridges* Penguin 2018

Bishop, Patrick *Operation Jubilee: Dieppe 1942 The Folly and the Sacrifice* Penguin 2021

Brooke, Alan *War Diaries 1939–45* ed. Alex Danchev and Alan Todman Weidenfeld & Nicolson 2001

Bruce Lockhart, Robert *Diaries 1939–45* ed. Kenneth Young Macmillan 1980

Churchill, Winston *The Churchill War Papers* Vol. 3 *The Ever-Widening War 1941* Heinemann 2000

— *The Churchill Documents* Vol.17 *Testing Times 1942* Hillsdale College Press 2020

Fergusson, Bernard *The Watery Maze: The Story of Combined Operations* Collins 1961

Foot, M.R.D. and Langley, J.M. *MI9: The British Secret Service That Fostered Escape and Evasion 1939–45* Bodley Head 1979

Ford, Keith *Swift and Sure: 80 Years of No. 51 Squadron RAF* T'otherside 1997

Ford, Ken *The Bruneval Raid* Osprey 2010

Forster, Margaret *Daphne du Maurier* Kindle edition Random House 2015

Frost, John *A Drop Too Many* Cassell 1980

Frost, John *Nearly There* Pen & Sword 1991

Gale, Richard *Call to Arms* Hutchinson 1968

Gillois, André *Histoire secrète des Français à Londres* Hachette 1973

Guerin, Alain *Chronique de la Résistance* Omnibus 2000

Hastings, Max *Das Reich: Resistance and the June 1944 March of the 2nd SS Panzer Division to Normandy* Michael Joseph 1981

— *Armageddon: The Battle for Germany 1944–45* Macmillan 2004

— *Finest Years: Churchill as Warlord 1940–45* HarperCollins 2009

— *The Secret War: Spies, Codes and Guerrillas 1939–45* HarperCollins 2015

Hinsley, F.H. and others *British Intelligence in the Second World War* Vol. 2 HMSO 1981

Jackson, Julian *France: The Dark Years 1940–44* Oxford 2001

Jeffery, Keith *MI6: The History of the Secret Intelligence Service 1909–1949* Bloomsbury 2010

Jones, R.V. *Most Secret War* Penguin 2009

Kerrand, Philippe *L'étrange colonel Rémy* Champ Vallon 2020

Lecompte-Boinet, Jacques *Mémoires d'un chef de la Résistance* Felin 2021

Mead, Richard *Commando General: The Life of Sir Robert Laycock* Pen & Sword 2016

Millar, George *The Bruneval Raid* Cassell 2002

Millet, Alain and Bucourt, Nicolas *Raid de Bruneval et de La Poterie: Mystères et vérités* Heimdal 2012

Neillands, Robin *The Raiders: The Army Commandos 1940-46* Fontana 1989

Oldfield, Paul *The Bruneval Raid* Pen & Sword 2012

Petropoulos, Jonathan *Royals and the Reich: The Princes von Hessen in Nazi Germany* Oxford 2006

Pollack, Guillaume *L'armée du silence* Tallandier 2022

Powell, Geoffrey *The Devil's Birthday: The Bridges to Arnhem 1944* Buchan & Enright 1984

Price, Alfred *Instruments of Darkness* Granada 1977

Rémy, Colonel *Le Refus: Mémoires d'un agent secret de la France Libre* France Empire 1998

Saunders, Hilary St. George *The Red Beret: The Story of the Parachute Regiment at War 1940-45* Michael Joseph 1952

Smith, Adrian *Mountbatten: Apprentice War Lord* I.B.Tauris 2010

Terraine, John *The Life and Times of Lord Mountbatten* Arrow Books 1968

Thomas, Cédric *Etretat 1939-1945: De l'occupation allemande au camp Pall Mall* Self published 2009

Ziegler, Philip *Mountbatten: The Official Biography* Collins 1985

Zuckerman, Solly *From Apes to Warlords* Hamish Hamilton 1978

Index

All ranks given are those held in February 1942

Abdication Crisis (1936), 27
Aberdeen University, 245–6
Abwehr (German intelligence service), 147
Addison, Air Commodore Edward, 11
aerial photographic reconnaissance, 10, 13, 120; 'dicing' technique, 14, 15, 16–17; Lannion photos, 7, 9; Photographic Reconnaissance Unit (PRU), 14, 15–17, 18, 38, 54, 236, 240; RAF interpretation centre at Medmenham, 6, 14, 15–17; of site at Bruneval, 13–14, 38, 54, 126, 133, 240; Wavell's 'Altazimeter', 16
airborne assault, xix; aircraft used for, 40–1, 43, 116–17, 121–2; British as slow to adopt paratroop concept, 39–40; British descent on Caen canal bridge, 251; choice of landing zone for paratroopers, 130–1, 175, 250–1; era of massed parachute drops as brief, 259; First Allied Airborne Army (1944–45), 259; German commandos' rescue of Mussolini, 251; German gliderborne descent on Eben Emael, 89, 130, 251; gliderborne units, xvi, 45, 89, 130, 247–8, 251; Luftwaffe's paratroops (*fallschirmjäger*), 22, 39, 89, 136, 258; need for speed and surprise, 89–90, 134–6, 250–1; operational parachute drops in darkness, 38, 154–6, 158–63, 248; paratroop training centre at Ringway, 40–5, 90–2, 108; RAF's failure to provide aircraft for, 40, 115; Tragino aqueduct raid (Colossus, February 1941), 44, 89, 116, 247
Airborne Assault Museum, Duxford, xvii
Alton Priors, Wiltshire, 98–100
Amery, Leo, 254
Amouroux, Henri, 57
amphibious assaults: landing-craft capable of carrying tanks, 22; as not possible at Bruneval, 38; shallow-draught landing-craft, 34; St Nazaire and Dieppe raids, 33–4, 151–2, 231, 254, 255*, 255–6; war effort turns towards (from 1942), 256

Anderson, Édith, 58–9, 61–2, 68
Anquetil, Bernard, 70–1
Arndt, Cpl. Max, 201, 203, 224
Arnhem (Market Garden, September 1944), 51, 131, 239, 243, 244, 246, 250–3
d'Astier de La Vigerie, Emmanuel, 57, 68
Auchinleck, Gen. Sir Claude, xiii
Australia, 34, 35, 245

Bader, Group-Captain Douglas, 120
Barratt, AM. Arthur 'Ugly', 144
Battle of Britain, 1, 6, 8
BBC, 55, 61, 71–2, 221
Beatty, Admiral of the Fleet Earl, 26
Benson airfield, 14, 15, 16–17
Bletchley Park, 'Station X' at, xv, 6, 7, 10, 12, 19, 66
Boer War, Second (1899–1902), 21
Boulogne, 21–2
Bourne, Lt. Gen. Alan, 21, 22
Boxer Rising (1901), 22
Boyd, Sgt. Johnny, 204, 240
Branwhite, Charlie, 190, 191, 244
Braun, Karl Ferdinand, 8
Breit, Gregory, 8
Brereton, US Gen. Lewis, 251
A Bridge Too Far (Richard Attenborough film, 1977), 251
British Army: manning of weapons in Biting ALCs, 101; rearming and training (1940–44), xiv; slow to adopt paratroop concept, 39–40
British Army units
  Eighth Army, 35–6
  1st Airborne Division: and 38 Wing, 115; briefing to C Company on Biting, 129; Browning appointed to command, 39, 45–6, 50, 51; Browning's staff, 94–6; Frost in all four major operational drops, 246; gliderborne units, 45, 247–8, 251; landing site at Arnhem, 250–1; shoulder badge, 51, 92; Syrencot House (divisional HQ), 54, 95, 110, 122; Urquhart's command of, 252
  6th Airborne Division, 252, 253
  1st Parachute Brigade, xvi, 45, 53, 87–8
  8th Monmouth Regiment, 101
  Black Watch, 83, 96, 243
  Cameronians (Scottish Rifles), 85, 86–7
  King's Own African Rifles, 118
  Parachute Regiment, xviii–xix, 45, 144, 239, 246, 259
  Royal Engineers, 38, 53, 97, 101, 109–10, 113, 127, 131, 132, 175; dismantling of Würzburg by, 176–8, 180–2, 186–7, 233; dispersed between different 'sticks', 160; and mine-detectors, 96, 136, 156, 169, 206–7; transport of Würzburg parts to beach, 187, 196, 198, 208–10, 217
  Seaforth Highlanders, 122, 131, 202
  Special Air Service, 259
  1st Parachute Battalion (formerly 11th Special Air Service), 42, 44, 45, 53, 88, 89
  2nd Parachute Battalion (2 Para), xviii, xix, 45, 53, 88, 97, 101, 134, 144, 160, 222, 239–40, 243, 244, 251. *See also* British Army units: C Company, 2nd Para
  3rd Parachute Battalion (3 Para), xix, 241–2
  3 Commando, 137
  10th Parachute Battalion TA, xviii–xix

11th Bn. Royal Fusiliers, 101
Long Range Desert Group, 259
1st Parachute squadron RE, 97
C Company, 2nd Para, xix, 82–5, 88–92; Browning inspects, 93–4; chosen for Biting, 53–4; Frost's command reorganized, 94, 96, 186; as overwhelmingly Scots, 53, 82, 88, 146–7; singing by during Biting, 145, 148, 152; stay at Tilshead, 54, 91, 92, 93–7, 108–9, 121–3, 142–5 *see also* Bruneval raid (Operation Biting)
Broadlands (stately home), 26–7
Broadley, Alan, 118–19, 242
Bromley-Martin, Maj. Peter, 94–6
Brooke, Gen. Sir Alan, xiii, xiv, 32, 33, 92–3, 228, 254–5, 259
Brossolette, Pierre, 153, 245
Browning, Maj. Gen. Frederick 'Boy', xvi, xvii, xix; After-Action Report on Biting (March 1942), 279–96; ageing effects of wartime service, 121; and airborne assault concept, 114–15, 252, 253; ambition of, 52, 252; appointed to command airborne division, 39, 45–6, 50, 51; background/private life, 46, 47–52, 253; and Biting planning/preparations, 93–6, 97–8, 99, 100, 101, 115–16, 121–2; as chief of staff to Mountbatten in Ceylon, 257; First World War service, 46–7; impatience/impetuousness of, 139; and order to carry out Biting, 142–3; private demons, 47, 49, 51–2, 253; reputation of today, 253; role at Arnhem, 51, 250–3; service/life after Bruneval, 253, 257; and success of Biting, 222, 227, 228, 229, 249, 250–1

Bruneval raid (Operation Biting), xv*, xv–xx, 53; 18 wireless sets, 160, 200, 204, 206, 209, 216; 51 Squadron's involvement, 116–17, 121–2, 137, 139, 146–50, 152–8, 160–5, 222, 230, 240, 248; aerial photographic reconnaissance of site, 13–14, 16–17, 18, 38, 54, 126, 133; Airborne Division HQ briefing (21 February), 129; appointed assembly place, 130, 162; army bureaucracy's complaints over, 237; arrival in Portsmouth after, 221–3; attack on Stella Maris, 200–1, 202–3; battle to break through to the beach, 172, 173–6, 183–8, 194, 196–8, 199–207, 230; BCRA intelligence gathering, 55–7, 74–81, 134, 173, 226, 240–1, 245, 247; beach pillboxes (Redoubt), 128, 131, 168, 169, 171, 173, 187, 196, 197, 198, 250; Beuzelin farm, 190, 193, 194, 197; British fatalities, 186, 199, 216, 219, 237–8; British prisoners taken during, 195, 224, 237–8, 248; British wounded, 174, 175, 184, 186, 187–8, 190–1, 200, 204, 208, 213, 214, 215, 219, 229, 237–8; Browning's After-Action Report (March 1942), 279–96; capture of Gosset chateau (Lone House), 198–9; combat during, 172, 173–80, 182, 183–8, 190–205; conditions on board Whitley bombers, 148, 149–50; Cook as naval CO of, 100, 211–12, 213; Cook's flotilla, 143, 150–2, 208–15, 217–22, 249–50; danger

Bruneval raid (*cont ...*)
of German reinforcements, 197, 199, 208, 209, 210, 215, 216–17; the defile, 78, 131, 172, 173–6, 184–6, 188, 196–8, 209–10, 214, 229, 230; designated parachute landing zone, 130–1, 154, 158, 160–3, 248; Drake group, 96, 132, 161, 162, 163, 168, 179–80, 182–6, 197, 200; dropping of weapons and equipment, 154–5, 156, 158, 160, 161–2; Échos farm, 191, 215, 238; and enemy vessels in Channel, 151–2, 213, 219; escort ships, 143, 150–2; evacuation from the beach, 212–15; evacuation rehearsals, 137–9; failure of photography, 181, 250; flight to Bruneval, 148–50; German beach defences, 38, 78–9, 124, 128, 169; German flak during, 152–3, 155, 164; German investigation into, 248–9; German lack of transport, 128–9, 167; German lassitude and incompetence during, 167–8, 179, 181–2, 188, 189–90, 195, 197, 198–9, 201–5, 213–17, 248, 256; German prisoners taken, 178, 181, 187, 202–3, 205, 210, 219, 220–1, 222–3, 226, 232–3, 234, 237; German propaganda response, 226; German uncertainties about British intentions, 163, 179, 189–90, 197, 198–9, 205, 215, 217, 248; Germans impressed by, 258; Gosset chateau (Lone House), 125–6, 129, 130, 131–2, 133–4, 168, 169–70, 172, 194, 198–9; Gosset farm as not among objectives, 182–3; Gosset farm (Rectangle), 77, 126–7, 129, 132, 166–8, 171–2, 175, 177–80, 181–4, 186, 197, 205; 'Guardroom', 128*, 128, 131, 173; Hardy group, 96, 132, 133, 176–8, 180–2, 183; Hill 102 east of village, 195, 250; initial proposals for, 19, 37, 38; intelligence brief, 134, 228–9; Isle of Wight mock attack subterfuge, 91, 93, 95, 98; Jellicoe group, 96, 131–2, 187; Jones as begetter of, 18–19, 229; jump at Syrencot (15 February), 106, 110, 121–2; jumping of paratroopers, 154–5; lack of briefing about wider countryside, 124, 155; lack of jump injuries, 162–3, 248; lack of medics, 143, 174; local inhabitants during, 163, 191; Lulworth exercise fiasco, 137; makes warlords overconfident, 249; medals/decorations awarded for, 229–31, 243; MI6's intelligence request to BCRA (January 1942), 55, 56–7, 71, 74, 75–81; MI9's escape techniques briefing, 136–7; missing 'sticks' attempts to reach battlefield, 189–96, *192*; modest size/objectives of, 258; need for a full moon, xvi, 54; need for participation of radar expert, 106–9; need for spies on the ground, 54; need to borrow planes, 115–16; Nelson group, 96, 131, 154–7, 162, 168–9, 172, 173–4, 175, 183, 184–6, 196–8, 199, 201–2; network of trenches near Stella Maris, 128, 129, 170–1, 173, 175, 184–6, 187–8, 196–8, 201, 203, 230; Norman as air supremo of, 121, 137, 145; offshore rendezvous with gunboat escort, 217; operational plan/order, 129–34, 182–3, 196, 249–50, 253, 261–9;

order of battle, 271–7; order to carry out (27 February), 142–3; paratroop landings, 155–6, 157–63; paratroops left behind in France, 215–16, 218–19; paratroops unable to urinate on planes, 150, 161; participants' deaths on later battlefields, 239–40, 242–3; participants' service/lives after, 239–40, 241–7; perceived windows of opportunity, 137–8, 139–40, 141–2; plan imposed on Frost, 94, 133; planning and preparation, xv–xvi, xix, 19, 38–9, 45–6, 94–105, 106–10, 121–4, 127–33, 136–9, 249–50, 253; plaster-of-Paris model of Bruneval site, 123–4, 149, 228, 229; 'Point X' offshore, 152, 211; Polet farm, 190, 194–5; press coverage of, 223–4, *225*, 230; RAF diversionary nuisance missions before, 145–6; RAF's choice of route, 148–9; rearguard in the defile, 209–10, 214; return across Channel, 218–22; return of lost paratroopers from the south, 206; Rodney group, 96, 131, 132–3, 157–62, 168, 182, 183–4, 187, 193, 196, 199–200, 201–2, 209–10; Ross as second-in-command, 96–7, 131; securing of access to the beach, 131, 168–9, 171, 173–6, 184–6, 188, 196–8, 230; as series of small miracles, 247–8, 249–50; significance of, xvi, 224, 236, 249, 259–60; and snow, 145, 146, 155, 156, 162–3, 166, 174, 248; Stella Maris (Beach Fort), 78, 79, 128*, 128, 129, 131, 160, 170–1, 174, 186, 197–8, 199–203, 250; 'sticks' dropped in wrong places, 155–6, 157, 158–60, *159*, 164, 219, 222, 230; surprise as vital to, 134–6; take-off from Thruxton (27 February), 146–8; topography/geography of site, 79–80, 123–4, 126–8, 129, *135*; training for pilots, 116–17; training in Wiltshire, 98–100, 106, 110–11, 121–3; training with the navy in Scotland, 101–5, 139; TRE report on technology captured during, xviii, 297–325; use of mine-detectors, 97, 136, 156, 169, 206–7; wait on the beach, 205–6, 208–11, 230; weather delays to (24–26 February), 139–40, 141–2; white snow smocks left behind, 145, 174; and wire entanglements, 78, 128, 129, 131, 137, 169, 171, 174, 180, 186, 200, 201–2; wireless failures, 133, 160, 184, 208–9, 212, 237 *see also* Würzburg radar at Bruneval

Bruneval village, xv*, xv–xvi; Beau-Minet hotel, 77, 79, 80, 134, 189, 216–17, 224–6, 238; buildings destroyed for Atlantic Wall, 226; Gosset chateau destroyed, 236; Pol and Charlemagne's intelligence gathering, 55–7, 74–81, 134, 173, 226, 240–1, 245, 247; replacement Würzburg at, 236

Bucourt, Nicolas, xvii–xviii, 104*

Calderwood, Jim, 174
Campbell, Cpl., 160, 193–4, 204, 206, 213
Cap d'Antifer, xv*, 74, 80, 151, 164, 166
Carrington, Col. Charles, 51, 114, 115, 144, 163–4, 218, 258

Casa Maury, Wing-Commander 'Bobby' Marquis de, 31–2, 33, 134, 228–9, 249–50, 253, 257
Cassel, Sir Ernest, 26
Charteris, Brig. John, 84, 239
Charteris, Lt. Euan, 98, 148, 154, 212, 221; arrival at Redoubt, 197–8; background and character, 84–5, 157, 239; and battle to break through to the beach, 199, 200–7, 229, 230; Biting tasks/objectives, 131, 173–4, 196; at Bruneval beach, 205–7, 208, 210, 213, 214; and capture of Stella Maris, 200–4; death of in North-West Africa campaign, 239–40; dropped in wrong valley, 155–6, 157, 168, 248; march towards beach defile, 190–6; Military Cross award for Biting, 229
Chauveau, Charles (Charlemagne), 76–81, 173, 245, 247
Churchill, Winston, xiv; Biting debriefing in Cabinet War Rooms, 227–9; and Biting delays/setbacks, 137–8, 139; commitment to airborne warfare, 40, 228; commitment to offensive action, 20–2; creates Combined Operations, 20; Jones impresses, 9–10, 231; Lindemann as scientific adviser, 6, 19; long passage with windows analogy, 12; love of adventure/military theatre, xv, xvi, xviii, 228–9, 256, 259; and Mountbatten, 23–5, 28, 33, 253–5, 256, 257; as over-impressed by Luftwaffe paratroops, 22, 89; peacetime government (1951–55), 246; presses for small-scale raids on the continent, xiv–xv, 20–2, 35–6, 105, 229, 256, 259–60
Clarendon Laboratory, Oxford, 3
Clarke, Col. Dudley, 21
Coates, F/Lt., 154–5
Combined Operations Command, xv*, xvii; badge of, 35; base and training centre (HMS *Tormentor*), 34–5, 100–1, 110; Bourne replaced by Keyes, 22–3; Bruneval assault proposed to, 19, 37, 38; Bruneval plan devised by, 94, 133–4, 249–50, 253; Churchill creates, 20; defies Dansey over escape information, 137; and Dieppe raid (August 1942), 33–4, 151–2, 231, 254, 255–6; and fanciful schemes, 36; HQ in Richmond Terrace, 19, 22, 28, 30; Keyes replaced by Mountbatten, 23–5, 30; Lofoten Islands raid (March 1941), 22; Mountbatten's appointments to, 31–2, 228–9, 249–50, 253, 254, 257; Operation Flipper (November 1941), 35–6; St Nazaire raid (March 1942), 231, 255*, 255, 256; Vaagso and Maaloy raid (December 1941), 35; and wider armed forces failures, 256–7

commando forces: 3 Commando, 137; ballooning of activities during war, 258–9; Boulogne and Guernsey fiascoes (1940), 21–2; first 'Commando' formed, 21; German rescue of Mussolini, 251; maroon beret of Parachute Regiment, 45, 144, 239, 259; Operation Flipper (November 1941), 35–6; raids as out of fashion in post-1942 period, 256
see also units under British Army

Cook, Sgt. Andy, 158, 162, 219
Cook, Lt. Cdr. Fred, 34–5, 46, 100, 141–2, 143, 150, 219; Distinguished Service Cross for Biting, 230; flotilla's return journey to Portsmouth, 218–22; report on Biting to Admiral James, 222; service/life after Bruneval, 245; waits offshore during radio silence, 211–12, 213, 230
Cornell, Private George, 160, 215–16, 238
Coward, Noel, 27–8, 257–8
Cox, F/Sgt. Charles, 137, 144, 146, 148, 211; background and character, xvii, 107, 108, 110–11, 113, 232; Biting parachute drop, 160, 161–2; as Biting radar expert, xvii, 106, 109, 113, 132, 133, 180–1, 183, 187, 217–18, 233–4, 248; and guarding/transport of radar parts, 196, 198, 208, 209–10; Jones briefs at Air Ministry, 110–13; Military Medal awarded for Biting, 229, 243; parachute training, 108; service/life after Bruneval, 232, 243; as uniquely blue-clad member of raiding force, 111–12; 'volunteers' for Biting, xvii, 107–8
Cunningham, Admiral Sir Andrew, 28

Dalton, Hugh, 34
Danesfield, 14, 15–17, 123–4
Dansey, Col. Claude, 62, 137
De Gaulle, Gen. Charles, xvi, 55, 57, 59, 60, 62, 71, 240, 245
De La Bardonnie, Louis, 64–5, 70
Deckert, Sgt. Karl, 180, 248–9
Deeley, F/Lt. Geoffrey, 124
Delamare, Paul, 191, 238

Delattre, Robert, 74, 79, 80–1
Dewavrin, Capt. André ('Passy'), 60–1, 62, 63, 64, 65, 66, 69, 71, 75, 153
Dieppe raid (August 1942), 33–4, 151–2, 231, 254, 255–6
Dill, Gen. Sir John, 21
Dishforth, Yorkshire, 120, 241–2
Doppler effects, 18
Du Maurier, Daphne, 46, 47–51, 121, 253
Du Maurier, Sir Gerald, 48
Duclos, Maurice, 66
Dumont, Roger (Pol), 72–4, 76–81, 134, 173, 226, 247; execution of (March 1943), 241; Rémy's fatal message to, 240–1

Eben Emael (Belgian fortress), 89, 130–1, 251
Eden, Anthony, 228
Eisenhart-Rothe, Col. Ernst-Georg von, 127–9, 197, 217, 249
Eisenhower, Maj. Gen. Dwight, 52, 259
electronic conflict, xv, 1, 9–13, 234–5 *see also* radar, British; radar, German (*Dezimeter Telegraphie*); radio communications
Elizabeth II, Queen, 253
Elworthy, Wg Cdr. Sam, 143–4, 218
Embury, Pte, Frank, 160, 215–16, 238, 244
Ermoneit, Willy, 169–70, 177, 248–9
Étretat, 125, 127–8, 166, 167, 172, 197, 248
Ewing, Archie, 146–7

Falklands war (1982), xix
Faraday, Michael, 8
Faure, Francois (Paco), 72

First World War, 1, 22, 39, 46–7, 84, 239
Flavell, Lt. Col. Edwin, 90–1
Fleming, Ambrose, 8
Forest, Lee de, 8
France: destruction of fleet at Oran (1940), 56; Le Creusot works, 240; puppet Vichy government, 56, 57; *Service du travail obligatoire* (STO), 56 *see also* Free France exile regime; French Resistance movement
Frank, Charles, 13–14, 16, 18
Free France exile regime: and British intelligence services, 71; Bureau Central de Renseignements et d'Action (BCRA), 55, 60–81, 240–1; *chasseurs* (corvettes) of, 221; Dewavrin as chief of intelligence, 59–62, 71; pioneer BCRA agents in France, 62–81; Rémy's reports to Carlton Gardens, 63, 65–6, 69, 70, 72, 79–80, 153; security of as notoriously porous, 55, 241
Freeman, Pte. Eric, 244
French Resistance movement, xvi, xviii, 54; coding process using books, 70–1; de Gaulle on, 240; difficulty of providing 'real time' intelligence for London, 73; gathering of Bruneval intelligence, 55–7, 74–81, 134, 173, 226, 240–1, 245, 247; German radio interception technology, 70, 73; helps Cornell and Embury, 238; and Operation Jericho (February 1944), 242–3; recruits in first years of war, 56, 57–8, 62–70; *Réseau* Saint-Jacques, 66; surge of recruits near end of war, 56, 68; treachery and betrayals, 67–8; wave of German arrests in Brittany, 75; wireless-operators, 56, 69, 70, 74, 79, 80–1
Freya radar system, 7, 8, 11–14, 233, 236; at Bruneval, xv*, 13, 16, 74, 75, 125, 166, 179, 181–2; and *himmelbetten* system, 234–5
Frost, Jean (née Lyle), 246–7
Frost, Maj. John, xvii; activity on the ground during Biting, 161, 162, 168, 169–70, 172, 176, 178, 184, 186–8, 196–9, 203–4; appointed to command of C Company, 85; appoints Ross as second-in-command, 96–7; and army bureaucracy's complaints over Biting, 237; at Arnhem, 246, 251, 252; background and character, 85–6, 92; and battle to break through to the beach, 197–8, 203–4; as best sort of British professional soldier, 247; Biting parachute drop, 160–1; Biting plan imposed on by Browning, 94, 133; briefs C Company on Biting, 123–4, 128*, 130, 132, 261–9; on British Airborne Forces, 40; and Browning's staff, 94–6; at Bruneval Würzburg, 176, 178, 180, 181, 186–7; on C Company's shooting accuracy, 174–5; capture of Gosset chateau (Lone House), 198–9, 203; chosen to lead Biting, 92–3; command reorganized by Divisional HQ, 94, 96, 186; commands 2 Para, 239–40, 251; departure from Thruxton (27 February), 147–8; and final hours before Biting, 144–7; and flotilla's return to

Portsmouth, 221–2; intelligence brief for Biting, 134; as last to leave Bruneval beach, 214; meeting with Mounbatten in Scotland, 103–4; meets Churchill at Cabinet War Rooms, 227–9; Military Cross award for Biting, 229, 231; and missing 'sticks'/sections, 168, 184, 197–8; on modest size of Bruneval raid, 258; moves towards defile, 186–8, 196; in North Africa, 134, 239–40, 246; parachute training, 90–2; and paratroops left behind in France, 218–19; played by Hopkins in *A Bridge Too Far*, 251; presented to the king, 242; service/life after Bruneval, 134, 239–40, 246–7, 251, 252; on singing by paratroopers, 148; on Strachan, 83; and training for Biting, 99–100, 101–4, 121–3, 136, 138; view of Browning, 227; volunteers for 'special air service', 86–9; and wait at the beach, 207, 209, 210–11, 212–13, 230; and weather delays to Biting, 139–40, 141–2; whistle signal, 131–2, 136, 172

Gale, Brig. Richard, 53, 87
Garrard, Derek, 12, 106
Gavin, Col. James, 251–2
George VI, King, 241–2
Gestapo, 66, 70–1, 74, 76–7
Gibbins, Sgt. Alex, 193, 197–8, 202
Gibson, Wing-Commander Guy, 118, 120
Goering, Hermann, 8–9, 11, 124–5
Gourock, 101, 106
Grafton, Pte., 204
Grant, Bill, 175

Gray, Sgt., 161, 162
Great Escape from Stalag Luft III (March 1944), 240
Grieve, Sgt. David, 122, 155, 193, 199–200, 206; death of in North-West Africa campaign, 239; dropped in wrong place, 156–7, 164, 240, 248; leads downhill charge on Stella Maris, 201–2, 203, 204, 230; Military Medal awarded for Biting, 230
Guernsey, 21–2

Habakkuk (iceberg aircraft-carrier), 33
Haig, FM. Earl, 82, 239
Hamburg, Battle of (August 1943), 234
Hammelburg PoW camp, 242
Hardwick Hall, Derbyshire, 54, 83, 87–8, 89
Harris, Air Marshal Sir Arthur, 10–11, 115–16, 255[*]
Haydon, P/O Jeff, 157, 164
Heard, Reg, 187
helicopters, 251, 259
Heller (radar operator), 178, 181, 232–3, 234, 237
Hérissé, Roger (Dutertre), 74, 76
Hertz, Heinrich, 8
Heslop, Cpl. Jeff, 186
Hill, Cpl. Tom, 82, 193, 195, 197–8, 247
Hill, S/Ldr. Anthony, 15–17, 38, 124, 133, 240
Hitler, Adolf, 8
Hopkins, Anthony, 251
Hormandinger, Fusilier, 201, 203, 226
Hughes, Gordon, 15–16
Hughes-Hallett, Captain John 'Jock', 100, 249–50, 254

Huhne, Lt., 170, 171, 176, 182, 184, 186, 190, 198, 199, 215, 249
Humphreys, Arthur, 223

Imperial War Museum archives, xvii
In Which We Serve (Noel Coward film, 1942), 27–8, 257–8
intelligence, British: Admiralty Intelligence Branch, 6; cross-pollination with scientific community, 3–4, 5–6; Jones returns to (1951–55), 246; MI9 personnel, 71, 136–7; and Operation Jericho (February 1944), 242–3; and pre-war holiday photographs/postcards, 55; Scientific Intelligence at the Air Ministry, xv, 2, 4–6, 12, 17–18 *see also* MI6 (Secret Intelligence Service)
Inveraray, 102
Iraq Levies, 82
Ismay, Maj. Gen. Hastings 'Pug', 20, 138, 231, 253
Italy, 44, 244, 251

James, Adm. Sir William, 141–2, 146, 222
Japan, 105, 228
Java, 228
Johnston, L/Cpl Ralph, 168, 214
Jones, Cpl. Sid, 136, 211, 229–30
Jones, Dr R.V. (Reg), xvii, 2–7, 9–13, 16–19, 92–3; as begetter of Biting, 18–19, 37, 38, 110, 229; belated receipt of CB, 231; briefs Cox and Vernon at Air Ministry, 110–13; Bruneval objectives of, 37, 113, 169, 178, 180, 183, 188; and Bruneval planning, 106, 109–13, 182, 250; Churchill impressed by, 9–10, 231; grasps 'big picture' of German electronic defences, 234–5; on Tony Hill's death, 240; information on Würzburg gained from Biting, 233–4, 235, 236; interrogates prisoners, 10, 232–3, 234; *Most Secret War* (memoir, 1978), 9, 246; post-war life, 245–6; questions Heller, 232–3, 234; requests only signals prisoners, 130, 136, 178, 202–3, 232–3; use of aerial photography, 6–7, 13–14, 15–18, 38, 54, 74
Jones, Susan, 246
Jones, Vera (née Cain), 6
Joubert, Air Marshal Sir Philip, 11
Judge, John, 172
Julitte, Pierre, 75, 153

Kaffurbitz, Paul, 172, 226
Kammhuber, Gen. Josef, 234
Kennedy, Maj. Gen. John, 115
Kenya, 118
Kerrand, Philippe, xviii, 58, 64, 67
Keyes, Adm. Sir Roger, 22–3
Keyes, Maj. Geoffrey, 35–6
Kiel Harbour, 8
Kilkenny, F/Lt. John, 42
Kipling, Rudyard, 'R.A.F. (Aged Eighteen)', 241
Kriegsmarine: 'Channel Dash', 104–5; *Seetakt* (naval radar), 12; U-47 sinking of *Royal Oak* (1939), 35; *Gneisenau* (battle cruiser), 104–5; *Graf Spee* (pocket battleship), 2; *Prinz Eugen* (cruiser), 104–5; *Scharnhorst* (German cruiser), 104–5

La Poterie, village of, xv*, 79, 125, 126, 194, 197; Eisenhart-Rothe arrives in, 217; German forces in,

126, 163, 182; Huhne based in, 170, 171, 182, 190, 198; intelligence on German forces in, 80; members of 685th's 1st Company in, 128, 129, 163, 170, 171, 180, 182, 198, 205; Paschke arrives in, 201; plan to block road from, 132–3, 168, 183–4, 196; stand-by section of 685th arrives in, 184
Lajoye, Maurice, 238
Lang, Rudy, 166
Langley, Maj. James 'Jimmy', 137
Lannion, northern Brittany, 6–7, 9
Laughland, Tom, 82, 197–8, 202, 244
Laycock, Brig. Robert, 31–2
Le Havre, 76–7, 151, 219, 245
Lebaillif, Joseph, 210
Lechevallier family, 238
Lecompte-Boinet, Jacques, 56, 57–8, 67
Lewis, Wilfrid 'Ben', 18–19
Lindemann, Professor Frederick (Lord Cherwell), 3, 6, 19, 231
Lloyd, Col. Cyril, 31
'Lord Haw-Haw', 100
Louis of Battenberg, Adm. Prince, 25
Luce, David, 100
Luftwaffe: awards Iron Crosses to Bruneval defenders, 248–9; blitz, 9–10; and captured British RDF, 9; defence of Freyas during Biting, 179, 181–2; electronic defences against RAF bomber offensive, 10–19, 234–6 *see also* radar, German (*Dezimeter Telegraphie*); failure to impede returning flotilla, 220; fatalities at Bruneval, 172, 177, 226; fighting at Bruneval, 172, 176–80, 181–2, 184–8, 198, 199; *himmelbetten* system, 234–5; initial disdain for defensive radar, 8–9; initial reaction to C Company landings, 163, 166, 167–8, 170, 172; men at Gosset farm during Biting, 77, 126–7, 129, 132, 166–8, 175, 177–80, 181–3, 197, 199, 205; messages decrypted at Bletchley Park, 7, 10, 12, 19; paratroops (*fallschirmjäger*), 22, 39, 89, 136, 258; radar crew at Brunevald, 77, 126–7, 129, 132, 166–8, 176–8, 232–3; Seeberg plotting table, 234–5; use of electronic guidance beams, 9–11; Wild Boar tactics, 235–6; 23 *Flugmelde*, 124–5, 167, 248; FW 190 fighter aircraft, 242; Junkers Ju-52 aircraft, 41
Lumb, Sgt. Tom, 158–60, 193–4, 204, 206, 215

MacArthur, Gen. Douglas, 24
Macmillan, Harold, 32
Mair, P/O, 161
Maitz, Friedrich, 76
Mansion, Sgt. Jacques, 63
Marshall, US Gen. George, 33
Martini, Gen. Wolfgang, 232–3
Matkin, Pte., 204
Maxwell, James Clerk, 8
Mayer, Hans Ferdinand, 4
McCallum, John, 200, 206, 209, 215–16, 237–8
McCormack, Peter, 191–3
McIntyre, Pte. Hugh, 123, 186, 199
McKenzie, Sgt. Greg 'Mack the Knife', 177–8, 202, 230, 237
Meade, S/Ldr., 161
Medhurst, AVM Charles, 11
Medmenham, 6, 14, 15–17, 124

MI6 (Secret Intelligence Service): Bruneval request to BCRA (January 1942), 55, 56–7, 71, 74, 75–81; critics of Jones in, 10; and the Free French, 55, 56–7, 71, 74; headquarters in Broadway, 6, 71; lack of sources in France, 71; and the 'Oslo report', 4; and Gilbert Renault, 62

Michel, Henri, 67

Millais, Sir John Everett, 142

Millar, George, xvii, 244

Millington, Pte. Jack, 198

Montgomery, FM Bernard, 52, 115, 251

Morgan, Stanley, 224

Mountbatten, Cdre. Lord Louis, xvi, xix; ambition/lust for recognition, xvii, 24–5, 26, 27–8, 29, 30, 32, 36–7, 52, 228; appointed Commodore of Combined Operations, 23–5, 30; appointment to Chiefs of Staff Committee, 32, 253–4; background and character, 23–7, 30, 31–2, 34, 139; celebrity and influence of, 23–4, 25–8, 29–30, 32, 257–8; chiefs of staff as wary of, 30, 254–5; critics of within Navy, 26, 27, 28; and Dieppe raid (August 1942), 33–4, 151–2, 254, 255–6; empathy with Americans, 23, 29–30, 33; enthusiasm for Bruneval plan, 19, 37, 38; entourage of, 31–2, 228–9, 249–50, 253, 254, 257; friendship with Churchill, 28, 253–5, 256, 257; German cousins of, 124; good luck signal before Biting operation, 142, 222; as hard worker, 33; inspects *Prins Albert*, 102–3; interest in new technology, 26; as last viceroy of India, 257; murder of by the IRA (1979), 257; promoted after Biting, 253–5; questions Peter Walker, 103–4; record in command of *Kelly*, 28–9; senior military view of, 30–1, 32, 254–5; service/life after Bruneval, 245, 253–8; sexuality, 29; shortcomings as naval/military commander, 28–9, 33–4, 255–8; and success of Biting, 228, 229, 249, 253–4; as Supreme Commander in South-East Asia, 257

Mountbatten, Lady (Edwina Ashley), 26, 29

Muir, Sgt. Rob, 161

Mussolini, Benito, 251

Naoumoff, Lt. Peter, 132, 161, 162, 163, 168, 182, 183–6, 196, 197, 199, 200; service/life after Bruneval, 244–5

National Archives, xvii

Norman, Air Cdre. Sir Nigel, 40, 115, 121, 137, 145, 240

Norton, Peter, 100

Norway, 28; Lofoten Islands raid (March 1941), 22; 'Oslo report', 4; Vaagso and Maaloy raid (December 1941), 35

nuclear fission, 3

paratroops, 22, 37, 39–40, 45, 86–7; 1st parachute squadron RE, 97; court-martial offence to refuse to jump, 42; dropped in the wrong places, 88–9, 155–6, 157, 158–60, *159*, 164, 219, 222, 230, 248; landing technique, 90–1; Luftwaffe *fallschirmjäger*, 22, 39,

89, 136, 258; need for speed and surprise, 89–90, 134–6, 250–1; and reserve 'chutes, 41; role in initial German success as exaggerated, 89; training of, 40–5, 90–2, 108
Paschke, Maj. Hugo, 167, 197, 201
Patton, Maj. Gen. George, 242
Peate, Lt. Cdr. Henry, 143
Peirse, Air Marshal Sir Richard, 115
Péri, Gabriel, 153
Pétain, Marshal Philippe, 57, 58, 245
Peveler, Donald, 248
Philippon, Jean, 65
Picchi, Fortunato, 44
Pickard, Dorothy (née Hodgkin), 118, 119, 242
Pickard, Wing-Commander Charles 'Pick', xvii, 117–21, 137, 145–7, 241–2; awarded bar to his DSO for Biting, 230; death of (February 1944), 242–3; drops Charteris' section in wrong place, 155, 162, 163–4, 222, 230; flight to Bruneval, 148–9, 150, 152–3, 154; and jump at Syrencot (15 February), 121–2; and success of Biting, 222
Pickard, Nick, 242
Pigeonneau, Jacques, 63–4, 70
Pohe, Sgt. John, 155, 162, 164, 240
Portal, Sir Charles, 106, 222, 228, 229
Portsmouth, xv, 141–2, 143, 218, 221–3
Pound, Adm. Sir Dudley, 33, 228, 254
Powell, Col. Geoffrey, 52, 259
Preist, Donald, 106–7, 113, 217, 218
Preussen, Capt. Prince Alexander-Ferdinand von, 124–5, 167, 248
Puttman, Lt., 102
Puxley, Christopher, 48, 51
Pye, D.R., 11

radar, British, 1, 3, 8; apparatus lost to the enemy, 9; development in parallel with Germany, 1–2, 7–8, 218; radar-controlled nightfighter interception, 18–19
radar, German (*Dezimeter Telegraphie*): and defence of Berlin, 13, 14, 17; development in parallel with British, 1–2, 7–8, 218; 'Giant Würzburgs' introduced, 235; Nazi leaders as dismissive of defensive radar, 8–9; and notion of the 'Window', 234; and the 'Oslo report', 4; radar aerial on *Graf Spee*, 2; scanner at Lannion, 6–7, 9; scanners on the north coast of France, 6–7, 9, 12, 13–14, 74, 75; *Seetakt* (naval radar), 12; short-range aircraft-mounted radar, 235–6; technical counter-measures to, 234, 235; Würzburg system, 8, 12, 234–5 *see also* Würzburg radar at Bruneval
radio communications: and Bruneval raid, 94, 133, 160, 184, 208–9, 212, 237; cathode-ray tube, 8, 233; development of technology, 8; and French Resistance, 69, 70, 73, 79
Raid de Bruneval: Mystères et vérités (Alain Millet and Nicolas Bucourt, 2012), xvii–xviii
Rake, Denis, 64
Regnier, Madame, 238
Reid, Sgt. Alex, 157, 193, 199–200, 204, 248

Renault, Gilbert ('Colonel Rémy'), xvii, xviii; background and family life, 58–9, 61–2, 66, 68–9, 74, 75, 245; and Bruneval intelligence, 55–7, 74–81, 134, 240–1, 247; codename, 55, 62*, 71; coding process using books, 70–1; escape to England (June 1940), 58–9; extraordinary luck of, 55–6, 66–7, 69; fatal message to Dupont, 240–1; fate of family of, 241; flies to London on evening of Biting, 153–4; Francoist connections, 58, 61, 67, 68; importance of to wartime intelligence, 69–70, 71–2, 81; life after Bruneval, 245; lingers in Madrid, 63–4; network of spies (*Confrérie Nôtre Dame*, CND), 56–7, 64–5, 66–7, 69, 71–81; recruited as Free French spy, 59–63; reports/messages to Carlton Gardens, 63, 65–6, 69, 70, 72, 79–80, 153

Rommel, Gen. Erwin, 35–6

Roosevelt, Eleanor, 28

Roosevelt, President Franklin Delano, 23, 29–30

Ross, Lt. John: absence from the list of decorations, 230; and battle to break through to the beach, 172, 173–4, 175, 183, 184–6, 194, 196, 198, 199, 202, 203, 230; Biting parachute drop, 154–5; Biting tasks/objectives, 131, 168–9; decorated later in war, 230–1, 244; fires Very cartridges, 209; force of as understrength, 162, 168–9, 173–4, 175, 230; as Frost's second-in-command, 96–7, 131; service/life after Bruneval, 244

Rowe, A.P., 8

Royal Air Force (RAF): air marshals, 10–11; Army Co-Operation Command, 144; and Arnhem, 250, 251; Bomber Command, 13, 114–20, 143–4, 235; bomber offensive, 11, 234–6; bombing of Renault factory outside Paris (March 1942), 56; bombing of submarine bases in French ports, 65; diversionary nuisance missions before Biting, 145–6; dropping of paratroopers into combat landing-zones, 88–9, 154–6, 158–63, 248; electronic eavesdroppers/listening units, 13; failure to provide aircraft for airborne forces, 40, 115; fighter umbrella for returning flotilla, 220; and Hitler's Channel coast defences, xv; introduction of parachutes, 39; Operation Jericho (February 1944), 242–3; personal initiative/creative indiscipline in, 17; Special Duties Squadron, 153; squadrons of the PRU, 14, 15–17, 18, 38, 54, 236, 240; trains soldiers to parachute, 40–5, 108; WAAF (female auxiliary), 14

Royal Air Force (RAF) aircraft: Albemarle aircraft, 115; C-47 Dakota aircraft, 41; 'Ferret' Wellington bomber, 13; Havoc bomber aircraft, 146; Lysander light aircraft, 153; Mosquito light bomber aircraft, 242; Spitfire aircraft, 10, 15, 16–17, 54, 220; Typhoon fighter aircraft, 242; Whitley bombers, 40–1, 43, 116, 120, 121–2, 137, 147–50, 152–3, 154–5, 160–4

Royal Air Force (RAF) units: 109 Squadron, 13; 23 Squadron, 146;

38 Wing, 115; 4 Group, 116, 146; 5 Group, 115; 51 Squadron, 116–17, 120–2, 137, 139, 146–50, 152–8, 160–5, 222, 230, 240, 241–2, 248

Royal Navy: Biting escort ships, 143, 150–2; Biting evacuation rehearsals, 137–9; C Company train with in Scotland, 101–5, 139; Cook as naval CO of Biting, 100, 143, 150, 211–12, 213; destroyer escort for returning flotilla, 221; landing support craft (LSCs), 101, 143, 150, 151, 212–14, 217, 219; landing-craft (ALCs), 100–1, 102, 138, 143, 150, 151, 212–14, 217, 219; MGBs (motor gunboats), 143, 217, 218, 219, 220, 221; Mountbatten's early career, 25–6; raid on Zeebrugge (1918), 22; responsibility for Bruneval evacuation flotilla, 46, 53, 106, 137, 138, 143, 150–2, 208–15, 217–22; *Royal Oak* sunk at Scapa Flow (1939), 35; tardy arrival at Bruneval beach, 208–13, 230

Royal Navy vessels: HMS *Blencathra* (destroyer), 143, 150–1, 221; HMS *Curlew* (light cruiser), 35; HMS *Exeter* (heavy cruiser), 228; HMS *Fernie* (destroyer), 221; HMS *Illustrious* (aircraft-carrier), 23; HMS *Kelly* (destroyer), 27, 28–9; HMS *King Alfred* (shore training centre), 34; HMS *Lion* (battlecruiser), 25; HMS *Prins Albert* (former cross-Channel ferry), 34, 101–5, 106, 110, 139, 143, 150–1, 221–3; HMS *Royal Oak* (battleship), 35; HMS *Warspite*, 26

Royal Patriotic Schools, Wandsworth, 232

Ruben, Lt. Joachim, 167, 172, 179–80, 186, 199, 248–9

Sainte-Adresse, 124, 125
Sandys, Duncan, 31
Saundby, AVM. Robert, 116
Schleich, Lt., 125
Schmidt, Georg, 201, 202–3, 205, 221
Schmidt, L/Cpl. Georg, 170, 171
Schmitz, Pte. Adolf, 193, 224
Schonland, Col. Basil, 109, 233
Schumann, Maurice, 61
scientific community, British, 3–4, 5–6
Scientific Intelligence, Air Ministry, xv, 2, 4–6, 12, 17–18
Scott, Alan, 160, 209, 215–16, 219, 237–8
Scott, Pte. Dick, 184
Seago, Edward, 51
Second World War: Battle of Britain, 1, 6, 8; D-Day, 151, 189, 253, 256; destruction of French fleet at Oran (1940), 56; Eastern Front, 89, 249; German Atlantic Wall (1944), 226; German invasion of Crete, 89; lulls in the slaughter, xiii, xiv; Normandy campaign (1944), 251, 252, 253; North Africa campaign, 35–6, 239–40, 244, 246; Norwegian campaign, 22, 28, 35; Operation Market Garden (September 1944), 51, 131, 239, 243, 244, 246, 250–3; Pacific War, 105, 228, 257; Phoney War, xiii–xiv; RAF bomber offensive, 11, 234–6; Sicilian campaign, 89, 239, 244, 246; surrender of Singapore, 105
Senge, Hans, 177, 226
Sharp, Sgt. Jim 'Shorty', 155, 169, 175, 202

Shaw, Les, 174
Sinclair, Sir Archibald, 228, 231
Singapore, surrender of, 105
Slessor, AVM John 'Jack', 115
Smith, Adrian, 25
Smith, Cpl., 107–8, 109
Sorge, Richard, 64
Sosabowski, Maj. Gen. Stanisław, 250
Soustelle, Jacques, 69–70
Soviet Union, 39
Spain, 61, 62, 63–4, 67, 68
Spanish Civil War, 58
Special Operations Executive (SOE), 34, 64, 71, 74, 130, 242
St Nazaire raid (March 1942), 231, 255*, 255, 256
Stern Gang, 246
Stever, Maj. Gen., 217, 238, 249
Stewart, Cpl. Vic, 156, 157, 193, 200
Stirling, Lt. Col. David, 42
Stirling, Rob, 157, 193, 200, 203
Strachan, CSM Gerry, 82–3, 134, 142, 160, 187–8, 204; Croix de Guerre with Palm award, 229; service after Biting, 243
Student, Gen. Kurt, 258
Sunley, Sgt. Bill, 174, 175, 186, 200, 204
Sutherland, Pte. Jim, 190–1, 215, 219, 238

Tait, Air Cdre. Victor, 107–8, 109
Target for Tonight (Crown Film Unit, 1941), 120
Tasker, Sgt. Dave, 169, 171
Taylor, Cpl. Sam, 145
Teichman, Maj. Philip, 91, 93
Telecommunications Research Establishment (TRE), Swanage, 12, 18, 37, 182, 217, 233; moved to Malvern, 236; report on technology captured at Bruneval, xviii, 297–325
Telefunken company, 8, 183, 218
Templer, Gerald, 101
Tewes, Fusilier Johannes, 201, 202–3
Thomas, Taffy, 200, 206, 209, 215–16, 237–8
Thornycrofts, 34
Thruxton airfield, 54, 121, 139, 140, 142, 144, 145–7, 163–4
Tilshead, Wiltshire, 54, 91, 92, 93–7, 108–9, 121–3, 142–5, 227
Timothy, Lt. John 'Tim', 83, 152, 161; forms the reserve and rearguard, 133, 198, 209; lack of fifteen Rodneys, 158, 162, 168, 184; protects the eastern flank at Bruneval, 132–3, 168, 172, 182, 183–4, 196; service/life after Bruneval, 243
Tizard, Sir Henry, 3, 5, 6, 8, 11
Todt Organization, 236
Toute, Cyril, 224
Towsey, F/Lt., 155
Tragino aqueduct raid (Colossus, February 1941), 44, 89, 116, 247
Treinies, Sgt., 170, 171, 173, 184–6, 198, 200–1, 203, 205, 249
Tunisia, 239–40
Tuve, Merle, 8

United States: Central Intelligence Agency (CIA), 246; Churchill and public opinion in, xiv; Mountbatten's popularity in, 23, 29–30, 33
Urquhart, Col. Roy, 252

Val aux Chats (near L'Enfer), 155–6

the Venniers (Bruneval hotel owners), 77, 78, 134, 216–17, 224–6, 238
Venters, Peter, 191–3
Vernon, Captain Dennis, 109, 117, 137, 138, 163, 196; awarded Military Cross, 244; commended for Biting, 230; commissioned to photograph the Würzburg, 109, 136, 181, 183, 250; 'Demounting party' of, 109–10, 132, 133, 136, 180–2, 183, 186–7, 208, 209–10, 233–4; Jones briefs at Air Ministry, 110–13; service/life after Bruneval, 244
HMS *Victory* (Nelson's flagship), 141–2
Vormschlag, Sgt., 190, 200

Walker, Pte. Peter (Peter Nagel), 103–4, 144, 160, 177–8, 180, 210, 243
Walsh, Lt. Col. Arthur, 95
Ward, Freda Dudley, 31–2
warfare: conduct of commanders in, 52–3; watches as trophies, 178, 230, 237
Watson-Watt, Robert, 8
Wavell, S/Ldr. Claude, 14, 15–17
weaponry: Bofors 40mm gun, 143; Boyes anti-tank rifles, 101; Bren light machine-guns, 101, 139, 169, 172, 173, 175, 183, 184, 212, 237; Chatellerault 7.5mm light machine-gun, 170–1, 174, 175, 183, 187–8, 201, 204, 230; Lewis guns, 143, 214; Oerlikon cannon, 101, 143, 212, 214; Sten sub-machine guns, 97–8, 139, 172, 173, 175, 237; Steyr sub-machine-gun, 177
Wedemeyer, Maj. Gen. Al, 33

Wehrmacht: Biting casualties, 193, 203, 224, 226; and Bruneval reinforcements, 197, 199, 208, 209, 210, 215, 216–17; combat during Biting, 173–4, 182, 184, 186–7, 190–3, 194–5, 198–9, 200–3; German military doctrine, xv; initial reaction to C Company landings, 163, 167–8, 170–1; and Luftwaffe defence of Bruneval, 180; whitewash report on Bruneval raid, 249; 336th Infantry Division, 127–30, 163, 179, 184, 190, 197, 200, 204, 215, 249; 685th Regiment of 336th Infantry Division, 127–30, 184, 190, 200, 204, 215, 249; 687th Regiment of 336th Infantry Division, 163, 179, 197; Beau-Minet platoon, 190, 200, 204, 215
Wellington College, 84, 85
Wenzel, Sgt. Gerhard, 176–7, 226
Wernher, Sir Harold, 31
'Whipcord' (plan to invade Sicily), xiii
Willoughby, John, 206, 215–16, 237–8
Wilson, Sir Horace, 231
Windsor, Duke of (formerly Edward VIII), 25–6, 27, 31
Winterbotham, Group-Captain Fred, 4
Winters, Lt. Dick, 92
Wood, Bill, 206, 210
Wood, Carmen, 84
Woolsey, James, 246
Wright, Maj. Henry, 43
Würzburg radar at Bruneval, xv*, xvi, 38, 125, 166, 168, *185*, 250; aerial photographic reconnaissance of, 16–18, 19, 54; Biting engineers tasked with

Würzburg radar (*cont ...*)
dismantling, 38, 53, 109–10, 113, 127, 132, 136, 160, 175, 180–8, 233; christened HENRY by the British, 130; 'Demounting party' (Vernon's team), 109–10, 132, 133, 136, 180–2, 183, 186–7, 208, 209–10, 233–4; dismantling of at Bruneval, 176–8, 180–2, 186–7; examination of equipment captured at Bruneval, 233–4; German failure to protect, 167, 175, 179–80, 182, 205; information on gained from Biting, 233–4, 235, 236; replacement set, 236; transport of parts across Channel, 217–18; transport of parts to beach, 187, 196, 198, 208–10, 217; TRE report on technology captured at Bruneval, xviii, 297–325

Young, Andrew, 175
Young, Lt. Peter, 84, 148, 161, 177–8, 180, 203, 222; Henry as Biting objective, 132, 169, 172, 176; mentioned in despatches for Biting, 229–30

Zeebrugge, naval raid on (1918), 22
Ziegler, Philip, 28–9, 30